LEGENDARY LOCALS

OF

GRAND PRAIRIE

TEXAS

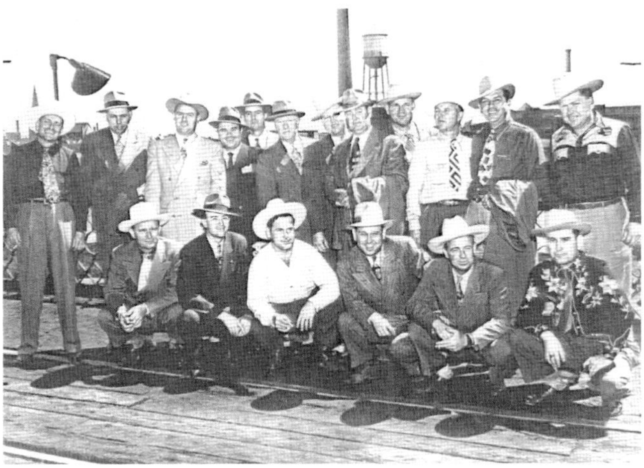

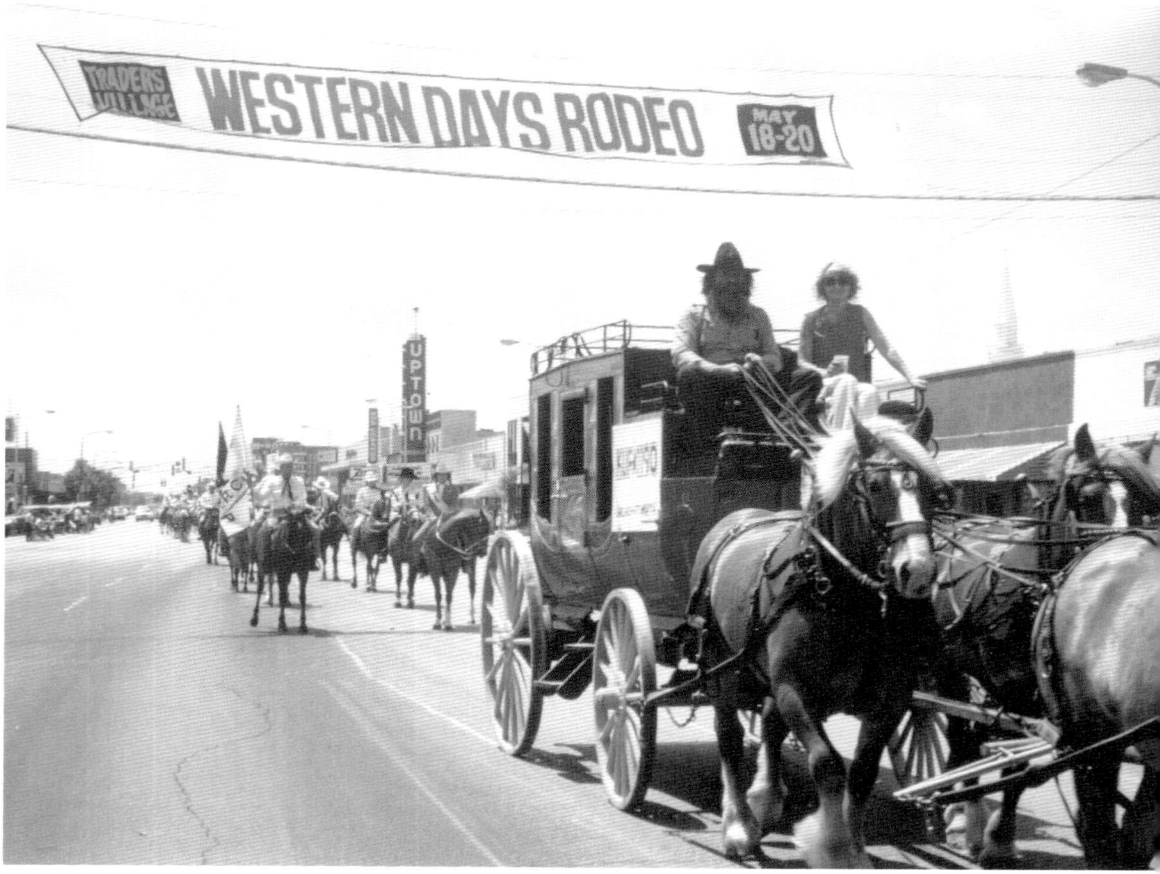

Stagecoach

Western Days was started by men like Tag Taggart and Wayne Hanks, working with the chamber of commerce as a way to promote Grand Prairie. Businesses and citizens gathered to celebrate their identity as a city. Breakfast was available all week, sponsored by businesses and churches. Folks only needed to show up. There was always a parade. The stagecoach rolled down Main Street, the Clydesdales were seen in all their grandeur, and businessmen and businesswomen could be found atop horses. Local personalities recruited to head up the procession could be found riding in a convertible or on a horse.

The climax of the week was a rodeo at Trader's Village. September still holds that Western flavor, with a big barbecue and the annual powwow at Trader's Village. (Courtesy of the Grand Prairie Chamber of Commerce.)

Page 1: Men in Hats

A group of Grand Prairie businessmen pose for a photograph. Pictured are Bill Jasper, Harold Bergstrom, Wesley Flinn, Bob Hancock, Walter Robinson, B.A. Stufflebeme, Gene Norton, E. Carlyle Smith Sr., Bill Davis, Anson B. Brundage, Dee Perkins, Frank Stanfield, Milton Fulton, Bob Barbier, H.N. Peek Jr., Cicero Floyd, W.A. Hotchkiss, and Buddy Ausburne. (Courtesy of the City of Grand Prairie Public Library Archives.)

LEGENDARY LOCALS

OF

GRAND PRAIRIE

TEXAS

RICHARD G. WALLER
AND PAMELA FLYNT KNIGHT

LEGENDARY LOCALS

ISBN 978-1-4671-0217-9

Legendary Locals is an imprint of Arcadia Publishing
Charleston, South Carolina

Printed in the United States of America

Library of Congress Control Number: 2015933920

For all general information, please contact Arcadia Publishing:
Telephone 843-853-2070
Fax 843-853-0044
E-mail sales@arcadiapublishing.com
For customer service and orders:
Toll-Free 1-888-313-2665

Visit us on the Internet at www.arcadiapublishing.com

Dedication
This is dedicated to the Grand Prairie Genealogical Society and the Grand Prairie Historical Organization, who are dedicated to the preservation of materials for future generations.

On the Front Cover: Clockwise from top left:
David Daniels, football coach (courtesy of the City of Grand Prairie Public Library Archives; see page 44), John Tull, fire control technician (author photograph; see page 30), Chance Vought, pioneer aviator (courtesy of the City of Grand Prairie Public Library Archives; see page 28), Ruthe Jackson, city leader and community volunteer (courtesy of Grand Prairie Chamber of Commerce; see page 79), Walt and Grace Minter, local business owners (courtesy of Grace Minter; see page 95), Emmadean Berry, real-estate agent and business owner (courtesy of the Grand Prairie Historical Organization; see page 106), Alexander Dechman, town founder (courtesy of the City of Grand Prairie Public Library Archives; see page 13), L.R. "Squat" Cannon, fireman and businessman (courtesy of Darcy Harris and L.R. Cannon family; see page 74), Dr. Bob Wilson, veterinarian (courtesy of the City of Grand Prairie Public Library Archives; see page 76).

On the Back Cover: From left to right:
Dr. William and Olga Colip, health advocates (courtesy of the City of Grand Prairie Public Library; see page 112), volunteer firemen on newly purchased 1925 truck (courtesy of the City of Grand Prairie Public Library; see page 8).

CONTENTS

ACKNOWLEDGMENTS

Several individuals have helped to pull together people, history, and photographs for this publication. It is with a grateful heart that we wish to thank them for their time and efforts. First, thanks go to the Grand Prairie Public Library system and its director, Amy Sprinkles, and the staff. Their efforts in maintaining historical information on people and places in Grand Prairie have made our research much easier. A hearty thanks goes out to the Grand Prairie Historical Organization and its president, Stephanie Moreno, who gave her time and help in searching files and photographs. Our appreciation also goes out to the chamber of commerce staff, especially to president and CEO Lynn McGinley and Alex Sprinkles, director of operations. Thanks also go to Angela Giessner for use of the Turner scrapbooks. They trusted us with facility keys for our research efforts. We appreciate the efforts of Jorja Clemson. Jorja's access to the collection and pictures of her mother, Ruthe Jackson, were invaluable. Thanks, too, to Mary Ann Hartsell, president-elect, and member Sharon Wilson of the Grand Prairie Genealogical Society. Mary Ann, who also was chairman of the committee that published the history of the First Methodist Church, came through for us at the last minute with needed pictures. Sharon provided necessary research notes from one of her own projects. Their vast knowledge and generosity of time is appreciated. We also would like to thank Stephen Knight of Phunky Street Designs for help with some of our images.

Countless individuals shared their stories or the stories of others. Taking that time to share added a personal touch and joy to tales told and untold. They will be remembered for a long time. And, thanks go to my coauthor. Without your input, countless hours, cooperation, and research, this book would not have been possible.

The following image sources are noted by abbreviations: Grand Prairie Chamber of Commerce (CofC); Grand Prairie Historical Organization (GPHO); and City of Grand Prairie Public Library Archives (GPML).

INTRODUCTION

From buffalo, Indians, and settlers to aerospace facilities and recreation sites, the open space of Grand Prairie has hosted them all! When settlers started coming to this area, there were large numbers of buffalo. Even today, land is dedicated to their history in this area. The Indians, fewer in number, were moving out of the area, but there were still occasional Indian raids.

Grand Prairie began long before a city was ever incorporated. In 1840, the Jordan family moved into the northeast area of what is now Grand Prairie. In 1846, the Republic of Texas gave land grants to the Goodwin and Bradshaw families. With 640 acres each, they moved into the area the same year. By 1861, Alexander McRae Dechman had heard that he could obtain land, and he had the first planned community, known as Dechman.

By 1877, the area had become known as Grand Prairie instead of Dechman, but it was not until 1909 that the town finally incorporated. In 1877, the first post office was established; it was listed as Deckman, because the handwriting was not clear on the application. The planned utopian community of Dalworth, which neighbored Grand Prairie, was finally annexed into the city in 1946.

Originally, this was a large farming area, and marketing to both Fort Worth in the west and Dallas in the east was facilitated by the railroad. Alexander Dechman gave land to the railroad in exchange for a guarantee that a depot would be established. The railroad was not the only mode of transportation with a stop in town. Grand Prairie had a port when the Trinity River was still a major waterway in the area. Early in the town's history, aviation arrived. An airport was just the beginning, as the booming hub eventually evolved into an aviation and aerospace industry. Grand Prairie was involved in the automotive industry as home to the Little Motor Kar Company. By the middle of the 20th century, the town between Dallas and Fort Worth was a booming city, still with the heart of a small town.

Before Grand Prairie was even incorporated, it focused on education. The Loyd family held school for family and neighbors in the late 1800s. The Grand Prairie Independent School District was formed in 1902. From its humble beginnings and its first brick building in 1905, it has grown to an organization with multiple schools and programs from preschool through 12th grade in both traditional and magnet schools. Grand Prairie had great innovators, such as Oma Braswell and Lloyd Boze, who worked hard for educational programs. Because of the amount of land and the number of counties Grand Prairie encompasses, students are also served by the Independent School Districts of Irving, Arlington, Mansfield, and Cedar Hill.

The economic identity of Grand Prairie has seen several changes in more than 150 years. What was once open prairie was boosted by incoming settlers. Planned communities rose up, and business grew around a vibrant farming area. The port, stagecoach, railroad, and interurban were the early incarnations of the transportation industry. Then, aviation arrived. When war broke out, the aerospace industry exploded in Grand Prairie. An entertainment district was developed, originally occupied by Ripley's Believe It or Not! and Louis Tussaud's Palace of Wax. Several other facilities were established, including a water park. Unfortunately, it was purchased by a nearby rival and demolished. The Lion Country Safari was lost through a flood, and the Texas Fire Museum became a teen club before closing. More recent recreation developments, clustered near I-30 and Beltline Road or the north side of town, are Lone Star Park, a thoroughbred horse-racing facility; an Independent League baseball stadium; and a public theater. To the south are Lake Joe Pool, Trader's Village, and the Summit senior center. Grand Prairie also has plans for a water park in the center of town, near the Summit.

The hometown appeal lingers in Grand Prairie, probably due to the many family legacies. The homes of early entrepreneurs, such as the Bowles, Trimbles, and Dr. Copeland, still stand, reminders of their contributions to the community.

Family businesses, such as Graff Chevrolet, continue from generation to generation, and Don Juan's and Theo's Drive Inn still serve generations of residents. The family connections in Grand Prairie can be found in every part of the community. Dr. Horace Copeland was the grandson of an early settler, Robert Copeland. Angela Giessner, a business and community leader, is the daughter of the former president of Grand Prairie State Bank, Durwood Sutton. He was the father of its current president, Marshall Sutton. Councilwoman Jorja Clemson was taught to serve the community by her parents, Vernon and Ruthe Jackson, who owned a business and served the city in numerous capacities. These are only a few examples of the families that drive the hometown spirit of Grand Prairie.

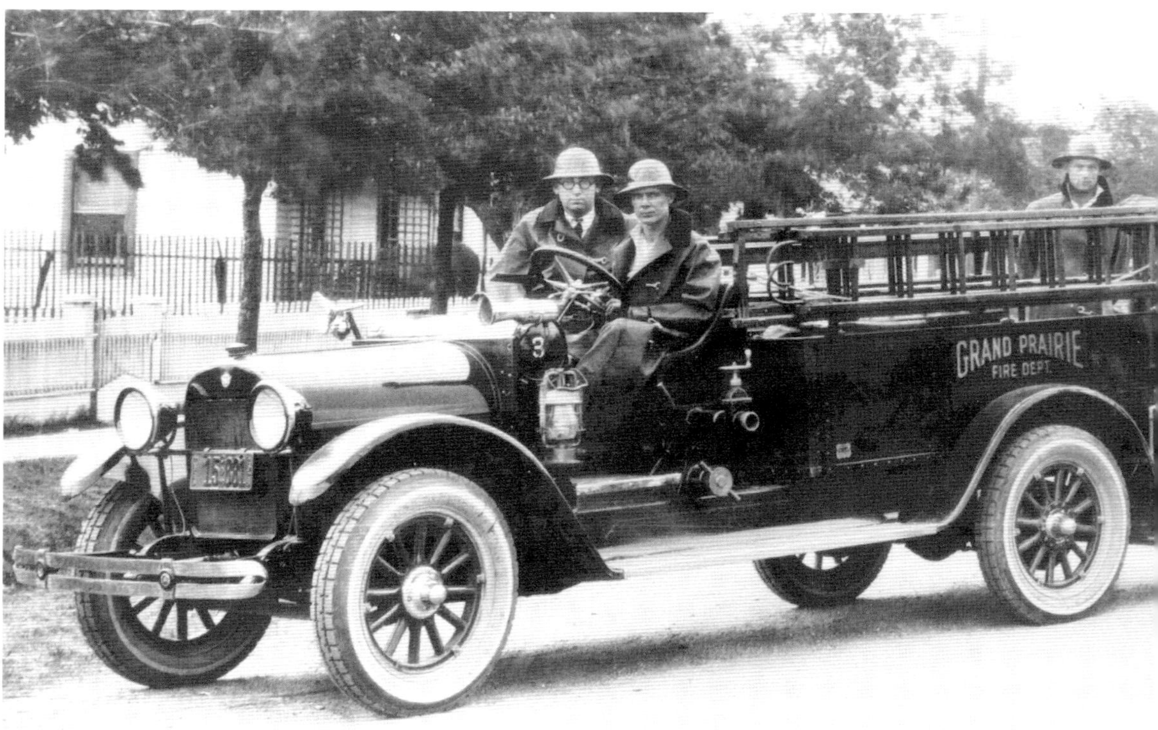

Grand Prairie Fire Department
It was a cause for great celebration when the Grand Prairie Fire Department was able to get a new fire truck. This 1925 engine replaced the prior truck, which had been used and fashioned by the firemen to provide services. The 1925 truck was the first new vehicle the department owned. (GPML.)

CHAPTER ONE

Early Grand Prairie

Grand Prairie began to be populated in the 1840s, when settlers came to the area because of Republic of Texas land grants. The Peters Colony was one of the first settled in the area, near what is now the vicinity of Interstate 30 and Highway 360. The Jordan family came to the area and settled in the northern part of town, just a few miles east of the Peters Colony. Other settlers, like the Bradshaws, Vernoys, and Loyds, soon followed, settling the area from north to south, all the way down to the current Joe Pool Lake area.

About 1855, Alexander Dechman learned he could obtain some land through a trade, and purchased over 200 acres in what is now downtown Grand Prairie. He laid out the initial plat for the city. Local train service was also secured by Dechman. It was not until after the turn of the 20th century that the town's name changed from Dechman to Grand Prairie. Businesses and schools sprang up, and city services were developed, but it was not until 1909 that the city incorporated. A development company laid out and began building a utopian community, Dalworth, adjacent to Grand Prairie. Dalworth had modern conveniences like water, gas, and telephone service. In 1945, it was annexed into the City of Grand Prairie.

Men like John and R.B. Stubbs, Dr. William Haskett, and Dr. J.E. Payne started businesses and provided services to the citizens of Grand Prairie. Industry began to bring more people to the area. Aviation, a big part of this early period, transformed into an aerospace industry in later years. People believed in the best for their community. Grand Prairie began to develop economically and to grow.

The town has not been without controversial people and issues. The Little Kar Company came to town with good intentions, but its president had more personal interests in mind. Cora Megrail was a local force behind the temperance movement and the war on alcohol.

Even today, descendants of Grand Prairie settlers live and participate in the community. Most of the early residents set aside property for a cemetery. Family members are still being buried in some of these family plots. Fortunately, the Grand Prairie Genealogical Society has surveyed and documented most of the cemeteries in town.

Grand Prairie is where East Texas meets West Texas. In the first 100 years, the area grew from a farming prairie to a city with a population of about 1,500. Today, this bustling city is home to nearly 200,000 citizens.

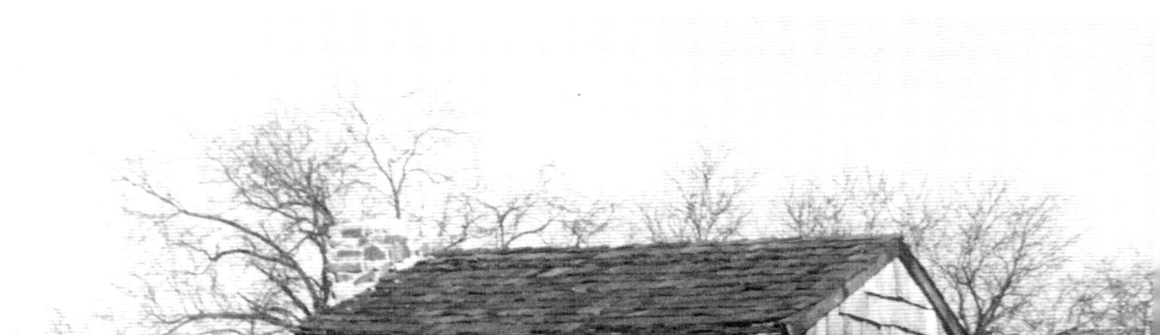

Micajah Goodwin

The Micajah Goodwin family was one of the first families to homestead in the Peters Colony, on a Republic of Texas land grant in the early 1840s. Mrs. Goodwin died just months after their arrival; she was the first white woman buried in the Watson cemetery. The Goodwin cabin (pictured) was reportedly the first permanent home built in Grand Prairie. It was moved to Cottonwood Park (now McFalls Park) in 1975. Designated a historic site, the cabin has both state and city historical markers.

Mrs. Goodwin's death shortly after arrival in Grand Prairie was not the only tragedy. In October 2003, vandals jumped the fence surrounding the historic cabin while it was being renovated and set fire to the structure. This thoughtless act destroyed 150 years of history. (GPML.)

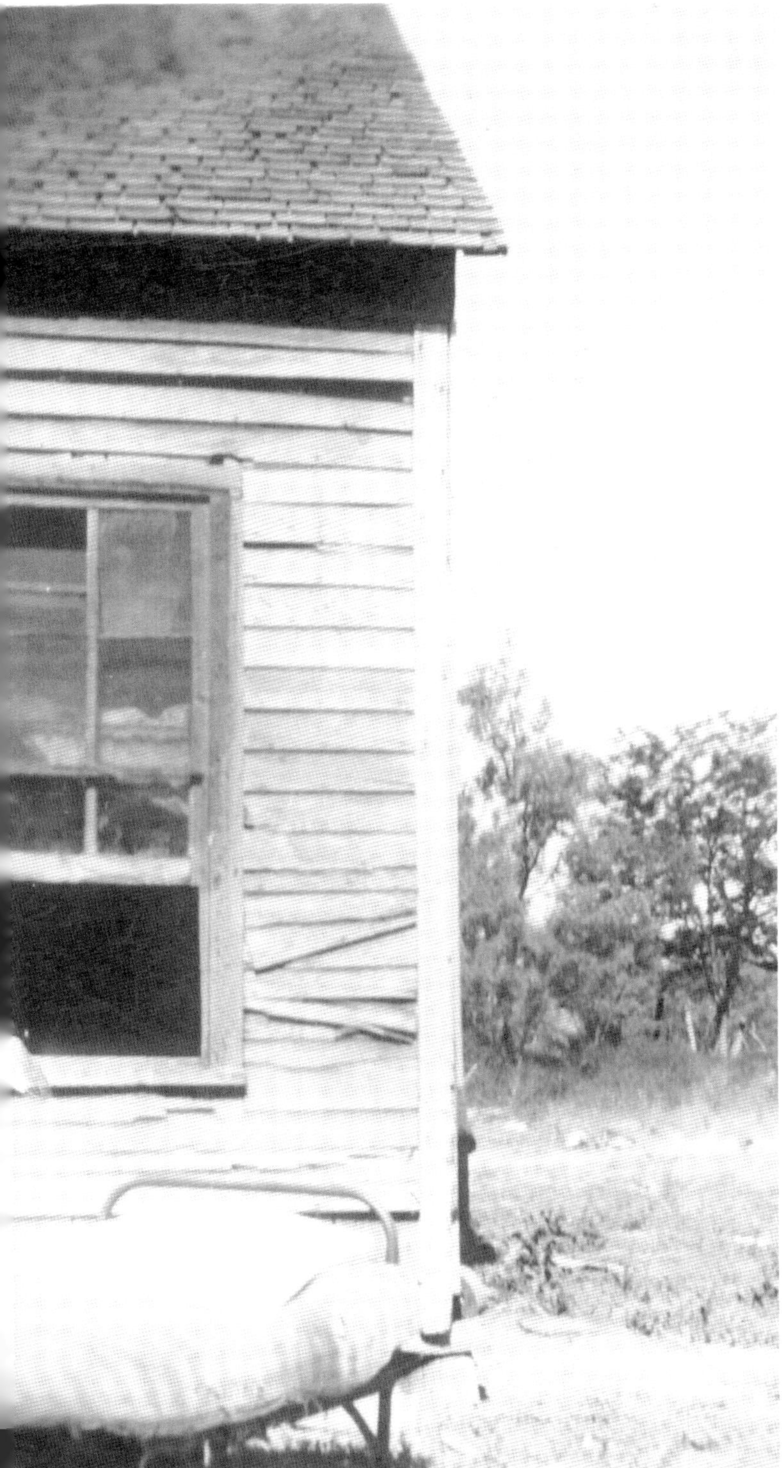

David Bradshaw
Bradshaw and his family were among the early pioneers to Grand Prairie. Arriving about 1849, they were recipients of 640 acres from the Republic of Texas as part of the Peters Colony land grant. The 1850 census lists David and Rebecca Bradshaw, ages 57 and 58 respectively, with three males in the household, ages 13 to 21.

The Bradshaw property was located in the north part of town, which is now the area of Bill Strong's llama farm and the intersection of Carrier Parkway and Highway 161. A family cemetery was established, but it has been lost. The last known record of the cemetery is from the early 1980s, when it was cleaned by a Boy Scout troop. The gravestones were not surveyed or photographed, and only one grave, that of a child, Leander Bradshaw, was noted. (GPML.)

Thomas Vernoy

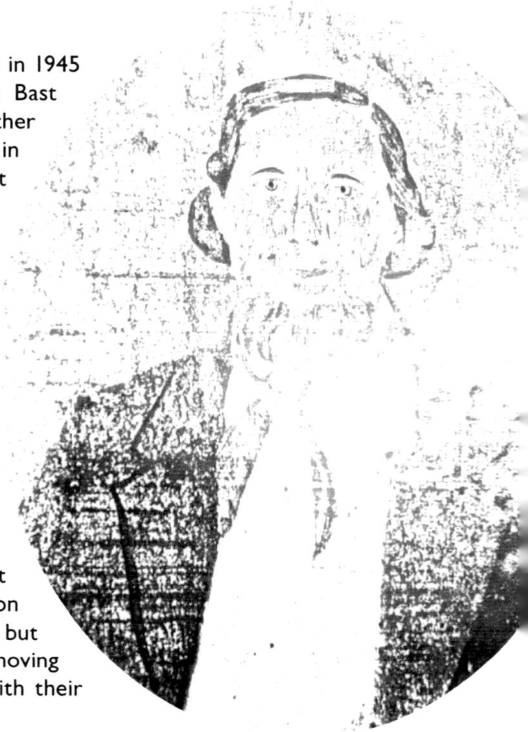

Vernoy, one of the first settlers in this area, arrived in 1945 from Peekskill, New York. He married Julia Ann Bast around 1946. She had come to the area with her father from Indiana. Thomas and Julia's ranch was located in the northwestern part of Dallas County. A merchant and a cattleman, Thomas Vernoy (right) was also adventurous. An original 49er, he had a successful trek to California during the Gold Rush. Upon his return, he used part of his profit to increase his cattle holdings.

The "Vernooy" spelling of their name is found only on the graves of Thomas and Julia. All other references to them or their relatives, including on gravestones, use the spelling "Vernoy." Once a single acre on an area ranch, Vernoy Cemetery in Grand Prairie is a small plot that sits nestled in a housing area and is protected by fencing. After Southland Cemetery was opened, the bodies of Thomas and Julia were moved from the family plot to Southland. The grave markers lay horizontally upon their graves. It is not clear why they were moved, but they had lived in the vicinity of Southland prior to moving farther south. Below, the Vernoy children pose with their bikes in front of the family home. (Both, GPML.)

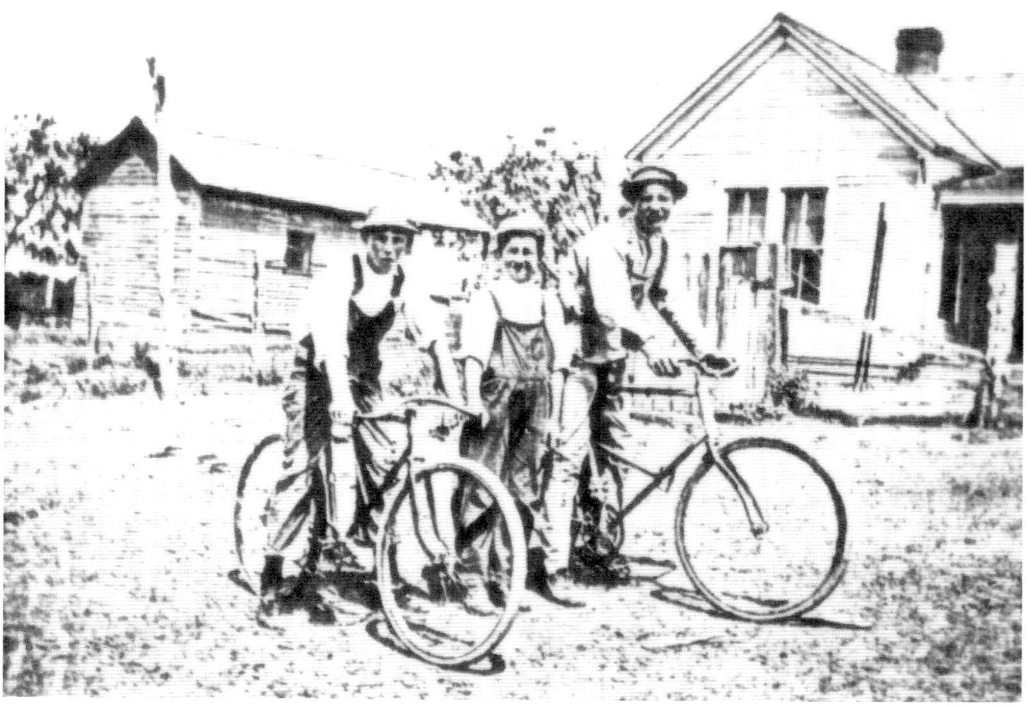

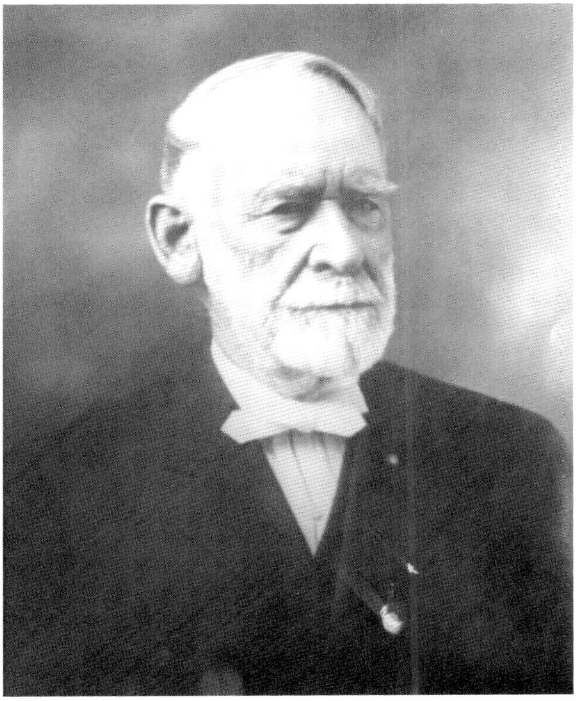

Alexander McRae Dechman

An adventurous man, Dechman began working at the age of 14 in a dry-goods store to help his family in Nova Scotia, Canada. At the age of 21, he was hired by John James to work in San Antonio, Texas, at the James R. Sweet & Company store. His duties were not limited to his position as a clerk in the store. He also traveled through risky territory, as far as El Paso, to transport goods. He was also involved in trading with Mexicans and Indians as part of his duties. At one point, he accompanied the Indian fighter "Bigfoot" Wallace on some expeditions.

By 1855, Dechman had become a good businessman. He set up a tent dry-goods store at Fort Belknap, but, by 1860, severe Indian attacks forced him to relocate his family to Leon County. He had married Mary E. Baker in Panola, Texas, on November 12, 1857. Their son Alexander was kidnapped by Indians while at Fort Belknap, but he was later rescued. The couple moved to Birdville, now Haltom City, in Tarrant County after the birth of their second son in 1861. Alexander was elected county tax assessor while there.

Dechman traded oxen, wagons, and $200 in Confederate currency for land in Dallas County. Preparing for his enlistment in the Civil War, he made a trade with the Caruth family. Dechman purchased 239 acres of land on one side of the Trinity River and another 100 acres of timberland on the opposite side. In 1865, he joined the Texas Cavalry and was a major in Parson's Brigade.

After establishing his land as a town by filing a plat with Dallas County in January 1863, Dechman guaranteed a depot by trading every other plot to the Texas & Pacific Railroad for the right-of-way going from Dallas to Fort Worth. There are different stories about the town's name, Dechman, becoming Grand Prairie. One story is that the railroad named it Grand Prairie when it built the depot stop, because the area was a grand prairie at the edge of West Texas. Another story recounts that the railroad named it Dechman, which prompted Alexander Dechman to move here. Yet another story is that a famous actress stepped off the train at the Dechman town depot and declared, "What a grand prairie!"

Alexander Dechman lived in Grand Prairie only from 1878 to 1879, but his son Alexander F. lived here and ran a trading post and farm. The Dechmans finally settled in Waxahachie. Mary died in 1905, and Alexander passed away in 1915. They are buried in Greenwood Cemetery in Dallas. (GPML.)

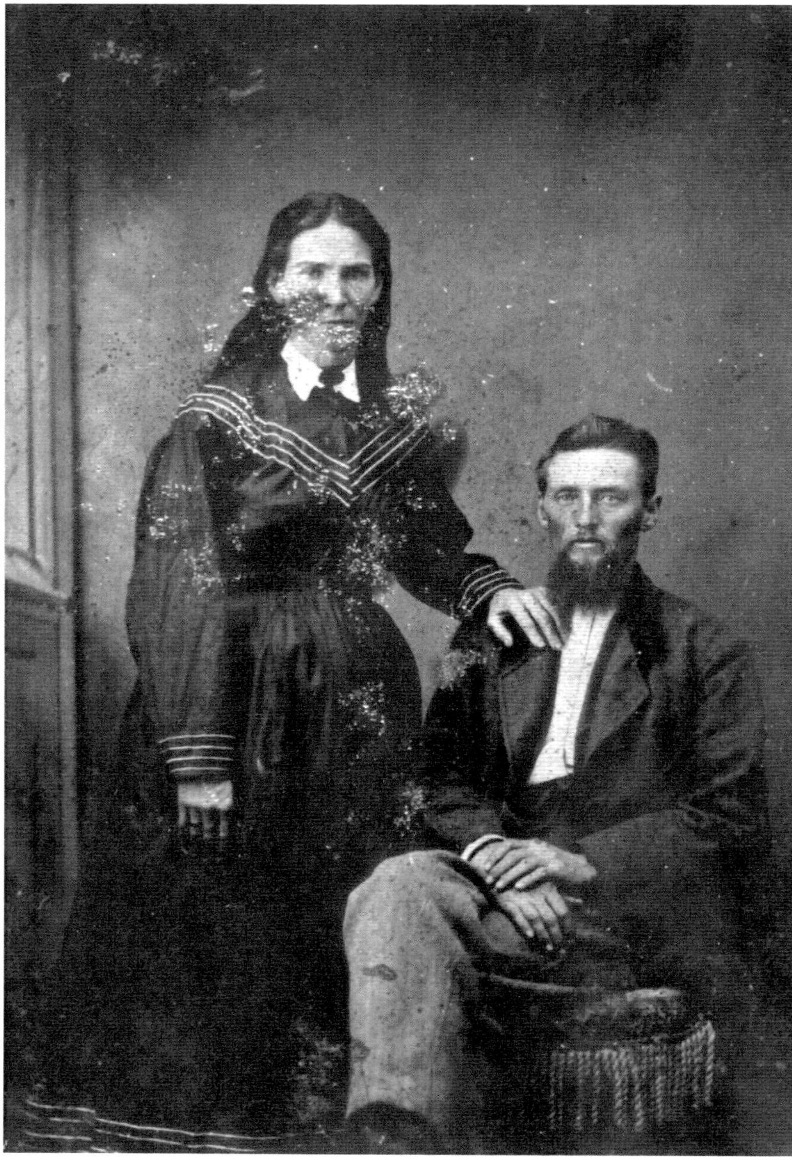

David and Alexander Jordan

Twin brothers from Murfreesboro, Tennessee, David and Alexander Jordan brought their family and some of their slaves in 26 carriages and wagons and settled in the area. The year was 1856. David's daughter Mary Elizabeth is pictured here in her calico wedding dress with her husband, James Curry. He was postmaster and had a grocery store.

The family provided all they needed from their farm, except for coffee and sugar, which they purchased. They grew wheat, corn, and a variety of fruit trees. A good hunter and fisherman, Alexander Jordan provided and cured a lot of meat and shared his bounty with neighbors.

Although the Jordans owned slaves, they may have been more lenient than other owners, giving them every Saturday to do as they wished. One slave sold ginger bread in town on Saturday afternoons, eventually purchasing his freedom. However, he chose to live with the Jordans for many more years. (GPML.)

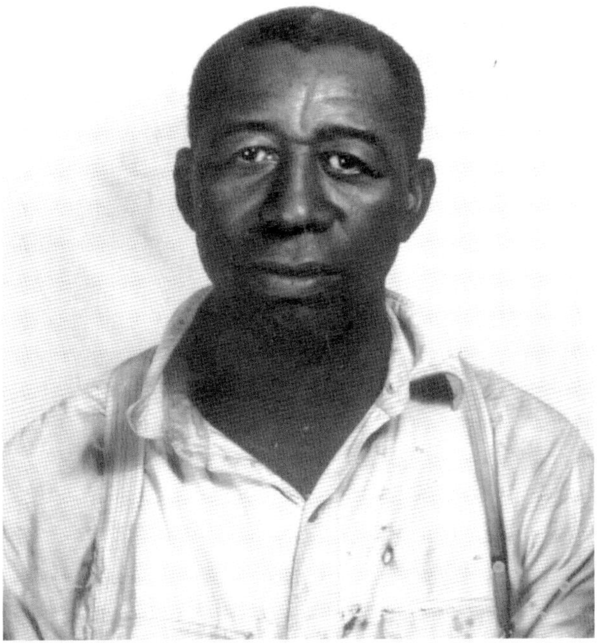

Mose Jordan

Mose Jordan (below), a former slave of the Jordan family, was freed after the Civil War. He was the first black man in Grand Prairie. Mose and two former slave families settled near Mountain Creek. He purchased a 125-acre farm, which he passed on to his son Mose Jordan Jr. (left). The elder Jordan was considered to be one of the best wheat farmers around, and many sought his advice.

Jordan Jr. was the first African American born in Grand Prairie. Besides being a farmer, he was a businessman, member of the Masonic Lodge, and president of the trustee board for the AME church. He organized the Dalworth Civic Club, which was responsible for bringing the urban renewal program to Dalworth.

Mose Jordan Jr. was described as a kind man who helped a lot of people. In 1990, a road in Tyre Park was named for him. He left a beautiful legacy for his family. (Both, GPML.)

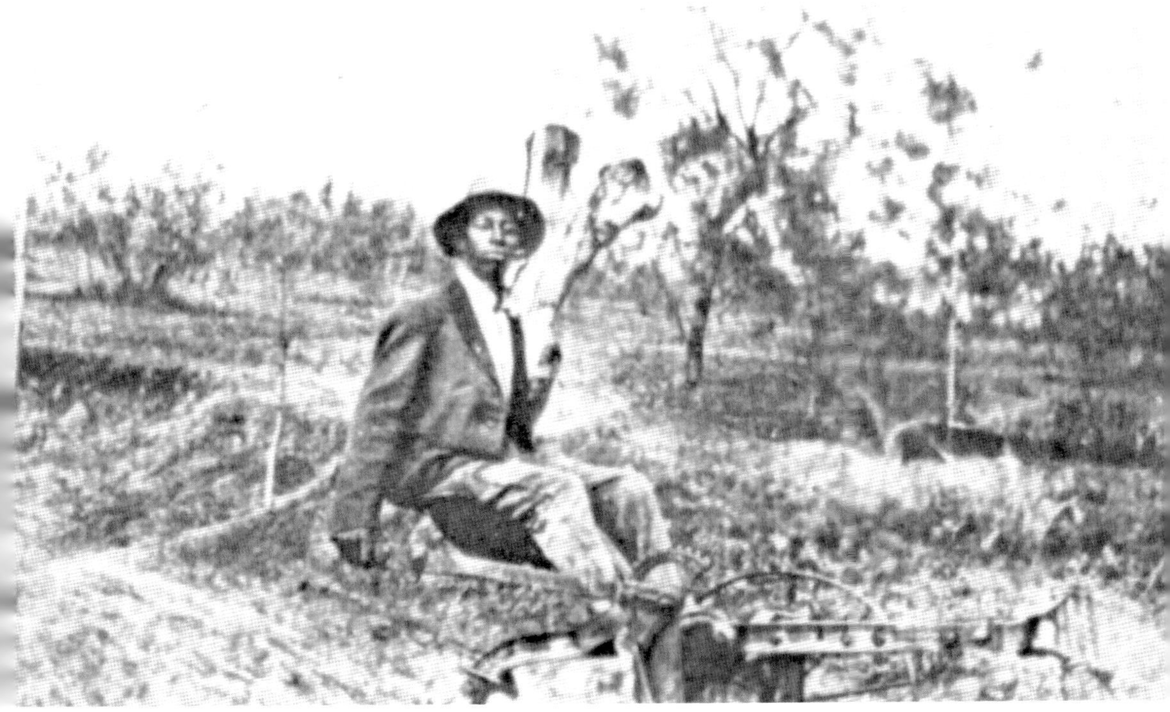

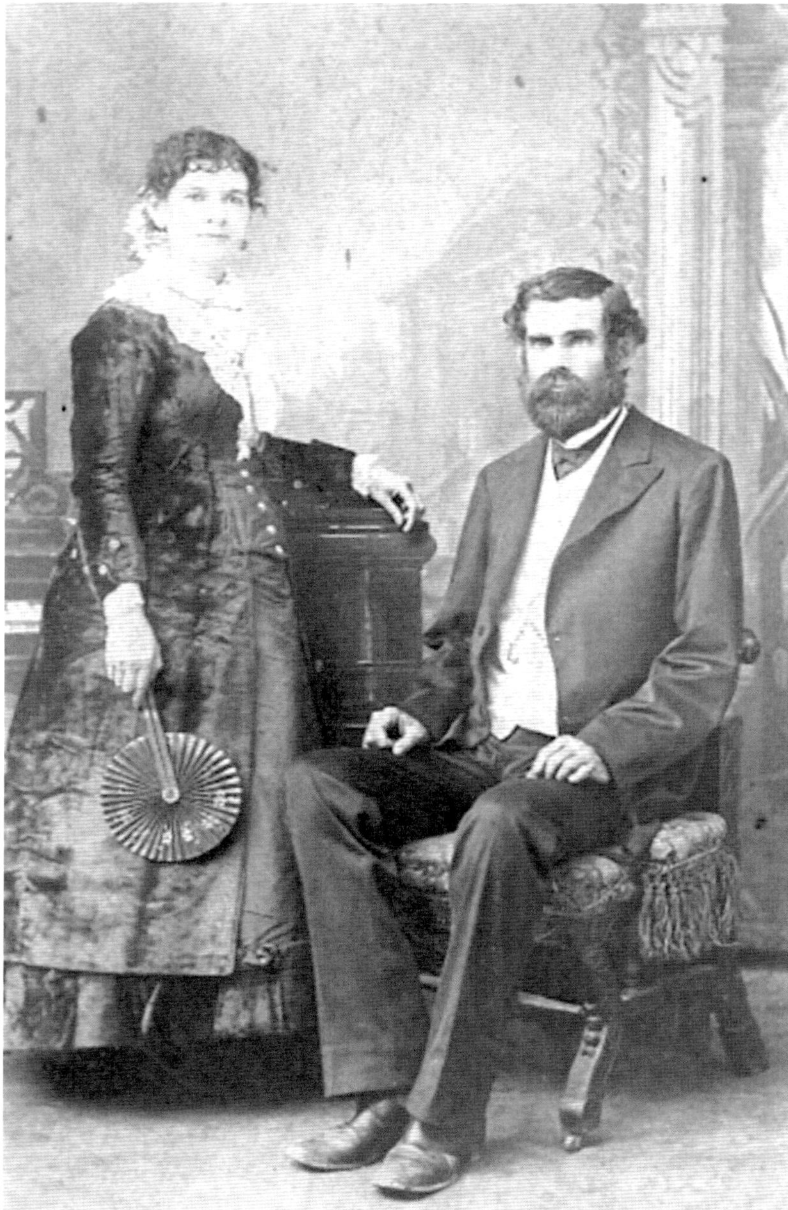

Dr. and Mrs. Haskett

Grand Prairie was not much more than a prairie in the late 1800s. The area was still dotted with buffalo, Indians, and pioneers. The roads were mud and gravel, and ranchers and farmers made up the community. Still, they needed a doctor. The first known doctor in the area was Dr. William Haskett. He and his wife, seen here, were early pioneers.

The sparse population meant that being a doctor was not sufficient to support a family. The first store was opened by Samuel Muggs in 1870. Dr. Haskett succeeded him in 1872. By 1874, the town had a post office, and Dr. Haskett served as the postmaster. (GPML.)

Richard Benjamin Stubbs

R.B. Stubbs, a resident of the Dalworth community, was elected a commissioner. In 1930, along with many other citizens, he signed a petition calling for the resignation of the mayor and two other Dalworth officials and for an accounting of funds. The point of contention seems to have been the extravagant spending of money on lighting.

Stubbs owned a blacksmith shop (pictured) in Grand Prairie and was married to Mary Alice Harston, the daughter of pioneer Dan Harston. Her grandfather came to Grand Prairie when her father was just a boy, and her father grew up here. R.B. and Mary Alice lost their son when he was a young man to pneumonia, developed from complications when he was in an automobile accident. (GPML.)

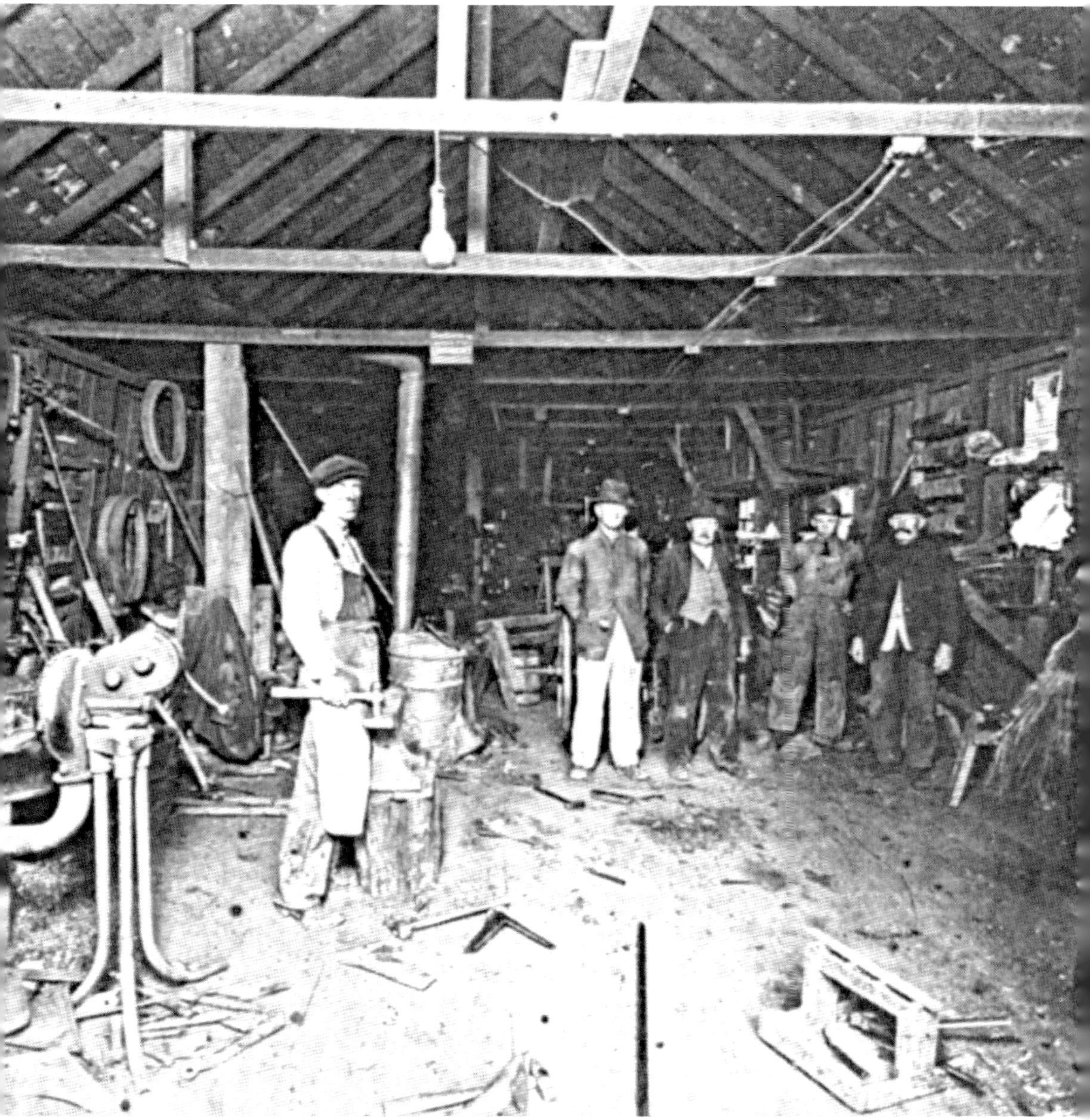

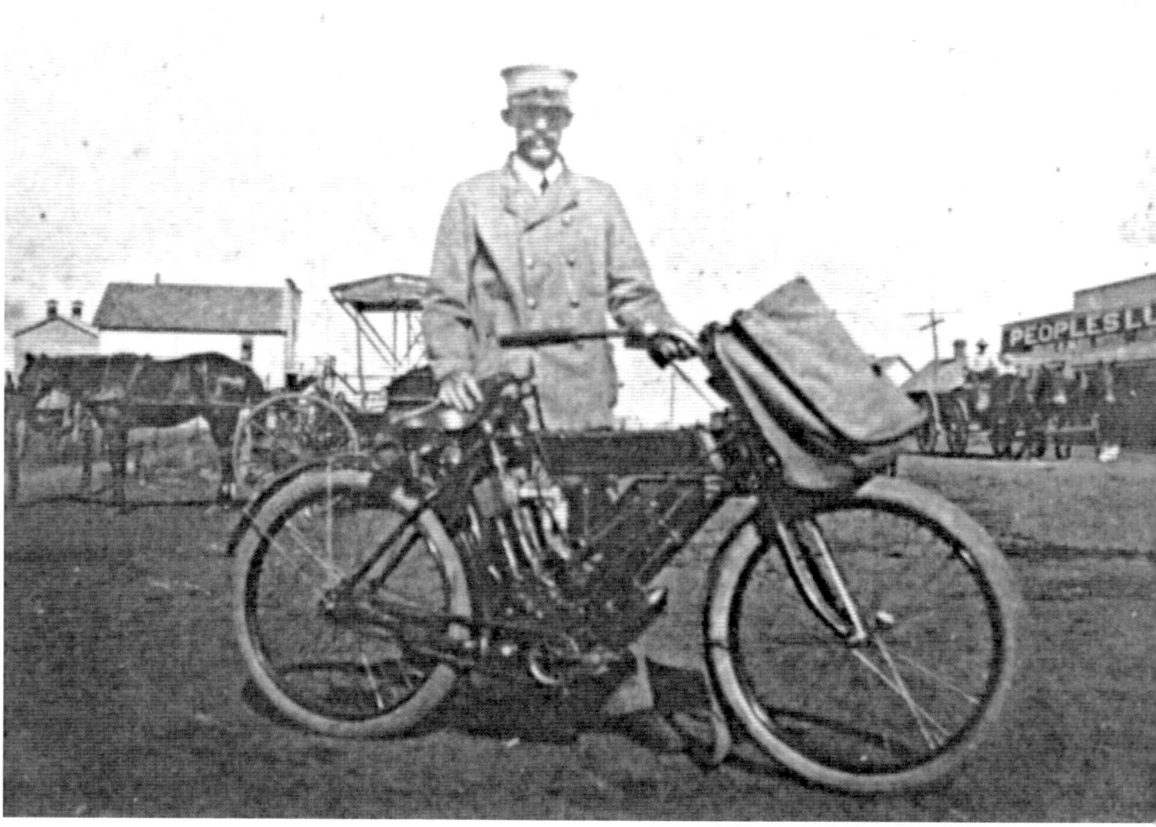

John L. Stubbs

John Stubbs did not depend only on the horse and buggy in 1900. He got around on his bike. An innovator, Stubbs was a printer and secretary for the town's newspaper, the *Grand Prairie Hustler*. In addition, he was the first mail carrier, and, when the first telephone was installed in town, he worked as the Southwestern Bell operator. The pay phone was installed in 1900 at Dr. Payne's Drugstore. Stubbs provided 24-hour service by sleeping in the store at night. When visiting, his brother George would assist him with duties as operator and with repairs. John Stubbs continued to work throughout the decades, retiring in 1956. (GPML.).

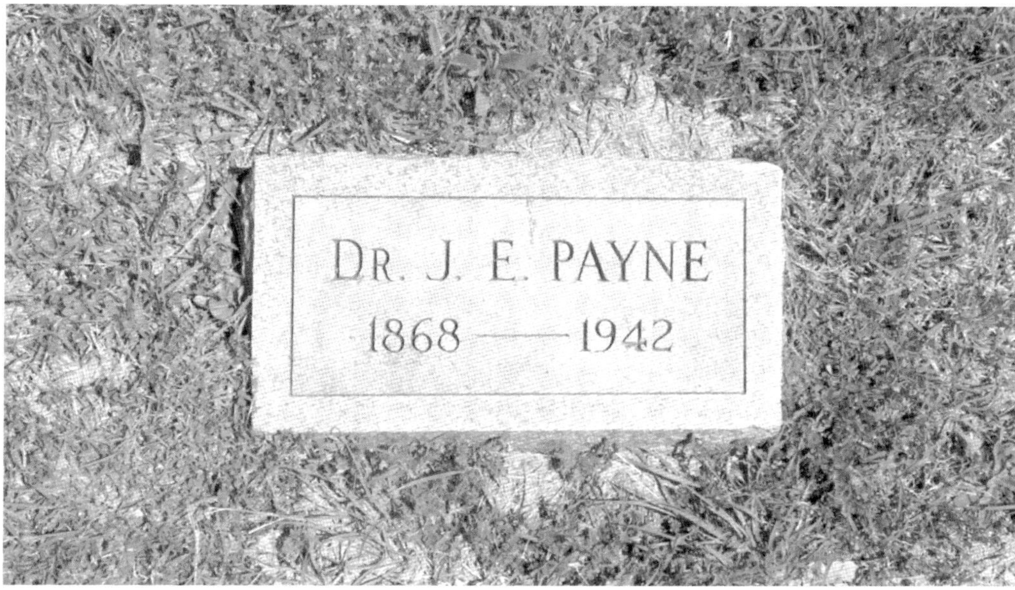

J.E. Payne

The *Grand Prairie Hustler*, the town's first newspaper, was owned by the Grand Prairie Publishing Company. Dr. J.E. Payne was the president, John L. Stubbs was the secretary, and W.P. Peed was the editor. The paper began in 1902 and ran until Monday, March 6, 1906. The full-sized newspaper was pretty progressive for a small town at that time. (Courtesy of Grand Prairie Genealogical Society.)

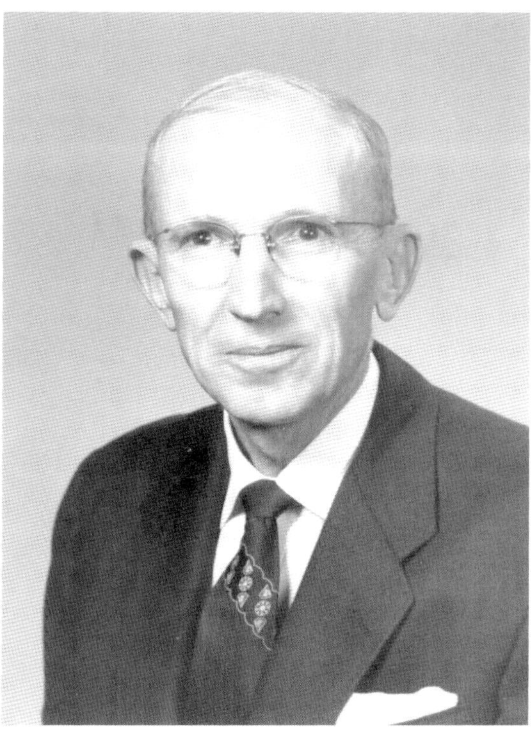

Dewey Millar

Millar Drug has been a Grand Prairie icon. It was opened in 1927 by pharmacist Dewey Millar and his wife, Ruby. They retired in 1950, but the establishment retained the Millar name for many years. The pharmacy closed long before the soda fountain, which grew into a restaurant.

Dewey Millar served the community beyond his work behind the counter. He was on the Grand Prairie Independent School board of trustees and the Dallas County School Board, and, in 1956, served as mayor pro tem. Millar was founder and charter president of the Grand Prairie Rotary Club, and recipient of Rotary's highest honor, the Paul Harris Fellow. Born in 1898, he died at the age of 95 in his Grand Prairie home. (GPML.)

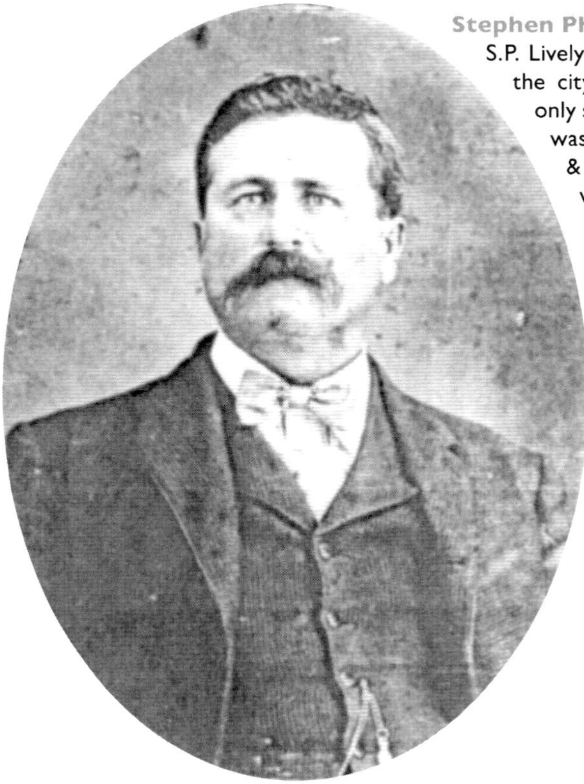

Stephen Phillip Lively

S.P. Lively was the first mayor of Grand Prairie after the city was incorporated in 1909. However, he only served for one year. A local businessman, he was the owner of a flour mill and the S.P. Lively & Sons Cotton Gin. He was born in 1862 and was married to Sarah Benton Lively. He died on his ranch near Mesquite in 1930. (GPML.)

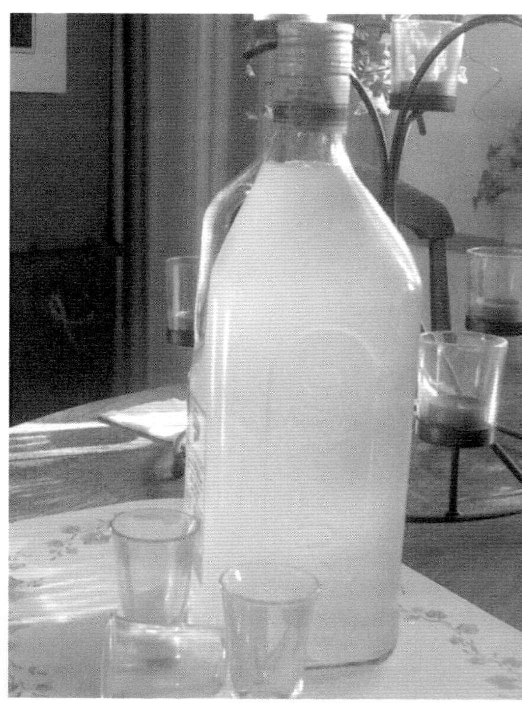

Cora Bell McPherson Megril

Cora Megril came to Grand Prairie in 1915 at the age of 50. For more than 30 years, she served the community. By 1920, Megril was president of the Texas State Women's Christian Temperance Union (WCTU). She worked to organize locally and statewide, serving as the state director of institutes and as chairman of the state board on education for the WCTU. She held a local institute at the First Presbyterian Church in 1935. The fight against alcohol was not the WTCU's only issue. It also spoke out against hasty World War I marriages and "bathing girl revues."

Megril was active in many endeavors. She was a founding member of the Grand Prairie Library and a charter member of the Grand Prairie PTA, and a member of the Grand Prairie Study Club and Grand Matron of Eastern Star. (Author photograph.)

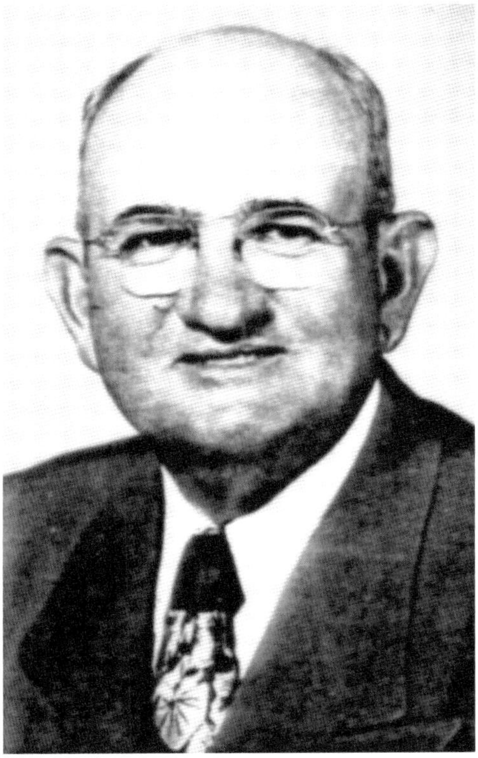

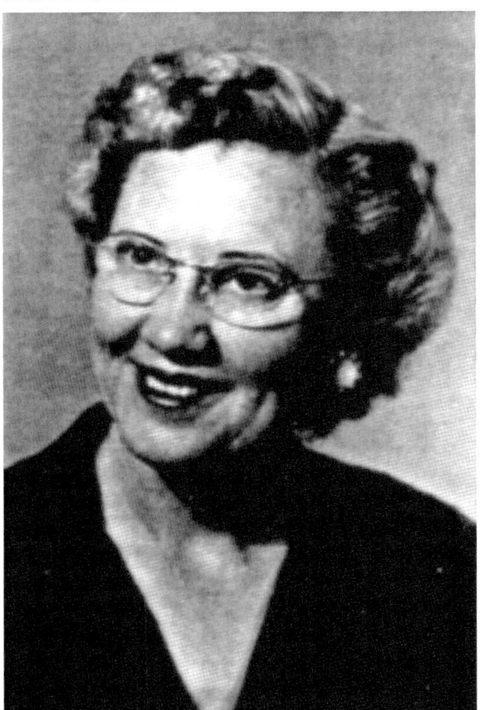

Lovel O. and Minnie Turner
L.O. Turner and his brother started in business together with a hardware store. Both men served as mayor of Grand Prairie and participated in many community activities. However, L.O. (top) seemed to have a quieter approach. He helped to start the first Boy Scout troop and served on the board for the First Methodist Church for 25 years. He served once as the director of the chamber of commerce, was an active Mason, and held a position on the school board. L.O. and his wife, Minnie (bottom), owned and operated the L.O. Turner Funeral Home, which was begun out of the back of the hardware store. He was also operator and director of the Southland Memorial Park cemetery for a time. (Both, GPML.)

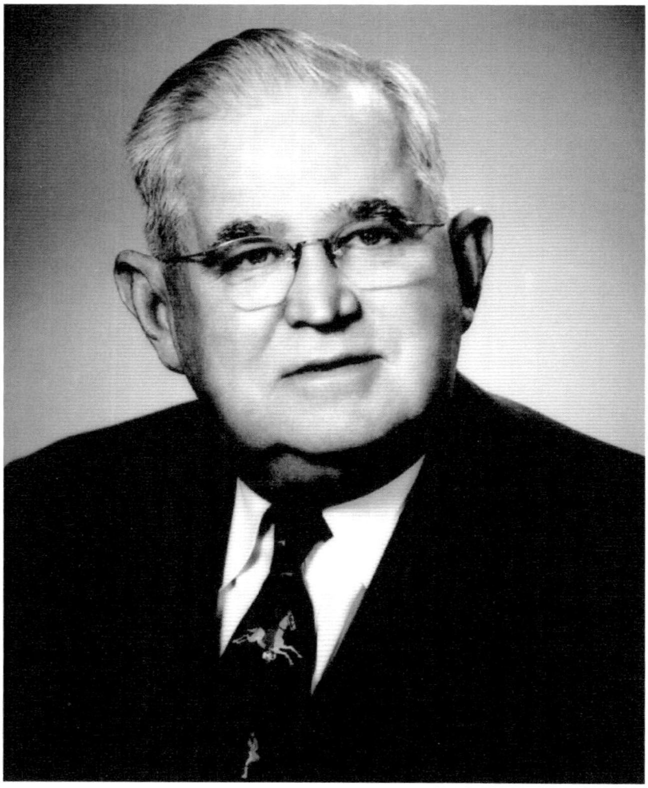

George Henry Turner

G.H. Turner had a more flamboyant approach than his brother L.O. He did things in a big way. As bank president, he hosted the largest Easter-egg hunt in the park that now bears his name. G.H. owned an insurance agency and a real-estate agency, and was also president of Grand Prairie State Bank. G.H. and L.O. were also owners of Turner Furniture (below). G.H. holds the distinction of being mayor for one of the longest periods on record, from 1923 to 1949, with the exception of one term (1935–1937). He was a member of countless organizations and was a colonel in the Confederate Air Corps. Turner promoted growth in every facet of the city.

The large collection of his scrapbooks boasts of his accomplishments and involvement. A seeker of unity, he once boasted that, during his long term in office, everything the city achieved was done through unanimous decision. (Left, GPML; below, courtesy of Angela Sutton Giessner and Sutton-Giessner family.)

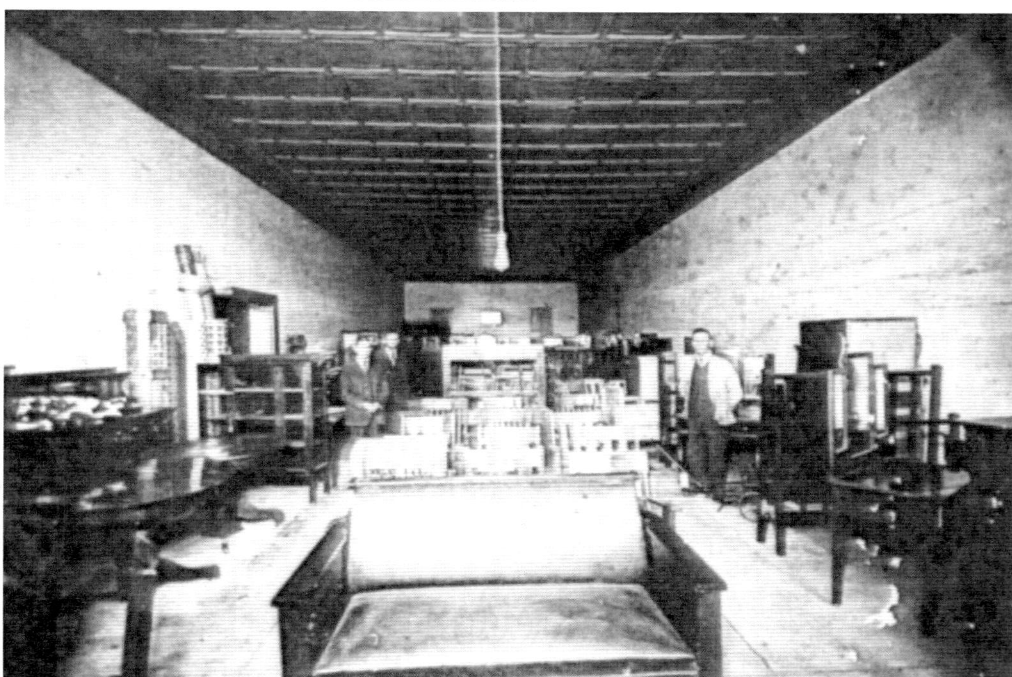

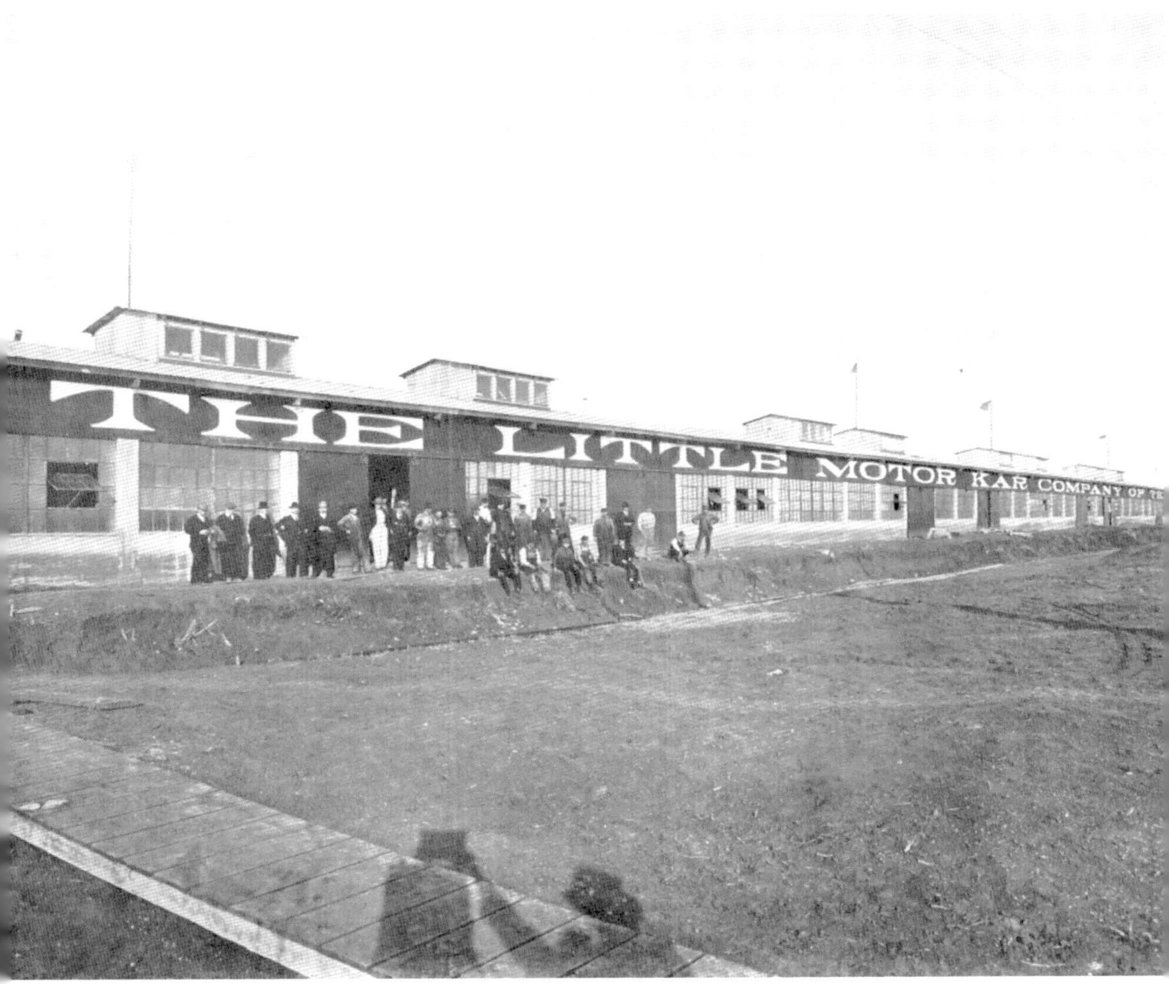

William S. Livezey

Born in 1889, William Livezey, president of the Little Motor Kar Company, wanted to produce sports cars and touring cars that were affordable to the average citizen. However, Livezey, along with R.L. McCoy and George Stricker, were arrested for mail fraud. Allegations of the misuse of funds for as much as $80,000 were dropped by the state for lack of evidence, perhaps related to missing stock transactions. However, in 1921, the charges for misuse of the mail earned Livezey five years at Leavenworth.

Despite allegations of embezzlement from the company, a large number of friends and stockholders wrote letters requesting a pardon for William Livezey. The Little Motor Kar Company did produce small trucks at the plant for a short period, but it was bankrupt by 1928. (GPML.)

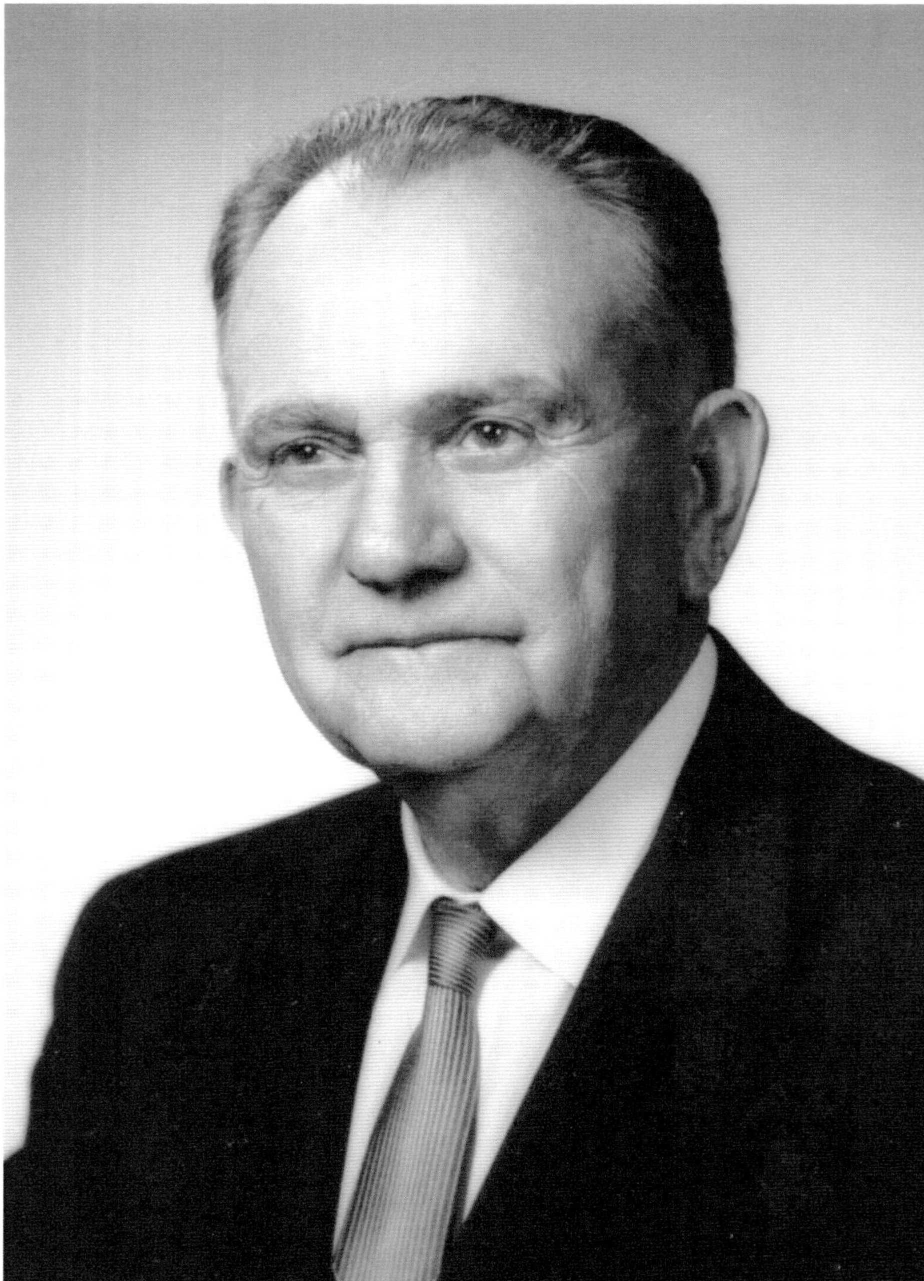

Dr. H.H. Milling

Considered to be one of the biggest-hearted men in town, Dr. Milling was a rancher, a member and past president of the Grand Prairie Chamber of Commerce, and owner of the Milling Sanatorium. He helped organize a big barbecue for the sponsors, managers, and boys of the local baseball league. He also hosted a barbecue for a meeting of the Rock Creek Barbecue Club at his sanatorium the year he was club president. (GPML.)

CHAPTER TWO

Transportation, the Military, and Religion

When the Jordan family settled in the area, they made sure there was a stagecoach depot. Alexander Dechman saw to it that horses and buggies were not the only mode of transportation. He used part of the land he acquired to negotiate a railroad depot, assuring modern transportation for the future town. The interurban was an electric train that ferried individuals to Dallas and Fort Worth before the use of buses. Dr. Horace Copeland bought the first car in 1910, ushering modern transportation into the city.

The aviation industry had the greatest impact on Grand Prairie. The influence of Orville and Wilbur Wright was felt across the nation, including in Grand Prairie. The Wright Aeronautical Corporation merged with Glenn Curtiss's Aeroplane and Motor Company to form Curtiss-Wright. The Curtiss-Wright Flying Service Corporation out of New York purchased 275 acres of property just one mile from Grand Prairie. Mayor G.H. Turner was present, along with dignitaries from both Dallas and Fort Worth, for the ground breaking of the new airport in late 1929. By mid-April 1930, the Curtiss-Wright Airport was open for business.

The airport was intended for advanced training of pilots. The highlight of its opening ceremony was Margaret Thomas, 18, winning a race against veteran pilots. Airplanes, demonstrations, and stunts drew a crowd of 10,000 people for the dedication weekend.

The Curtiss-Wright Flying School was not the success that was hoped. By 1940, Lou Foote had purchased the airport and founded the Lou Foote Flying School. Eventually, the airport fell under the control of the US Navy.

The military, a big part of Grand Prairie's aviation industry, served the town well until the next century. And Grand Prairie citizens were a big part of military history as well. The first Selective Service draftee from Grand Prairie was W.R. Tullos. John Tull served as a fire control technician in the Pacific during World War II, and served again during the Korean conflict. Gen. Mike Mosley served in the US Air Force for more than 30 years.

The men and women who participated in the community also served the many churches. First Methodist and First Baptist Churches have been around since 1880, but it was the West Fork United Presbyterian Church that first opened in Grand Prairie, in 1857, and is still attended today. Earl Odom pastored Calvary Baptist for nearly 50 years, and his associate pastor, Emil Balliet, served for around 35 years. Balliet is now the police department chaplain. Ernest Duncan spent 40 years at Fairview Baptist Church. Although Methodist pastors were often moved by the denomination, Corky McGee served 18 years at Inglewood Methodist Church.

The spiritual development of individuals is important in preserving integrity and character, traits that are needed in leaders. Innovation, dedication, defense, and faith have existed hand in hand with the citizens of Grand Prairie.

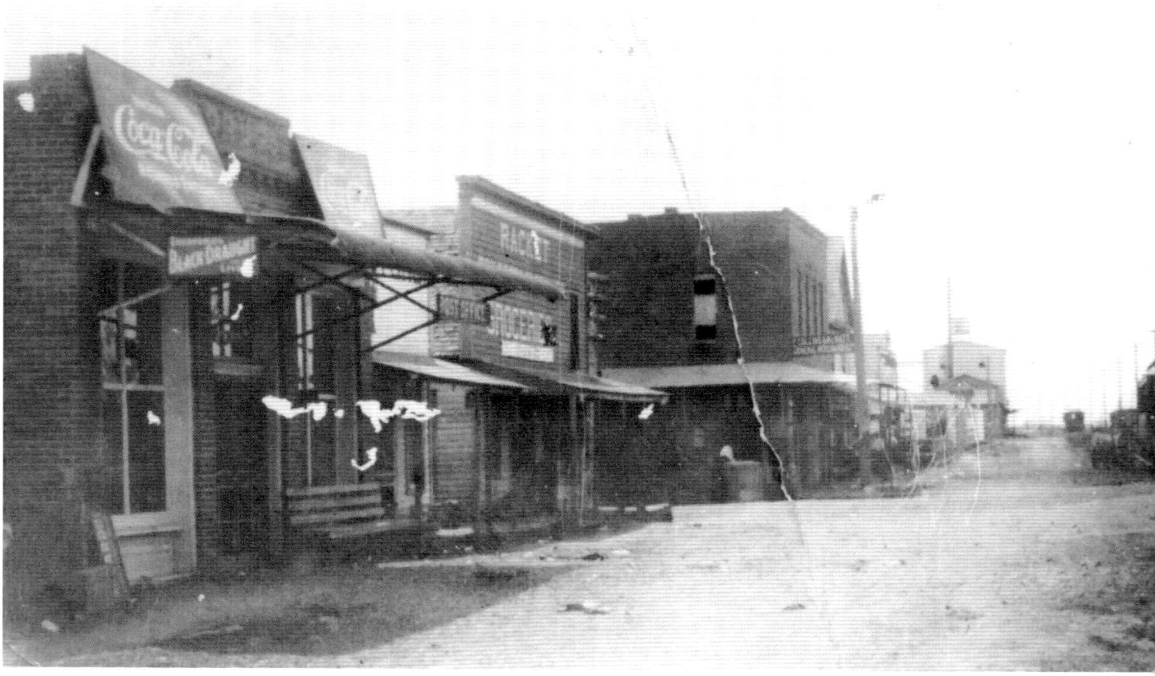

William R. Tullos

The son of S.S. and Katie Tullos, William Tullos served with the 359th Infantry, 90th Division in the Headquarters Company in the US Army. His company was involved with the Army's occupation of Germany during World War I. Tullos entered the service in 1917, and was discharged in 1919.

Shadrac Sylvester "S.S." Tullos studied medicine and began his work as a druggist in Mississippi. Arriving in Grand Prairie in 1893, he worked in a general store. It was not long before he dealt exclusively with the drug department, eventually purchasing the City Drug Store. According to First Methodist's history book, *125 Years in the Heart of the City*, he would hire ladies from churches to work during the Christmas season and then donate 10 percent of their cash sales to their churches. In 1901, he was appointed postmaster (the post office was inside the grocery store pictured here). S.S. Tullos also served on the Grand Prairie School Board and was a member of the Masons, Knights of Pythias, and the Modern Woodmen of America. (GPML.)

Airport Terminal

The influence of early aviation was felt in Grand Prairie. The accomplishments of men like William Boeing and Chance Vought inspired others, including Curtis Wright, Al Graff, and Robert McCullough. The Curtiss-Wright Airport opened for advanced pilot training in mid-April 930. It was only 10 years before the airport was bought by Lou Foote to open a flying school. Eventually, the Navy took charge, and the facility was moved to a naval base closer to Dallas.

But that was not the end of an airport in Grand Prairie. Today, the airport is a few miles southwest of its original site. It has been used by Aerospatiale for helicopter production processes. Hosting smaller private aircraft, the facility upgraded several years ago to handle more traffic. It a so facilitates some operations for the medical helicopter transportation in the Dallas–Fort Worth Metroplex. (CofC.)

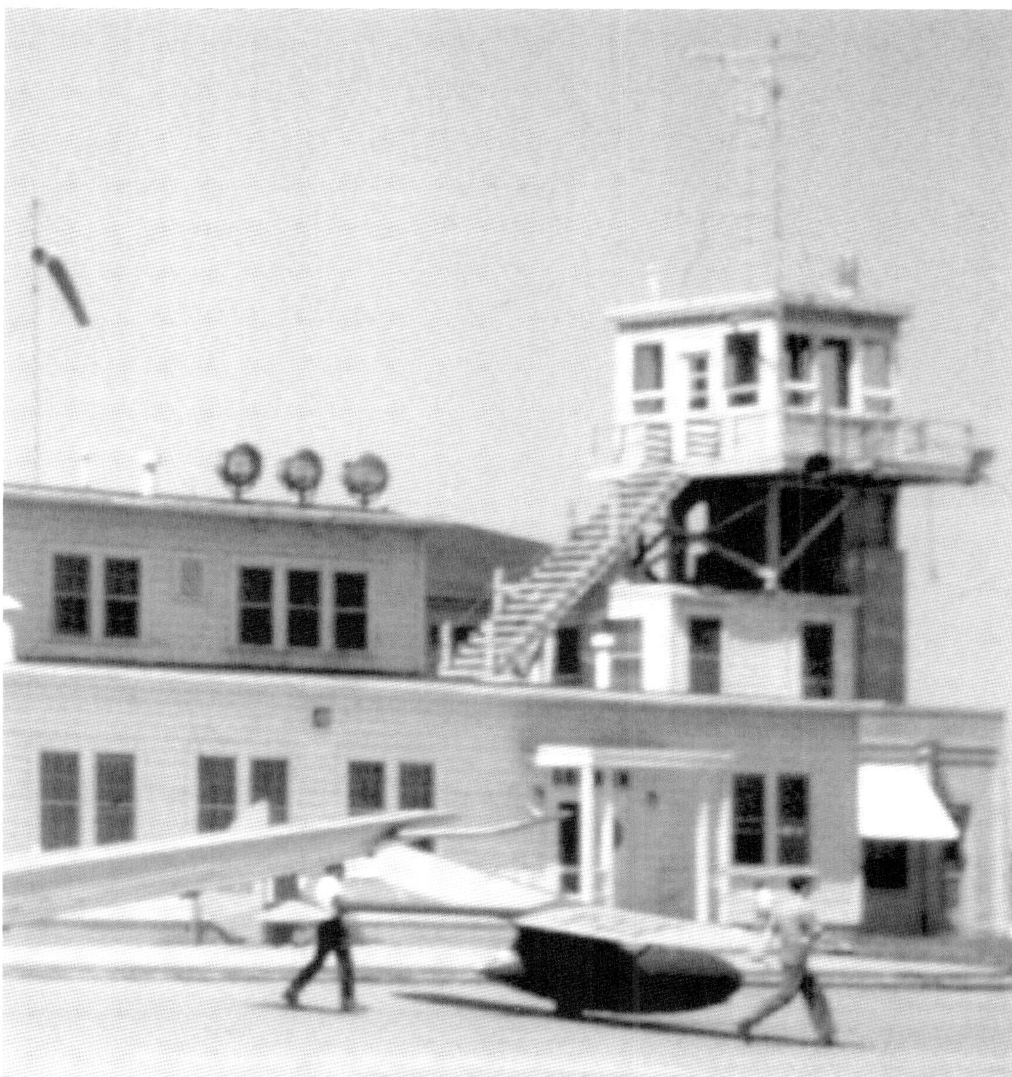

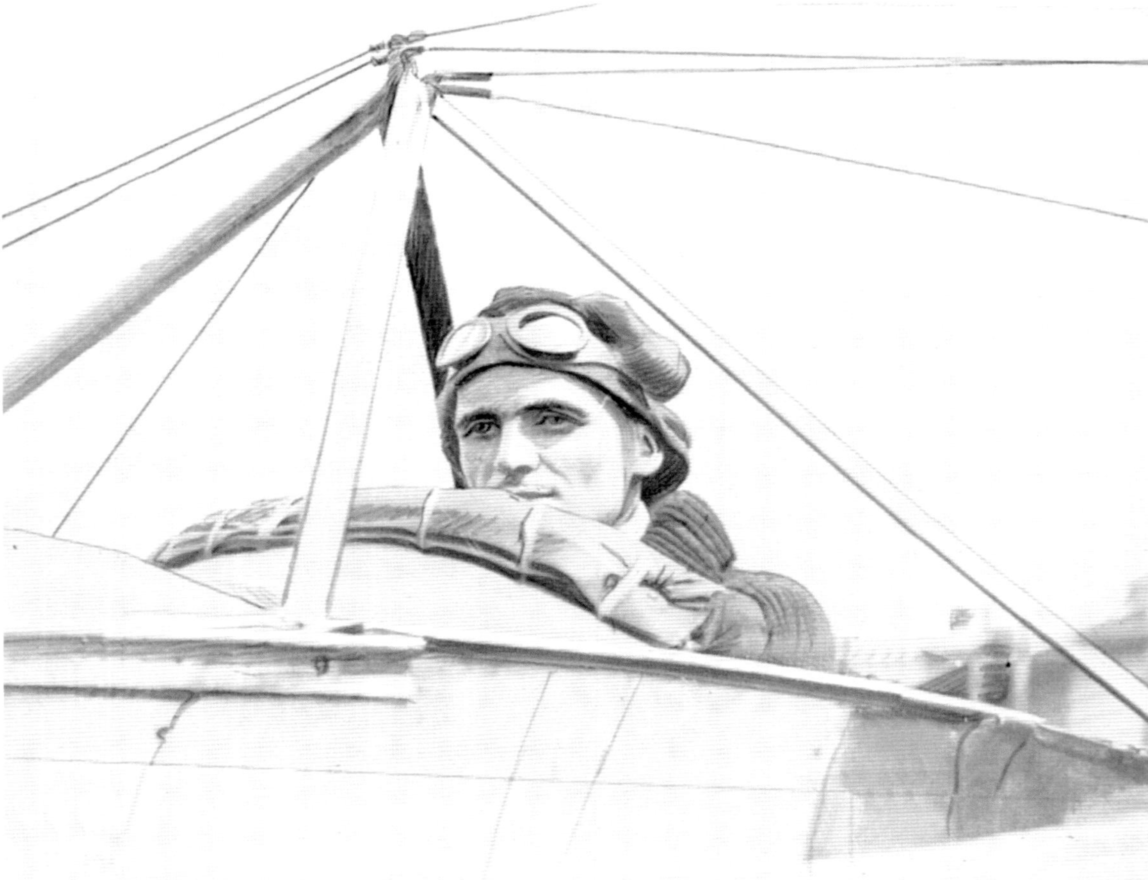

Chance Milton Vought

Aviation has played a major role in Grand Prairie. Several men from outside the city played a big part in its growth, including four individuals who merged their efforts in the early 1960s to form the aerospace company Ling-Temco-Vought (LTV). Although James Ling, Robert McCullough, his partner, H.L. Howard, and Chance Vought did not all reside within the city limits, their influence was felt in Grand Prairie for decades.

Chance Vought is probably the most famous of the Ling-Temco-Vought founders. Born in 1890, this aviation pioneer learned to fly in a Wright brothers biplane in 1912 with the FAI (Fédération Aéronautique Internationale, or World Air Sports Federation), with license No. 156. As an aeronautical engineer, his first solo design proved to be very successful. By 1916, he was designing for the Wright-Martin Company. By mid-1917, in a move to please his bride, Ena Lewis, Vought gave up flying and concentrated on manufacturing aircraft. Backed by his father-in-law, the Lewis and Vought Corporation was born. Chance Vought served as president and chairman of the board. A true pioneer, his influence touched the industry, from biplane trainers used by the British, to the aerospace industry at LTV in Grand Prairie. (GPML.)

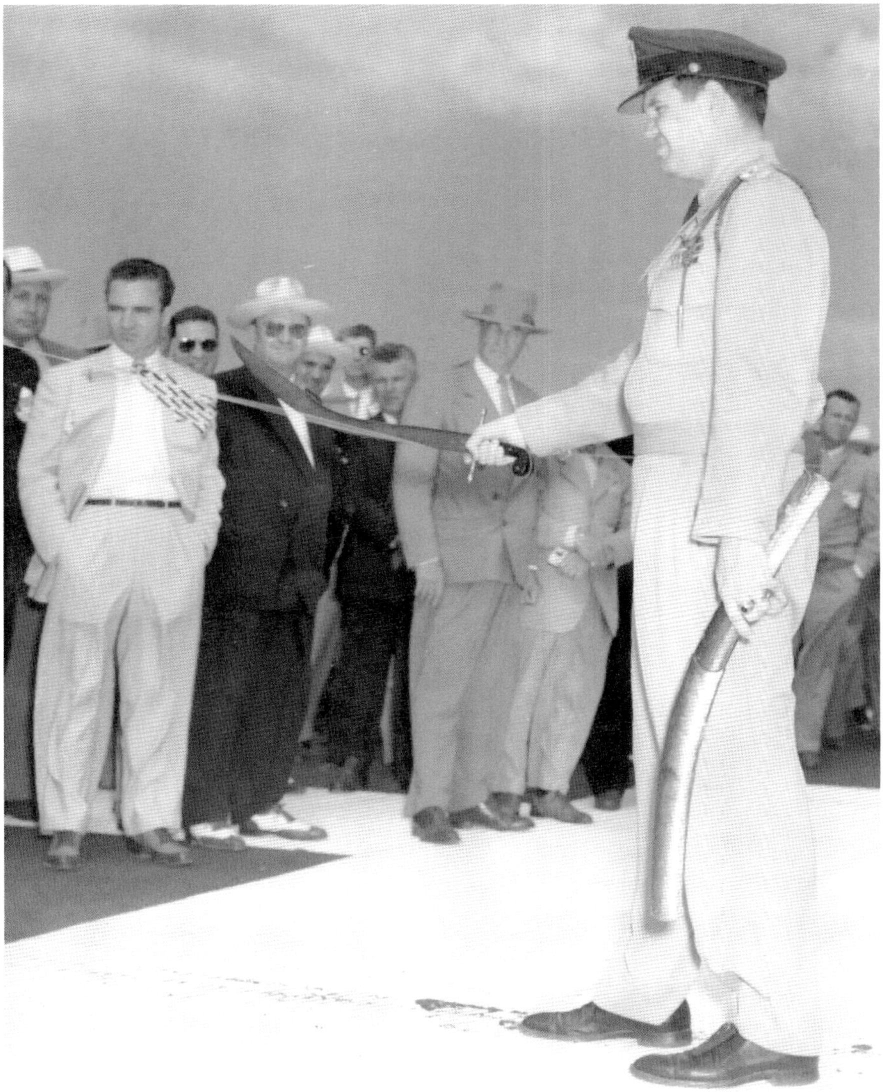

Ling and TEMCO

James Ling became a master electrician through his training with the US Navy, but he did not graduate from high school. Born in 1922, his childhood was less than appealing. His mother died at an early age, and his father was said to have murdered a fellow railroad worker. In 1956, after forming Ling Electric Co., he purchased L.M. Electronics in Dallas. Ling's entrepreneurial spirit led him to acquisitions that would eventually form LTV, which he would head until leaving in 1975.

Robert McCullough and partner H.L. Howard's company, Texas Engineering & Manufacturing Company (TEMCO), began in 1952. McCullough, a Scottish immigrant, had a successful career in aviation. He began working in aircraft before coming to the United States in 1927. Atlantic Aircraft Corporation eventually became North American Aviation (NAA), where McCullough advanced to factory manager. After taking a position as general manager of Convair in Tennessee, he eventually managed its Grand Prairie location, which closed at the end of World War II. He and H.L. Howard formed Texas Engineering & Manufacturing, which would merge with Ling-Altec and become Ling Temco. (CofC.)

John Tull

Ordinary citizen John Tull was part of a blended family. A Sunday-school hayride was his first date with Virginia, who became his wife of 63 years. He served as a Navy fire control technician during World War II aboard the USS *Iowa*, which saw a lot of action and received the latest equipment after being damaged in a typhoon. During the war, the ship transported Pres. Franklin Roosevelt, shot down a kamikaze pilot, and was off the coast of Japan when the atomic bombs were dropped. John was present when the *Iowa* was alongside the USS *Missouri* when Gen. Douglas MacArthur signed the peace treaty with Japan. Tull was also called up during the Korean conflict.

Tull worked 19 years as a milling machine operator and finished his 42 years in aerospace as a tooling liaison. He enjoyed identifying and solving quality-control, engineering, and tooling problems. (Author photograph.)

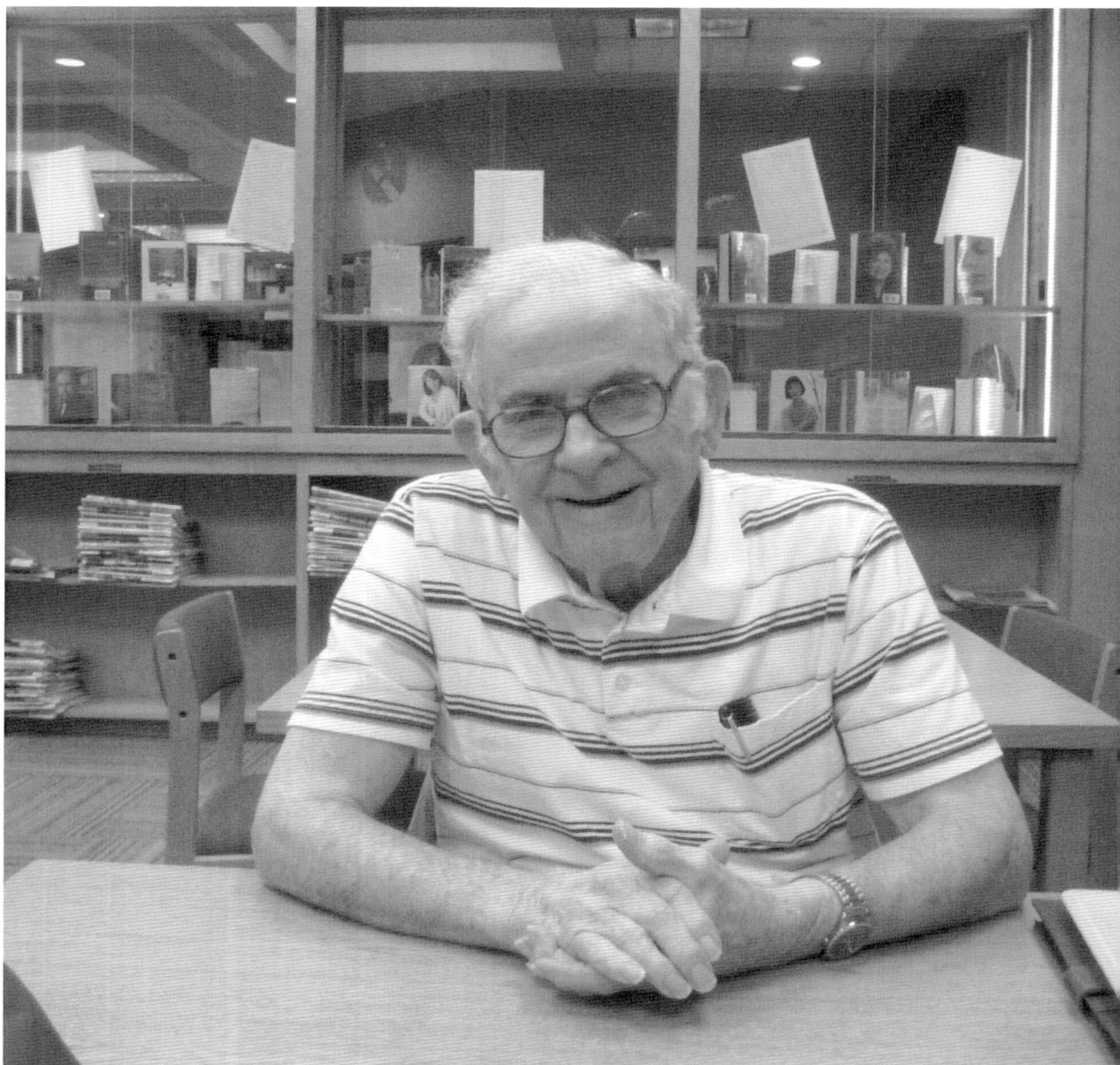

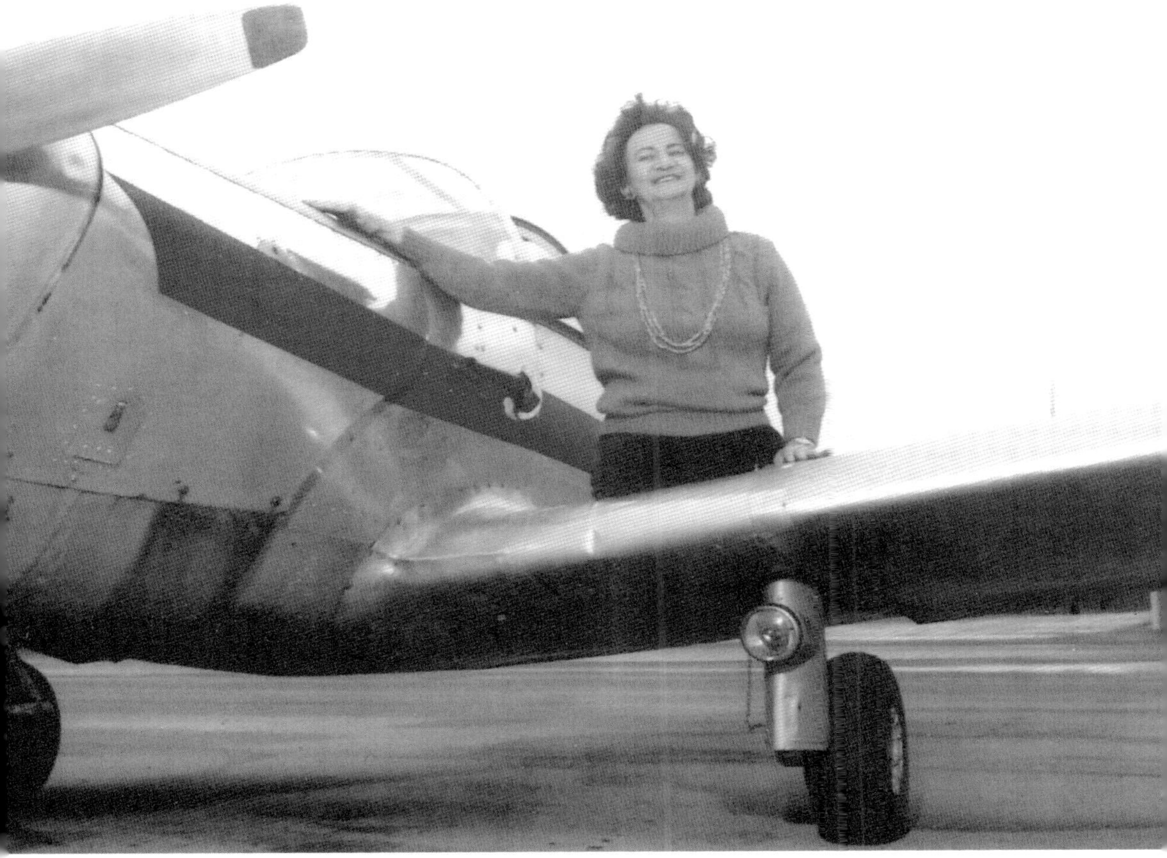

Alverna Williams

Alverna Williams settled in Grand Prairie with her husband. Having lost both legs at the age of one, her spirit was not daunted. She learned to do anything she wanted with her hands, including tap dancing and wearing heels. Prosthetic legs were too painful for her. A 1997 article in the *Herald Journal* reported that Williams, as a child, would respond to adults commenting on her not having legs by saying, "I have legs. They're in the closet."

Williams took on every challenge. She performed in the circus, skied in Colorado, and learned to drive a motorcycle, swim, cook, and clean. She also raised children. Her spirit finally got her a permit at the age of 16. When she was ready to get her license, she had to take on the FAA. She paved the way by becoming the first disabled person to receive a pilot's license. (Courtesy of the Amputee Coalition.)

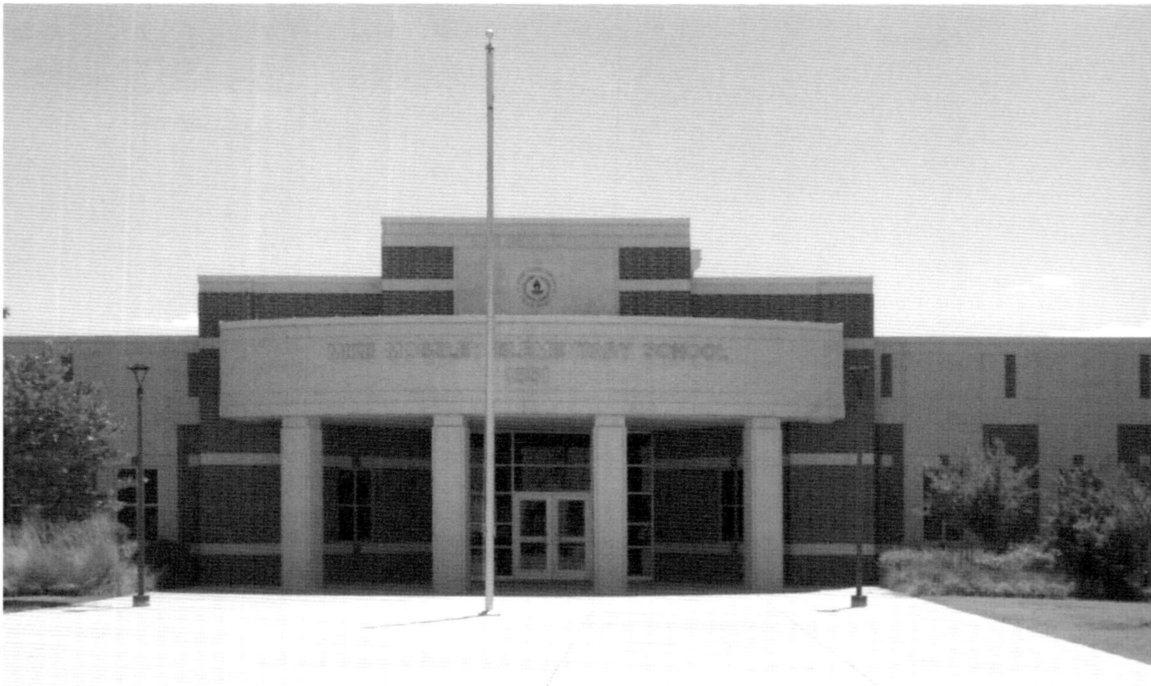

T. Michael Mosely

General Mosley had an outstanding military career in the US Air Force. He graduated from Texas A&M with a master's degree in political science in 1972, and by 2003, had reached the rank of general. By 2005, he was the chief of staff for the Air Force. Among his many commendations were the Distinguished Service Medal, Meritorious Service Medal with three oak leaf clusters, and a Joint Service Commendation Medal. The City of Grand Prairie named an elementary school after the four-star general (pictured).

However, this distinguished career has a blemish. General Mosley, who had served since 1971, was asked to resign in August 2008 in the wake of Air Force scandals. After he officially resigned and retired, the investigation was completed and he received a Letter of Admonishment in Retirement. (Author photograph.)

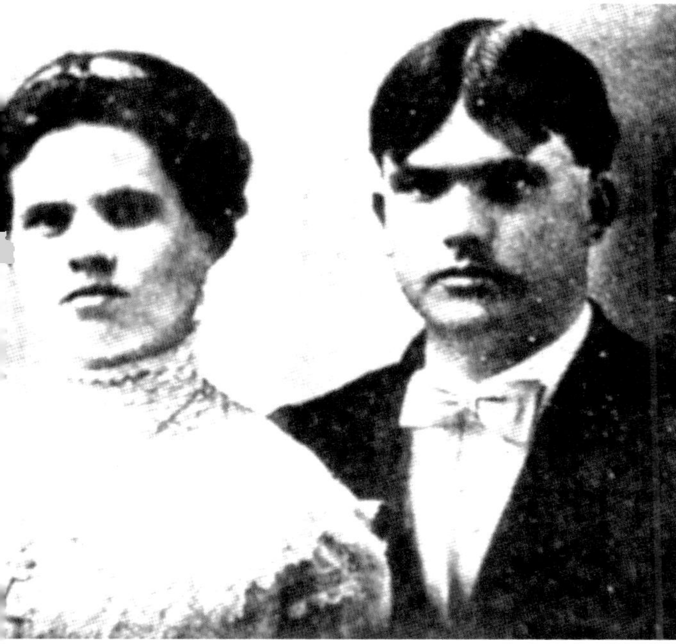

Sam and Lottie Sanders

When interviewed by the *Grand Prairie Daily News* concerning their 50th wedding anniversary, Sam and Lottie Sanders humbly admitted that their 1909 wedding was "the social event of the year." Sam Sanders and Lottie Witherspoon (left) were the first couple to have a church wedding in Grand Prairie. The ceremony held at the First Methodist Church, was attended by most of the 300 residents of Grand Prairie. Lottie met Sam during a visit to her cousin in 1908. Sam had come to Grand Prairie from Denton County in response to an advertisement for a barber. They are pictured below with family celebrating their 50th anniversary. (Left, GPML; below, courtesy of Susie Garrett.)

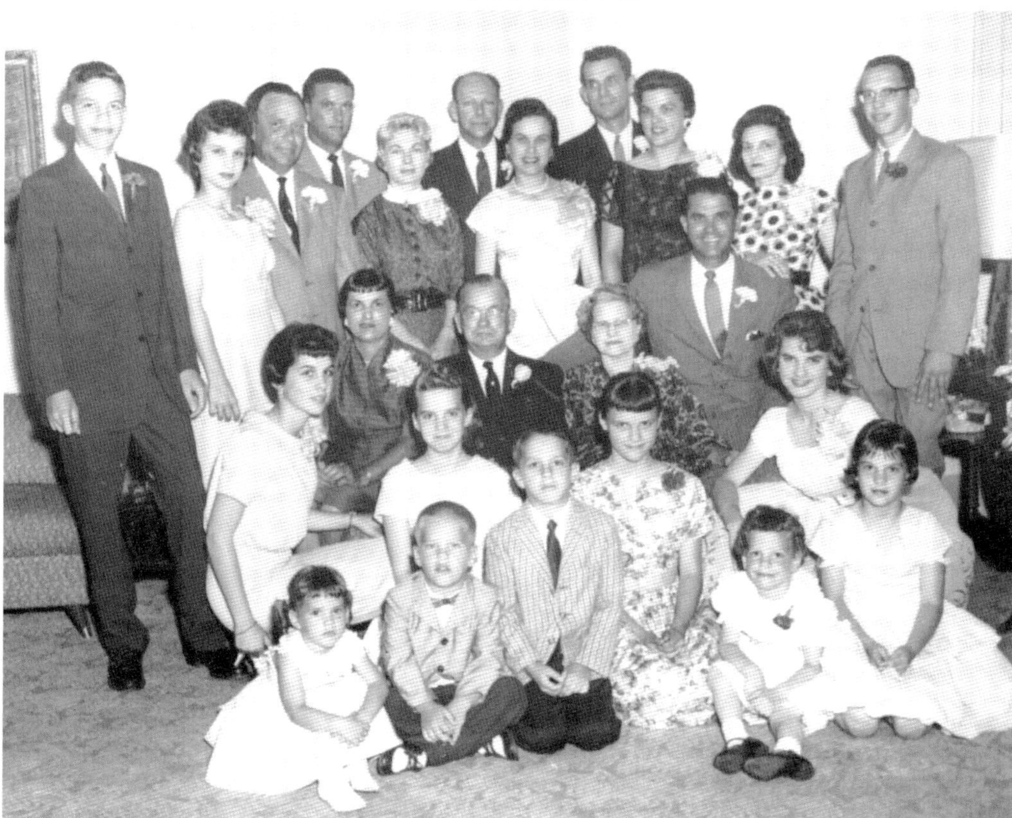

Dr. and Mrs. Earl K. Oldham

The New Testament Baptist Church was begun on March 31, 1935, with only 24 people. They met in a small building on the corner of Northwest Fourth and Church Streets. The first pastor, Woodson Mims, grew the little congregation to over 100 people within a year, and they opted to change the name to Calvary Baptist Church. Earl K. Oldham was a seminary student in Lubbock, Texas, when he was called to pastor Calvary Baptist in 1945. He stayed for another 45 years. In the 1950s, congregants began to attend the Silver State Youth summer camp in Colorado (below). By 1990, the church had grown to over 700 people, and Pastor Oldham had become president of Arlington Baptist College, the board of directors for Arlington Baptist College, and Minnetonka Christian Camp. (Both, courtesy of Calvary Baptist Church.)

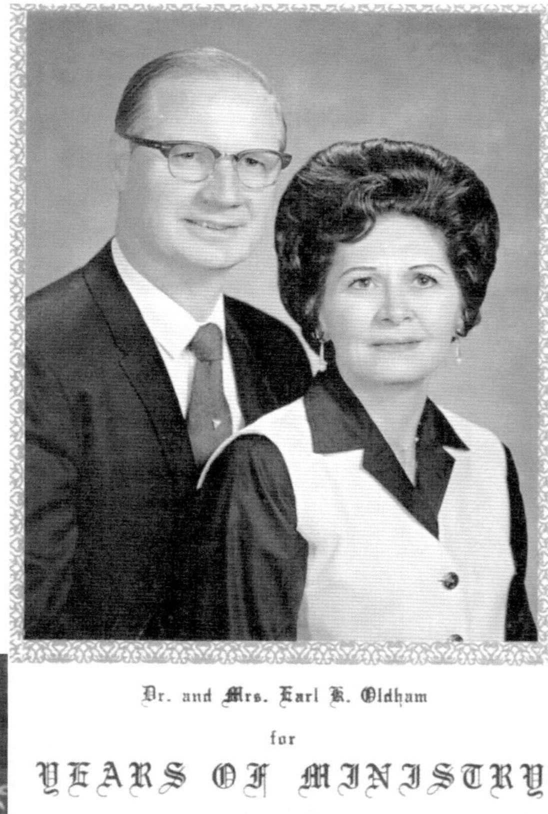

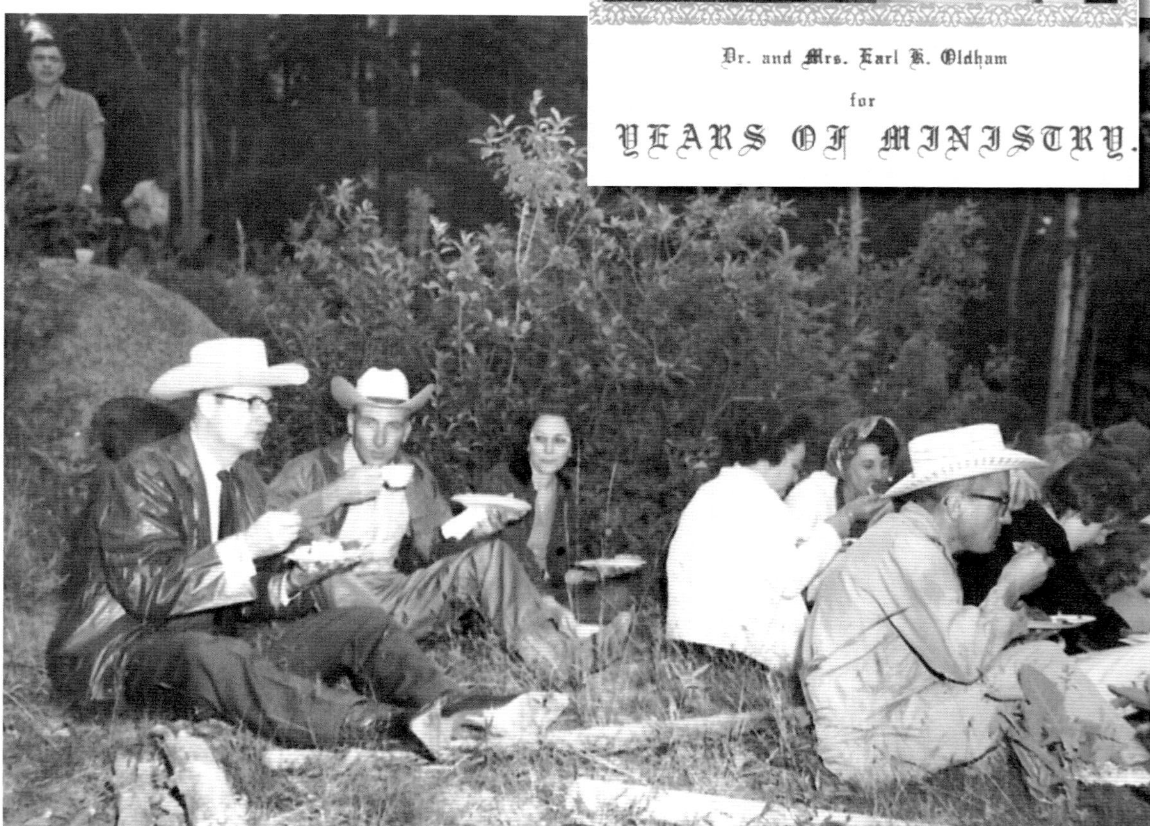

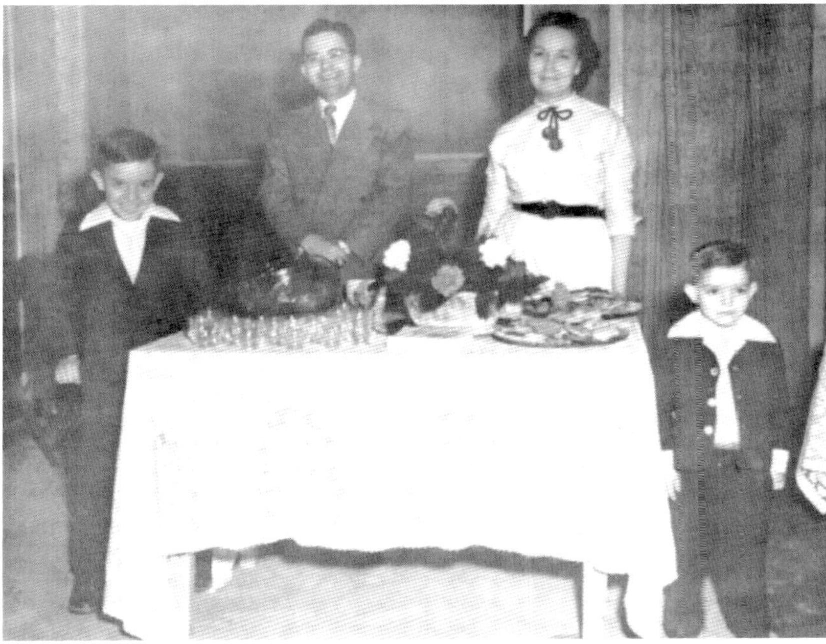

John Allen

Indian Hills Baptist Church was established in 1953 as a mission church through First Baptist, the Dallas Baptist Association, and the Baptist General Convention of Texas. By 1954, the congregation (below) had called John Allen (pictured above with his family) to come and serve as the first pastor. By the following year, the church had grown to 200 members and took ownership as a stand-alone church. John Allen served as pastor for 24 years. Other pastors then filled the position until Doug Simon arrived. He recently retired, having served as pastor for 27 years. (Both, courtesy of Indian Hills Baptist Church.)

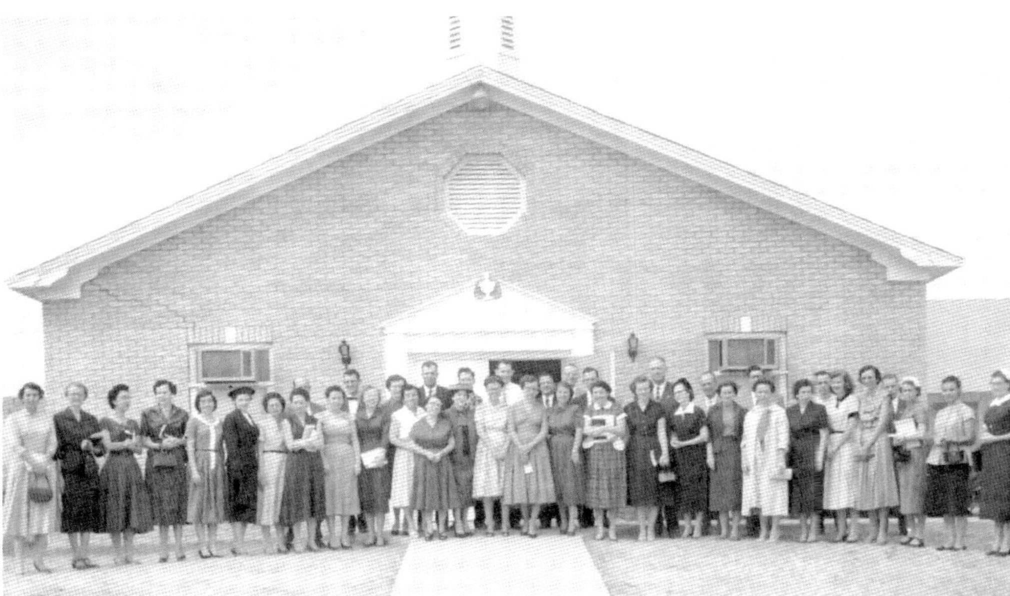

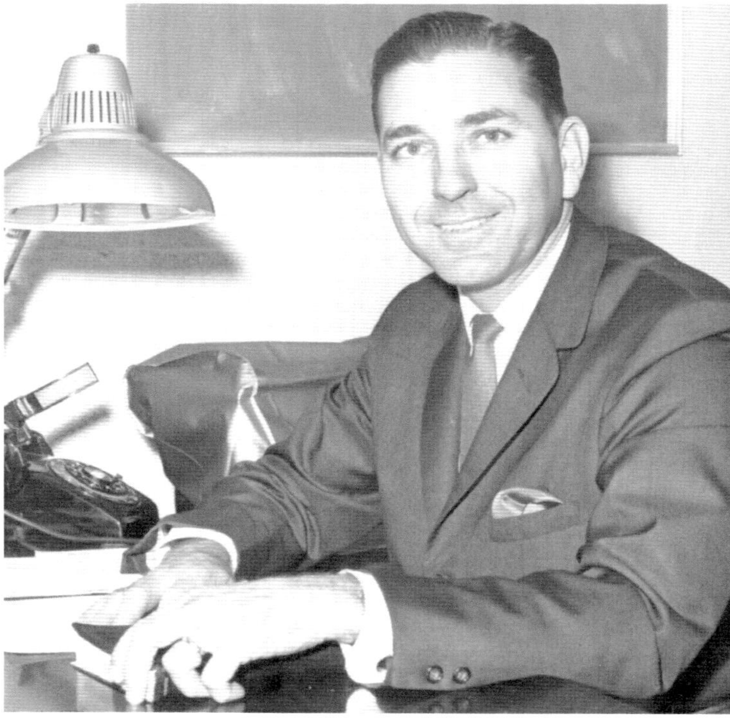

Ernest Duncan

Dr. Duncan (above) was pastor at Fairview Baptist Church (below) for 40 years, beginning in 1952. He had a heart for people. Because of this, Matthew Road Baptist grew out of one of Fairview's missions. Perhaps one of the greatest compliments a pastor can receive are the kinds words of another pastor. Pastor Carl McGee from Inglewood Methodist said, "Ernest Duncan was the most gracious, kind pastor you could ever have." (Both, courtesy of Fairview Baptist Church.)

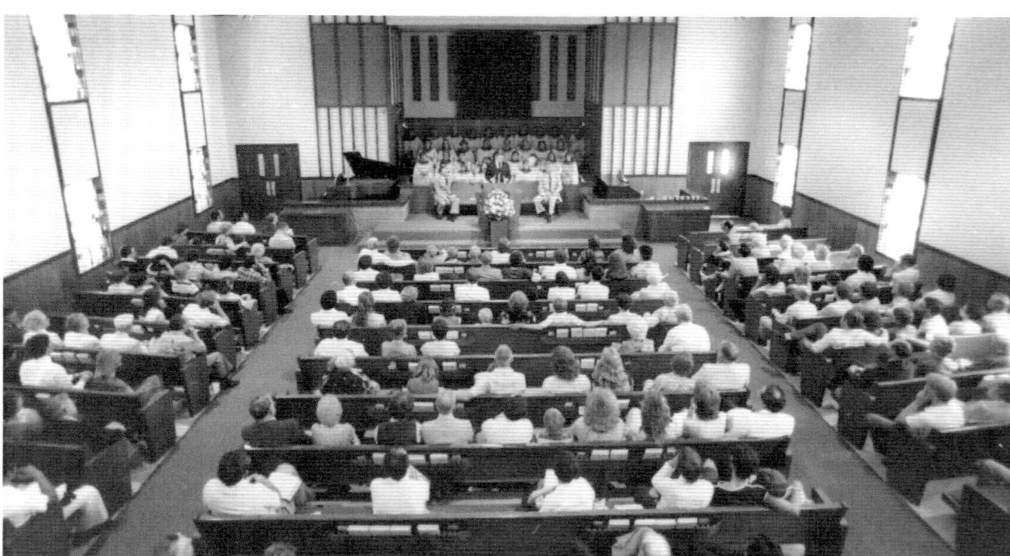

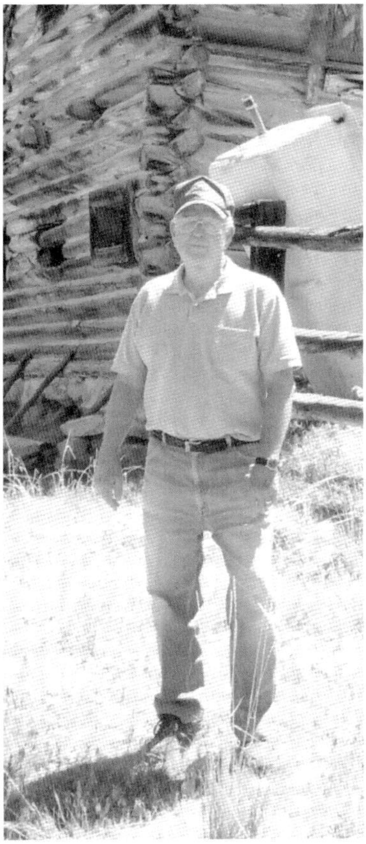

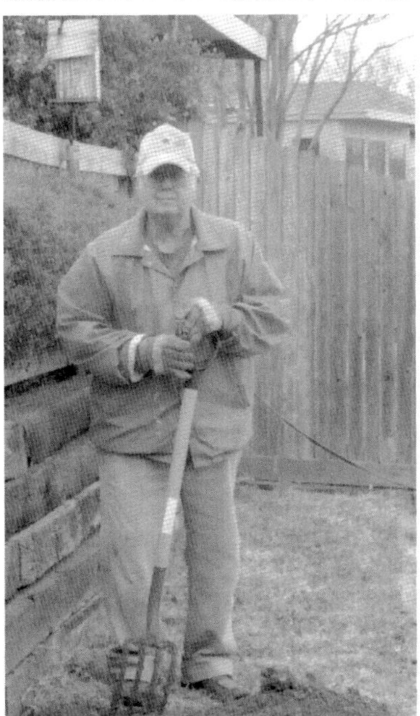

Carl Marshall McGee

Dr. "Corky" McGee was pastor at Inglewood United Methodist Church for 18 years. Married to his wife, Barbara, since 1956, he began attending the Methodist church after they met. Dr. McGee served in some small churches before coming to Grand Prairie in 1971. His church had mostly young and active adults. Mayor Bill Bowles, one of the church leaders, exerted his influence, as members were politically active in the community. McGee was involved in Kiwanis and the Ministerial Alliance. After their Ministerial Alliance evening meetings, he and First Methodist pastor Jim Garrett would often head over to the ballpark for Rangers games.

After leaving Inglewood, McGee was pastor for Lover's Lane United Methodist Church in Dallas. In recent years, Inglewood and Trailwood United Methodist Churches have merged into one church, simply called The Woods. (Both, courtesy of Carl McGee.)

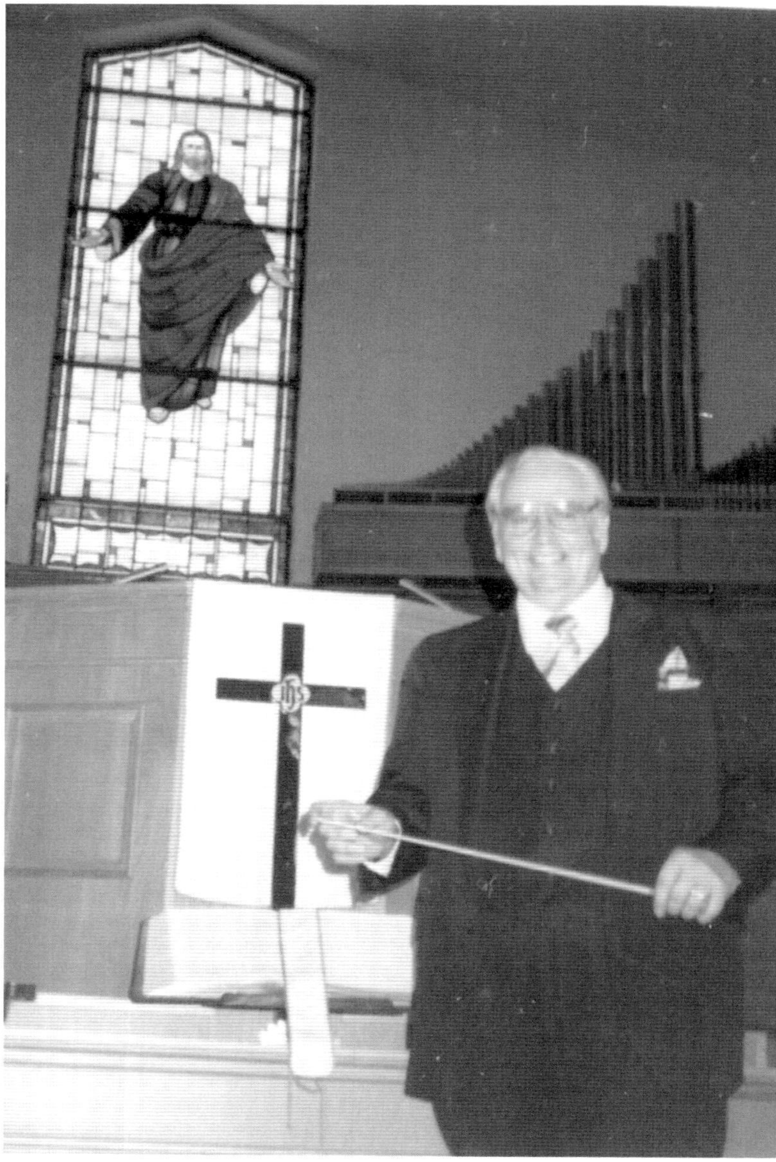

Earl Tom Keel

Keel, the son of an opera singer, left a legacy of music to more than three decades of students. He was the director of music and director of fine arts for the Grand Prairie Independent School District. He also filled the hearts of the members of First Methodist Church with worship as their minister of music for 30 years. He was known throughout the city as "Mr. Music." The theater at South Grand Prairie High School is named for him.

After Keel's retirement, he became the first dean for the fine arts department at Dallas Baptist University. His influence in music was widespread. He established the Grand Prairie High Capers, started the Texas Choral Director Association, and was awarded Outstanding Teacher of Texas for 1958. His great influence produced professional singers, movie actors, and a multitude of business professionals. (Courtesy of First United Methodist Church.)

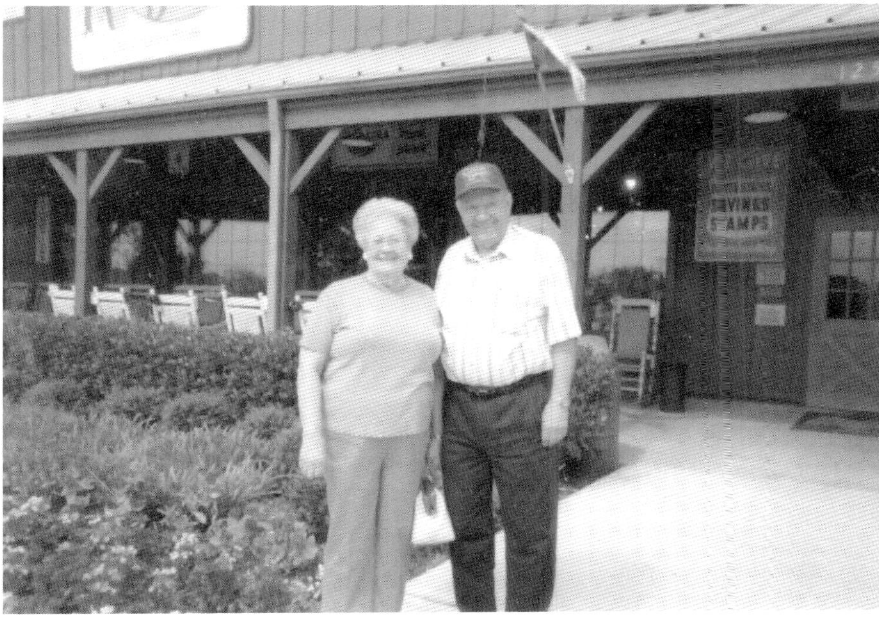

Helen and Cecil Bartel

A revival that swept across the country and was a major influence in California did not pass Grand Prairie without leaving its mark. Since many unconventional individuals needed discipleship, several families in the community, like the Bartels, Swains, Perkins, and Reeves, rose up to meet the need. A coffee shop, True Vine, was established downtown with the express purpose of ministering to this group. James Ryles received his salvation through the True Vine and went on to become a pastor and author. It was from this revival that Grand Prairie Bible Church was born. Pictured below from left to right are Earl and Louise Swain and Cecil and Helen Bartel. (Both, courtesy of Helen Bartel.)

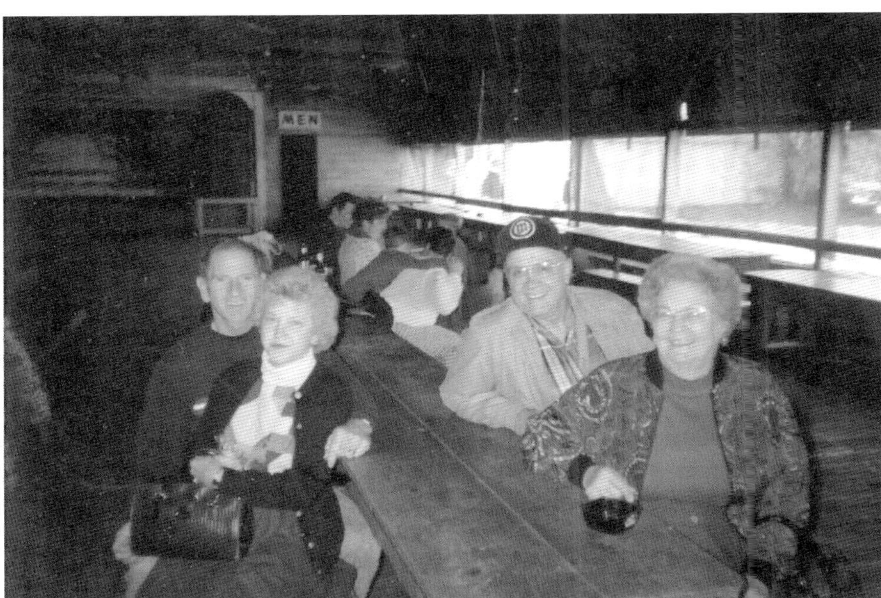

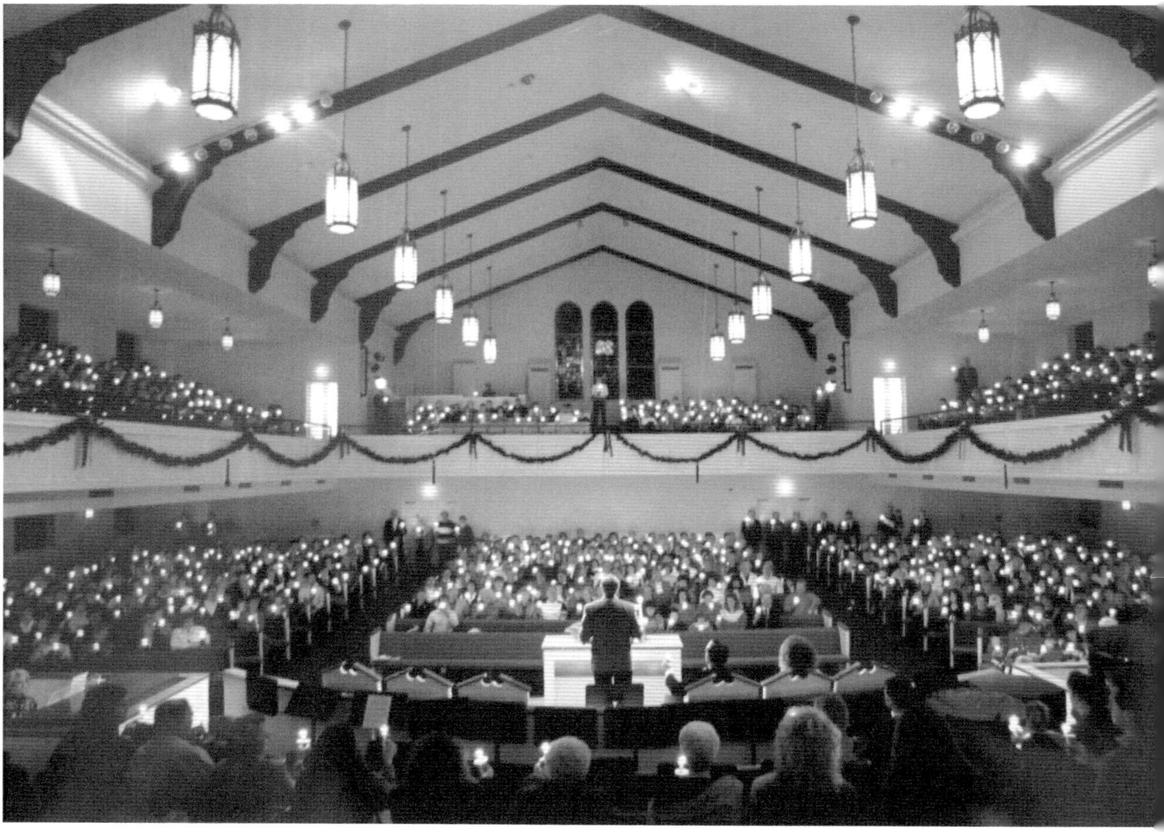

Dr. James W. Taylor, Dr. J.H. Wright, and Dr. Jerry Poteet

First Baptist Church, established in 1880 in Grand Prairie, has had three very memorable pastors. Each has had a building named in his honor. Dr. James W. Taylor, the first of these men, was pastor for 10 years. He fought on the side of temperance; it took a public vote to ban alcohol from the bars lining Main Street. Grand Prairie was dry for decades following that war on alcohol.

Dr. J.H. "Jay" Wright arrived in 1953 and was pastor for 23 years. His long and dedicated service was honored with the dedication of the children's wing to him.

Being without a pastor for a year, First Baptist called Jerry Poteet (pictured at the pulpit). Before retiring as a colonel, he had served as an Army chaplain for 32 years. He was pastor for 20 years at First Baptist. (Courtesy of Bob McCullough.)

CHAPTER THREE

Education

From shortly after the time settlers began to come to this area, education was important. The Loyds in the south part of Grand Prairie started a school for their family and friends. On the north side, the First Johnson Station Union Sabbath School was established in the Watson community. West Fork United Presbyterian Church opened the New Hope Cumberland Sabbath School. Churches established schools, and schools produced leaders to serve. These two elements of the community are part of its foundation. Many civic leaders and politicians have played integral roles in the education of children.

All aspects of education have been encouraged in this community by those who have participated in it. Men like Earl Tom Keel, whose focus was on the arts; Oma Braswell, who believed that music was important; and H.H. Chambers, whose influence cannot be forgotten. Reading, writing, and arithmetic are a good foundation, but developing the mind and body through arts and sports is also a vital aspect of childhood development. But the community's education system excelled in another way. Before desegregation, Grand Prairie was one of the first districts to build a high school in the community for black students so that they would not have to be bused out of town to go to school.

Education, a cornerstone of the community, has been responsible for and has supported several nonprofit organizations. The Crisis Pregnancy Center of Grand Prairie, now known as the Pregnancy Resource Center, was established and has been supported by local churches and individuals. It provides free services as well as educational information for any client. It has even participated in the many community fairs sponsored by the school district. Children First cares for the emotional needs of children, and Lifeline Shelter works closely with the schools and community to help house those who would otherwise be homeless.

Schools today teach those who are disabled and those who are talented. It serves artistic, theatrical, and musical students as well as those who like working with their hands or with computers. Grand Prairie schools provide the community's future leaders with intellectual development and emphasize sound practices and planning for today and the future.

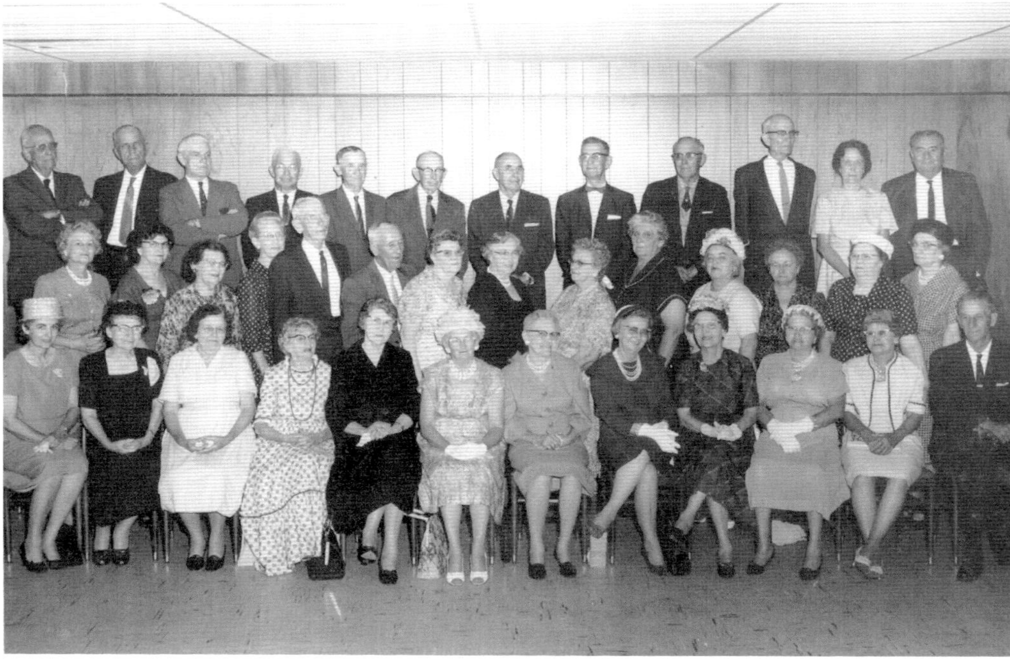

Friends of Yesteryear

The photograph above shows the Friends of Yesteryear at the Lennox Hotel in 1968. The Friends of Yesteryear was comprised of pupils in Grand Prairie prior to 1905. Pictured below is the class of 1906, featuring many of the same people. (Above, GPHO; below, GPML.)

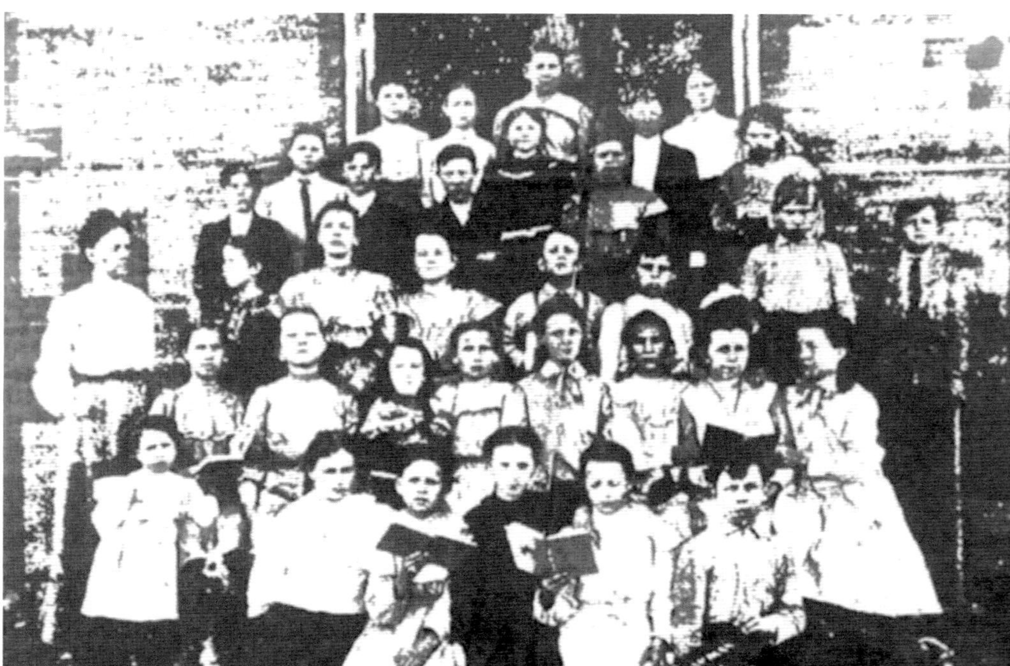

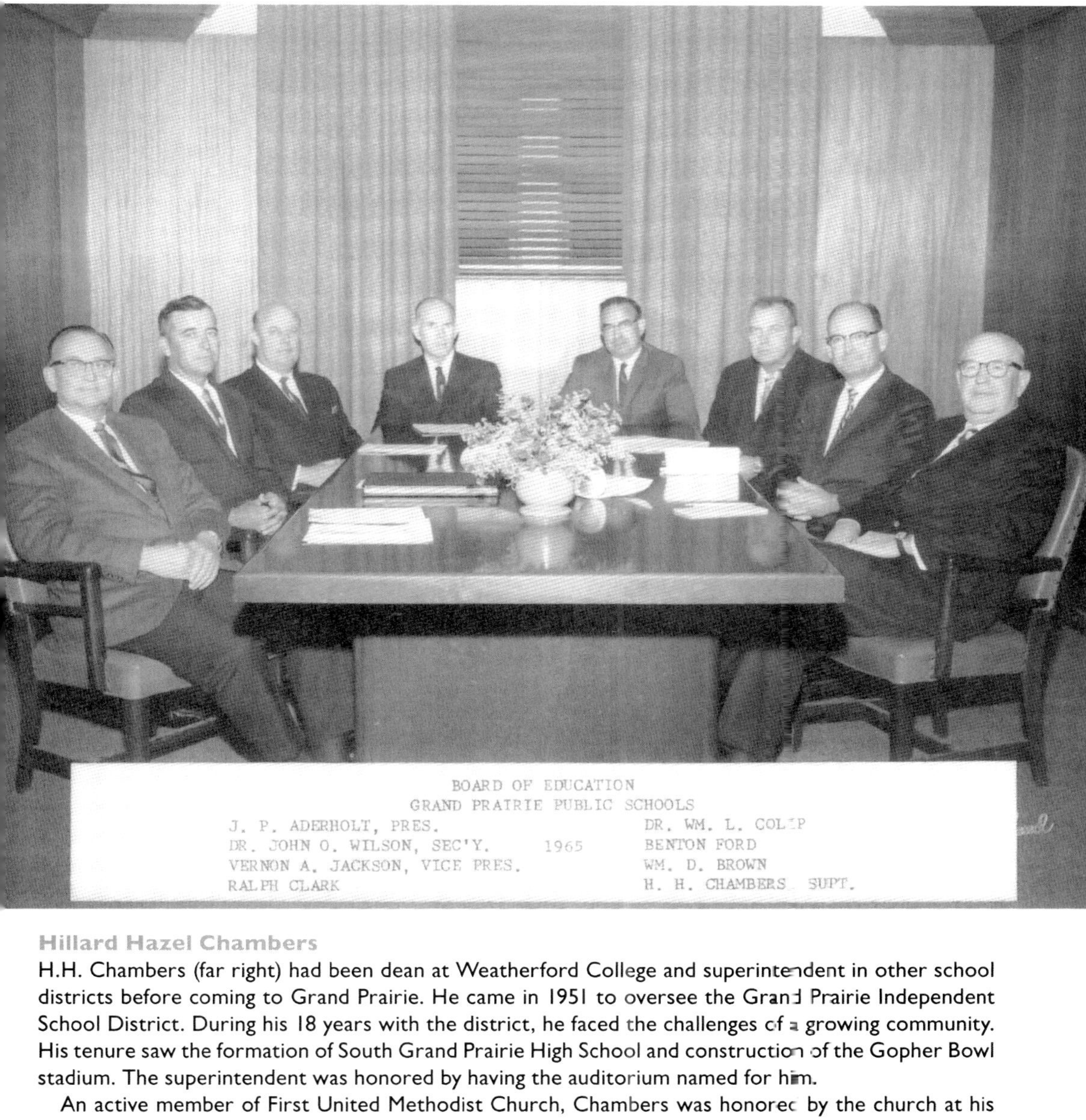

Hillard Hazel Chambers

H.H. Chambers (far right) had been dean at Weatherford College and superintendent in other school districts before coming to Grand Prairie. He came in 1951 to oversee the Grand Prairie Independent School District. During his 18 years with the district, he faced the challenges of a growing community. His tenure saw the formation of South Grand Prairie High School and construction of the Gopher Bowl stadium. The superintendent was honored by having the auditorium named for him.

An active member of First United Methodist Church, Chambers was honored by the church at his 10th anniversary as superintendent of schools. A bronze cross was placed in Baker's Chapel at the church. H.H. and his wife, Mildred, were active in the community. He was chairman of the YMCA board in 1959 and was a longtime supporter of Rotary. (GPML.)

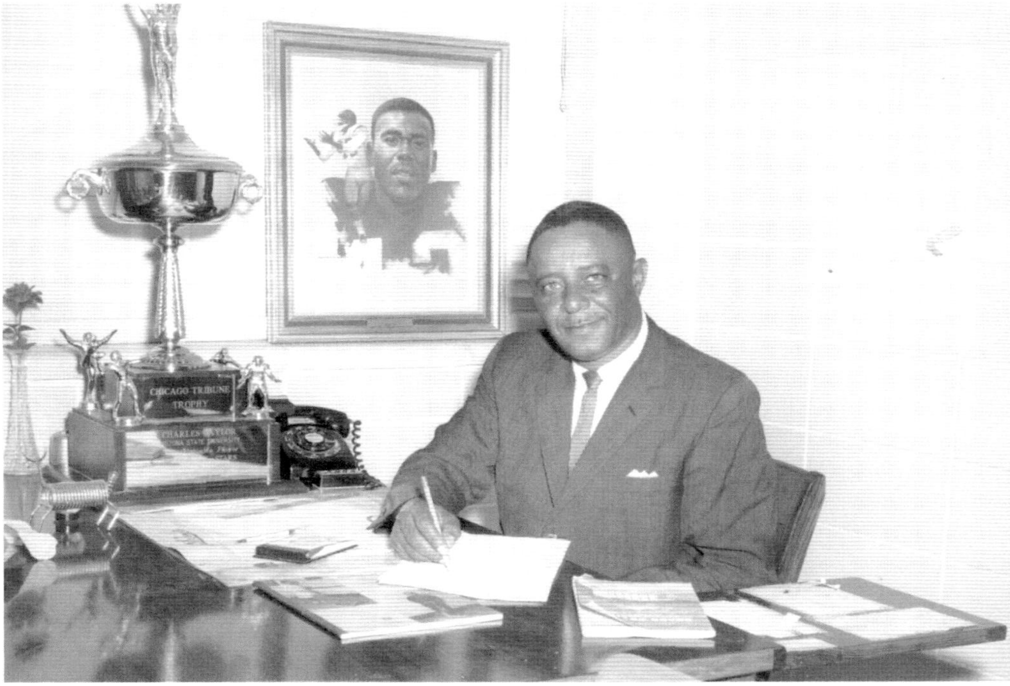

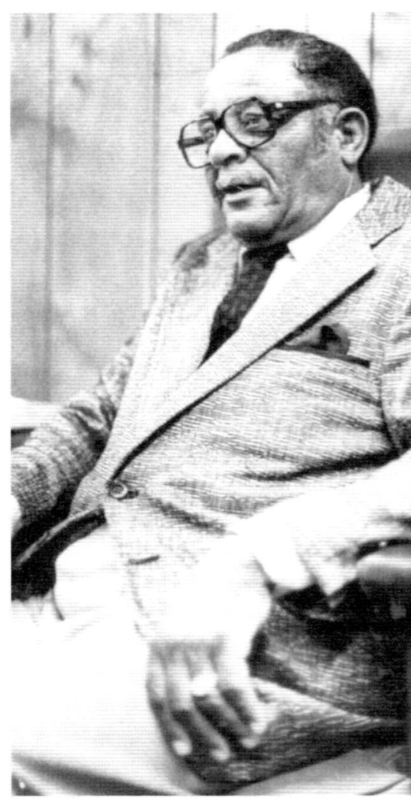

David Daniels

King David Daniels, an outstanding educator, was a teacher and principle at Dalworth. He cared for and encouraged students, including those who had to contemplate dropping out to help at home. His car was dubbed a taxicab because of the number of students to whom he gave rides.

He began the local Classroom Teachers organization and encouraged participation, which teachers were encouraged to join. He told them, "By being in an organization a person can assist in getting the improvements needed to the education system and better educate themselves professionally." He backed up this statement by being a member of several local, state, and national associations. The Grand Prairie Classroom Teachers was the only organization available to black teachers, who were invited to join the Texas Classroom Teachers Association.

Daniels worked toward unity and was involved with the urban renewal program. Leaders credited him with advocating with both blacks and whites to bring about improvements. His community service extended beyond the schools. Daniels held memberships in many civic organizations and in St. John's Baptist Church. He received many recognitions, including the Silver Beaver, the Boy Scouts' highest award. The city named a school after Daniels, and, in 1974, he was nominated for the Texas Administrator of the Year award. (Both, GPML.)

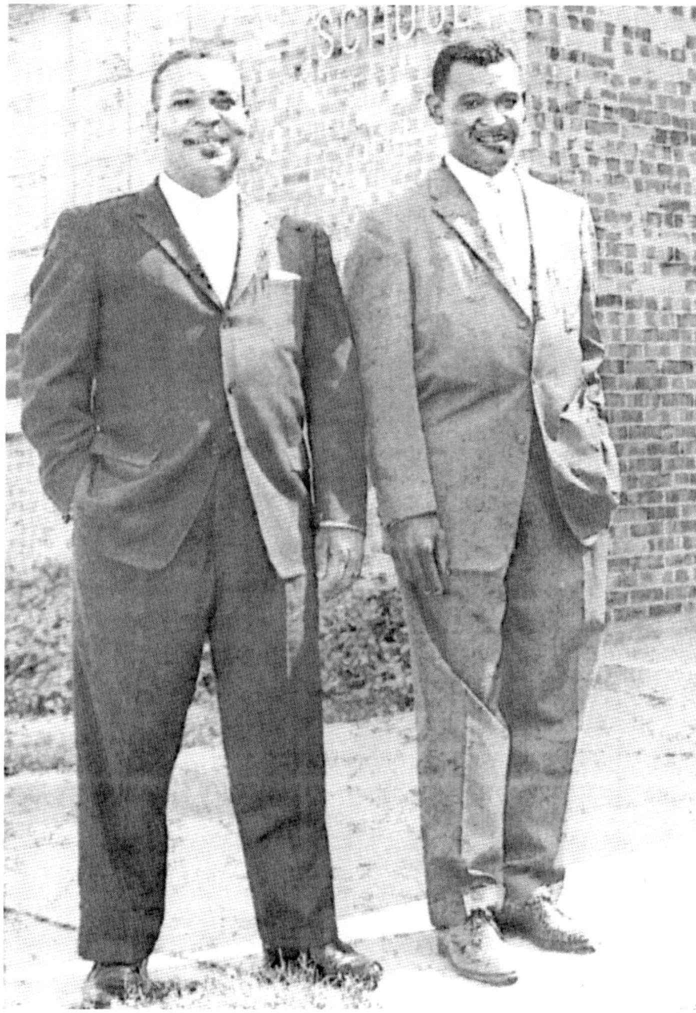

Randolph Reed
Reed took the Dalworth Dragons football team to the 1958 state championship playoffs. This accomplishment was recognized by the Grand Prairie City Council in the form of a resolution. During a playoff game, Reed (left) came up with plays that surprised the other team. This game was only one of Randolph's many accomplishments.

Besides playing with the NFL's Los Angeles Rams, Randolph Reed, in his role as a coach, produced professional athletes from Dalworth High School. Charley Taylor, Perry Pruett, and others from both Dalworth and Grand Prairie High Schools went on to be professional ballplayers. Reed was the only coach hired for Dalworth, where he ran the football, basketball, and track programs. After Dalworth was integrated with Grand Prairie High School, he continued as a coach. (Both, GPML.)

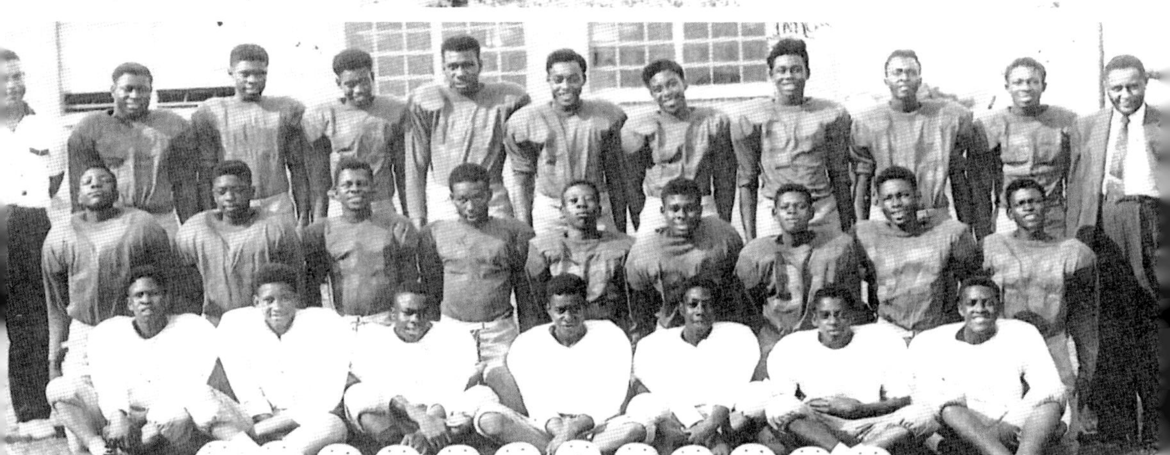

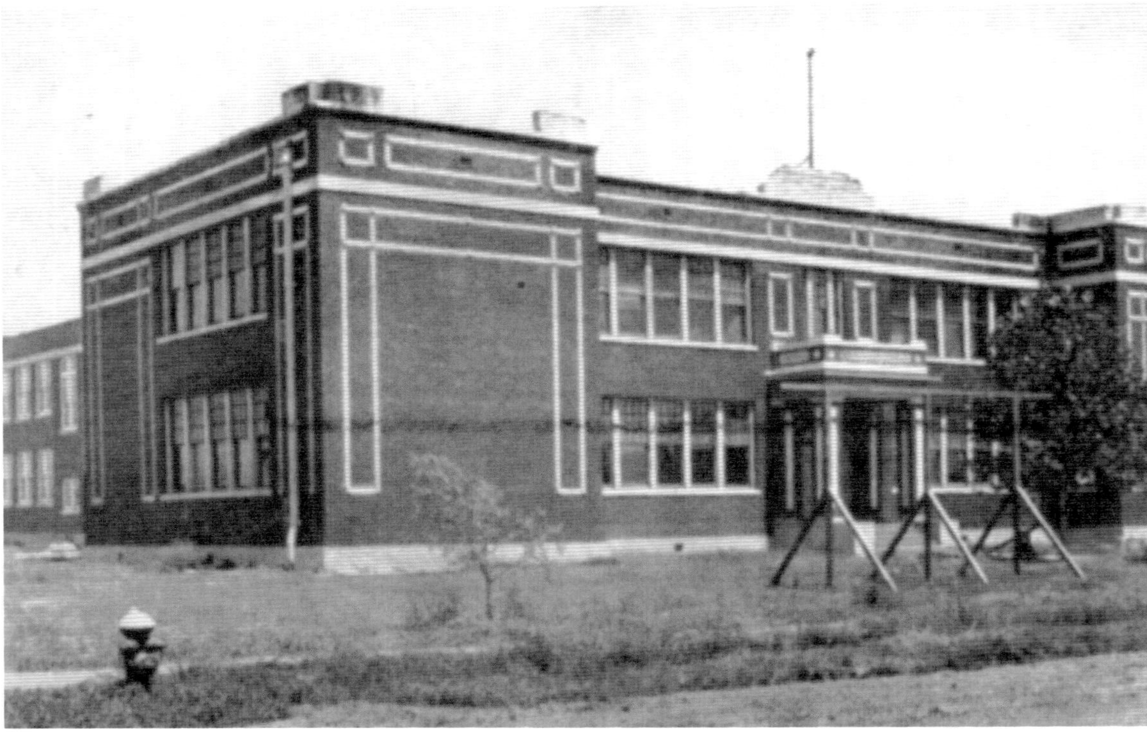

Lloyd Boze and Oma Braswell

A humble man, Lloyd Boze was a twin born in 1918 to a family that invested in education. An indication of the Boze family's involvement is the fact that eight of Lloyd's siblings had careers in education. He came to Grand Prairie in 1952 to be the principal of Grand Prairie Junior High, now Lee Middle School. He then served as principal of Grand Prairie High School (pictured). By 1958, he was the district deputy superintendent, his position for 19 years until he retired.

While with the school district, Lloyd Boze actively promoted the first adult education and special education programs. After retiring, he continued to serve the community. Boze was a Mason for 50 years and served as a member of the Lions Club. Upon his death in 2003, the newspaper reported Earl Tom Keel as stating, "He was a fine Christian man and one of the finest administrators we've ever had."

Fate holds sadness and blessings. If not for the death of Oma Braswell's parents at an early age redirecting her career, Grand Prairie could have missed out on this wonderful teacher. Coming to Grand Prairie in 1946, she began the district's music program, teaching at Grand Prairie High School. The many students who expressed their gratitude throughout her 93 years are a testament to her dedicated service. Oma served her church and community, too. She was a Red Cross volunteer, taught Sunday school, and served on the Grand Prairie Historical Commission. She was also a member of the Historical Organization, the Women's Club, the Music Club, and the Retired Teachers Association, and played music at church. (Author photograph.)

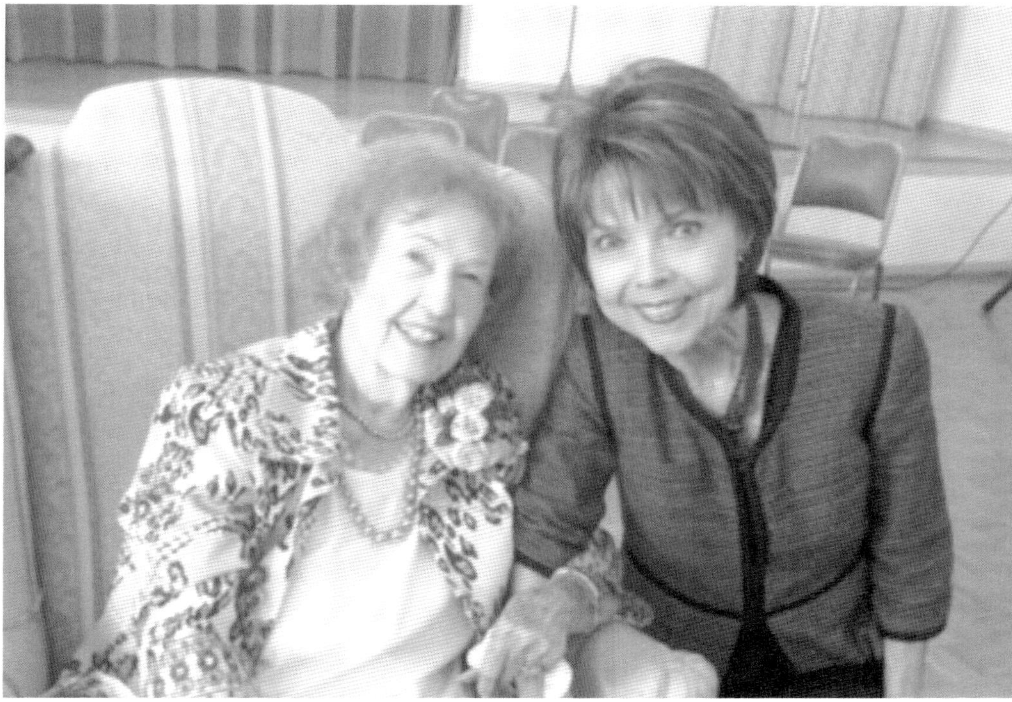

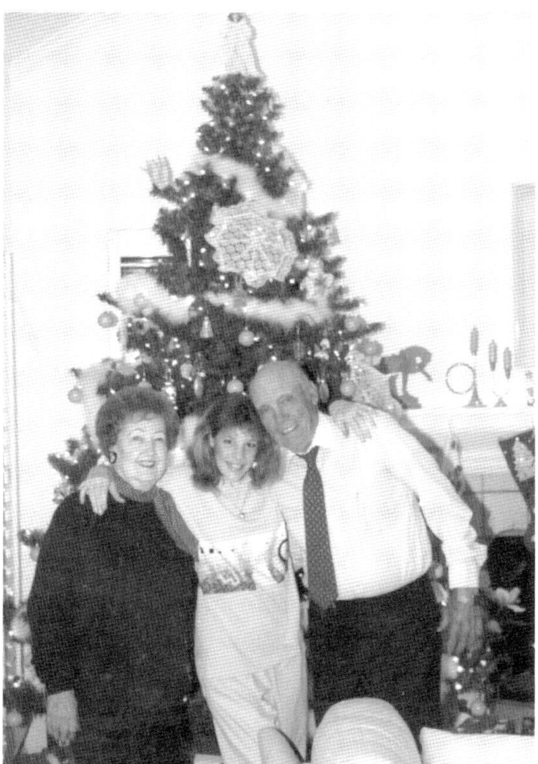

John and Beth Hill

Coach John Hill and his wife, Beth (pictured at left with their granddaughter), came to Grand Prairie in 1948 and taught school here. John's roommate from Hardin Simons in Abilene had encouraged them to move here, telling them that Grand Prairie was going to grow. Beth said, "There wasn't much here at the time," but she agreed that the town did grow. She celebrated her 100th birthday in 2014 (above, with Jorja Clemson), and says she has students from her elementary classes that now have grandchildren.

Beth Hill retired from teaching after 21 years and went into real estate with "Coach." After his death in 1996, she continued the business and has not completely retired from it. She still has a few properties she takes care of. (Above, courtesy of Jorja Clemson; left, courtesy of Beth Hill.)

Howard Leon Breeden

Breeden, band director at Grand Prairie High School, went on to award-winning accomplishments. He spent more than 20 years at the North Texas State College (now University of North Texas), where he directed the One O'clock Lab Band, bringing jazz into the mainstream of music education. Under his direction, the group became the first college band nominated for a Grammy. They played at the White House and opened for Ella Fitzgerald. (Courtesy of Leon Breeden Collection, University of North Texas Movie Library.)

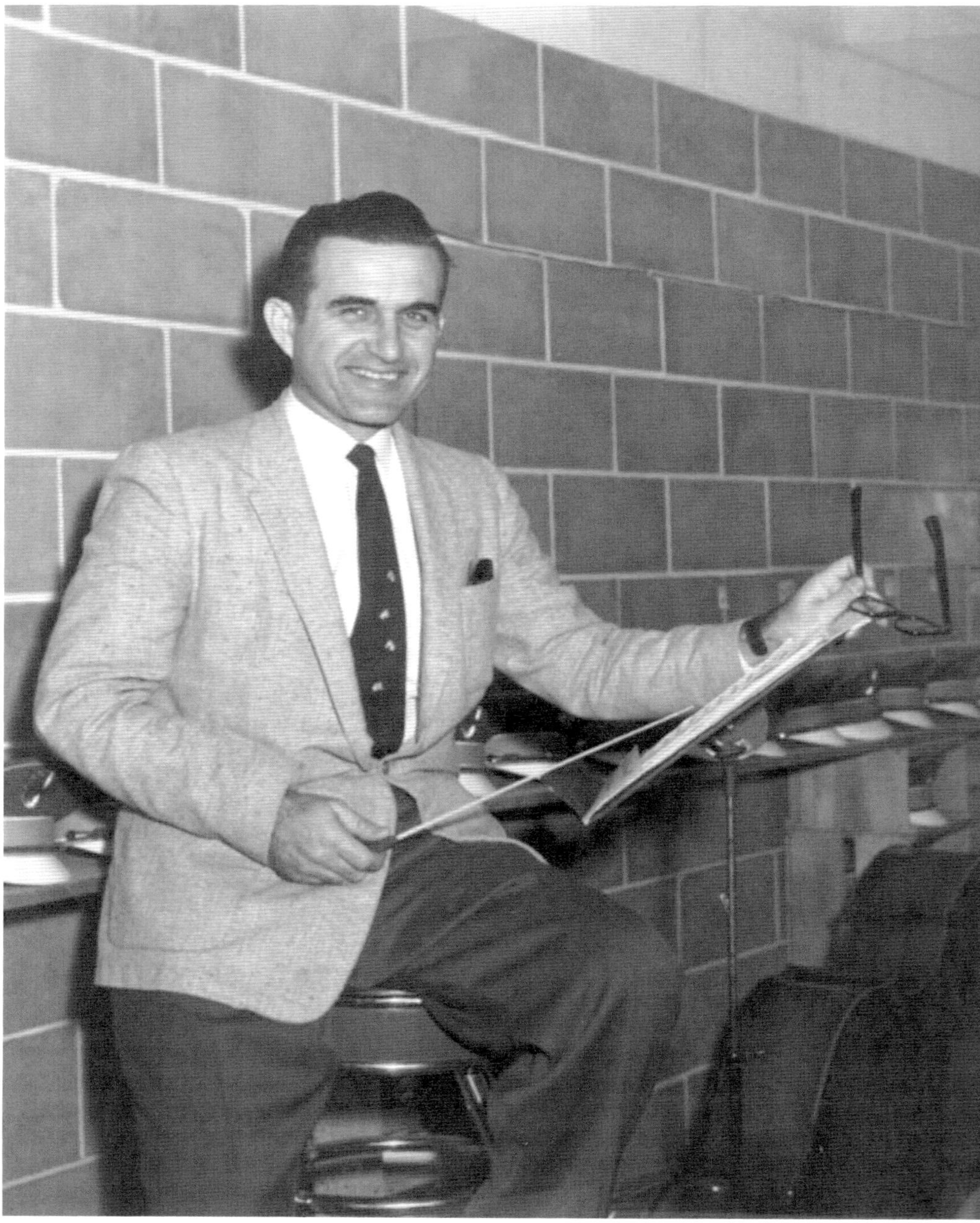

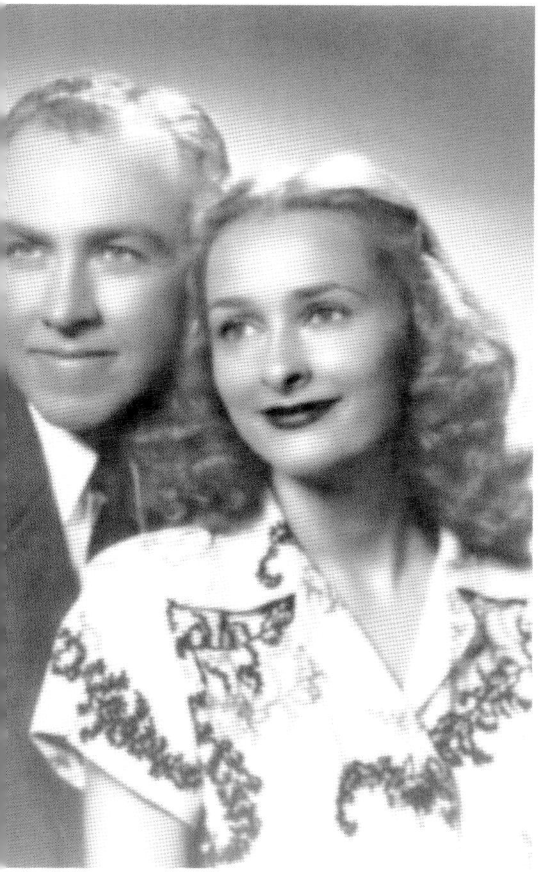

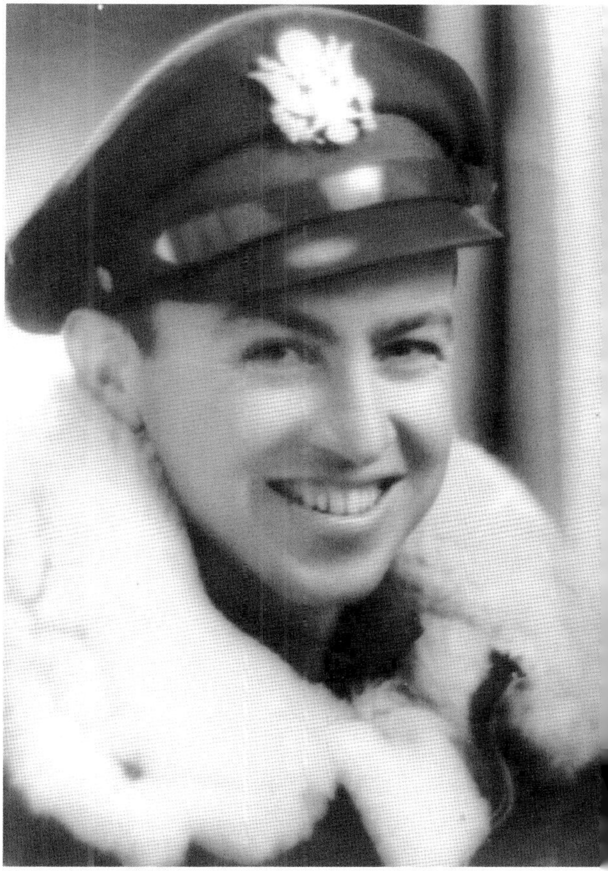

Amos Spurgeon Turner and Mary Evans Turner
Amos Turner and his wife, Mary, were well known on the basketball courts in Grand Prairie. Both were native Texans. They married and, in 1953, came to Grand Prairie. He was a teacher as well as a coach and an administrator for the Grand Prairie Independent School District. In all of his years of coaching, Mary was there to cheer on the team. She never missed a game and became well known to the athletes. They called her "Mrs. Coach Turner."

The Turners were devoted to one another and to others. It did not go unnoticed. In 1999, the new gym was named for Amos. Mary was honored with a pew at First United Methodist Church. (Both, courtesy of Pamela Ellis family collection.)

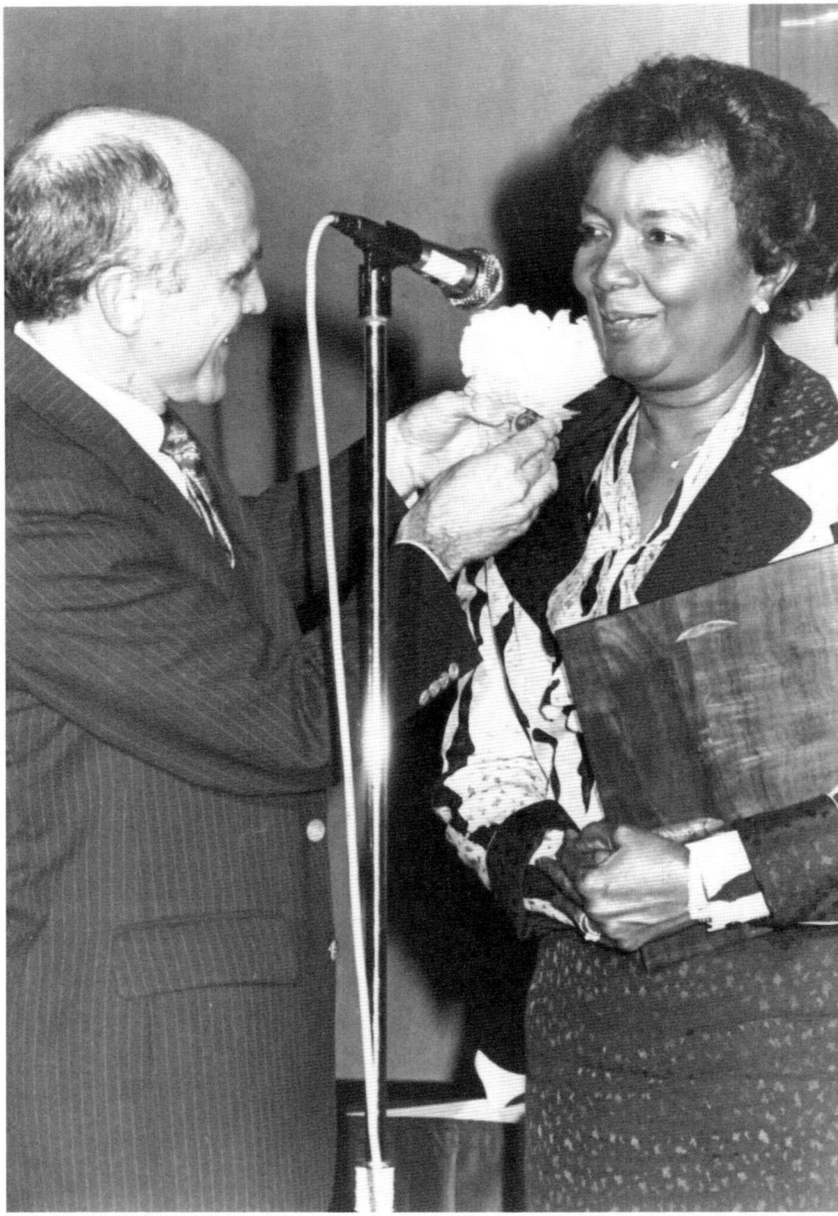

Sallye Ann Moore

Moore has been an important part of Grand Prairie Independent School District for more than 40 years. In addition, a local school has been named after her. She taught at both Dalworth and Grand Prairie High Schools and has been a principal. The values of education and family were instilled in her from an early age. Moore has left a valuable heritage to students over the years, evidenced by those who have become successes. It is a heritage passed on to her and her siblings, and that she has been able to share with students. She has received many awards through the years, including the Distinguished Educator award, Woman of Distinction award, Woman of History award, Thurgood Marshall Pioneers in Education award, and a merit award from students in 2007. (CofC.)

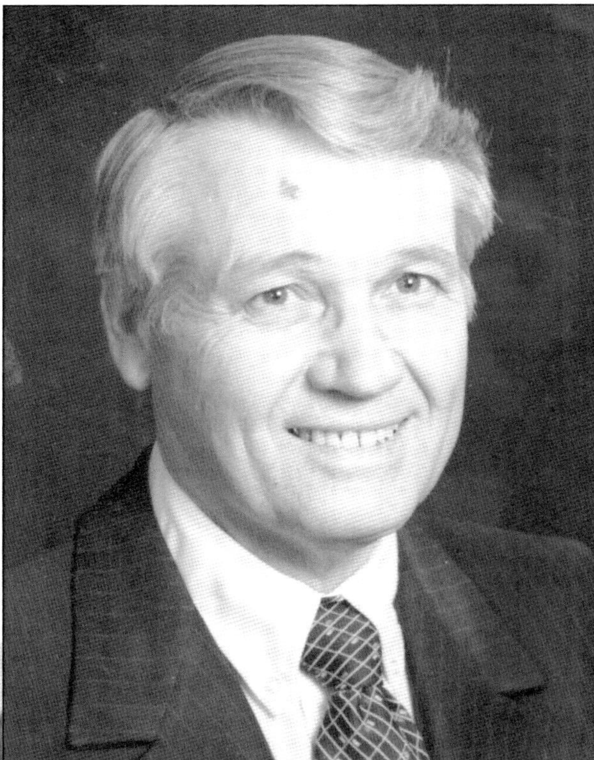

Bill Arnold

It is no wonder that when he was elected to the Texas legislature in 1989, Bill Arnold focused on education. He had been an outstanding educator and was the deputy superintendent for the Grand Prairie Independent School District. During his tenure with the Texas House of Representative (1989–1993), he served on the education committee and a special education committee. In 1995, he was named Outstanding Educator by the Grand Prairie Alumni Association. Bill Arnold is pictured below at left. (Both, CofC.)

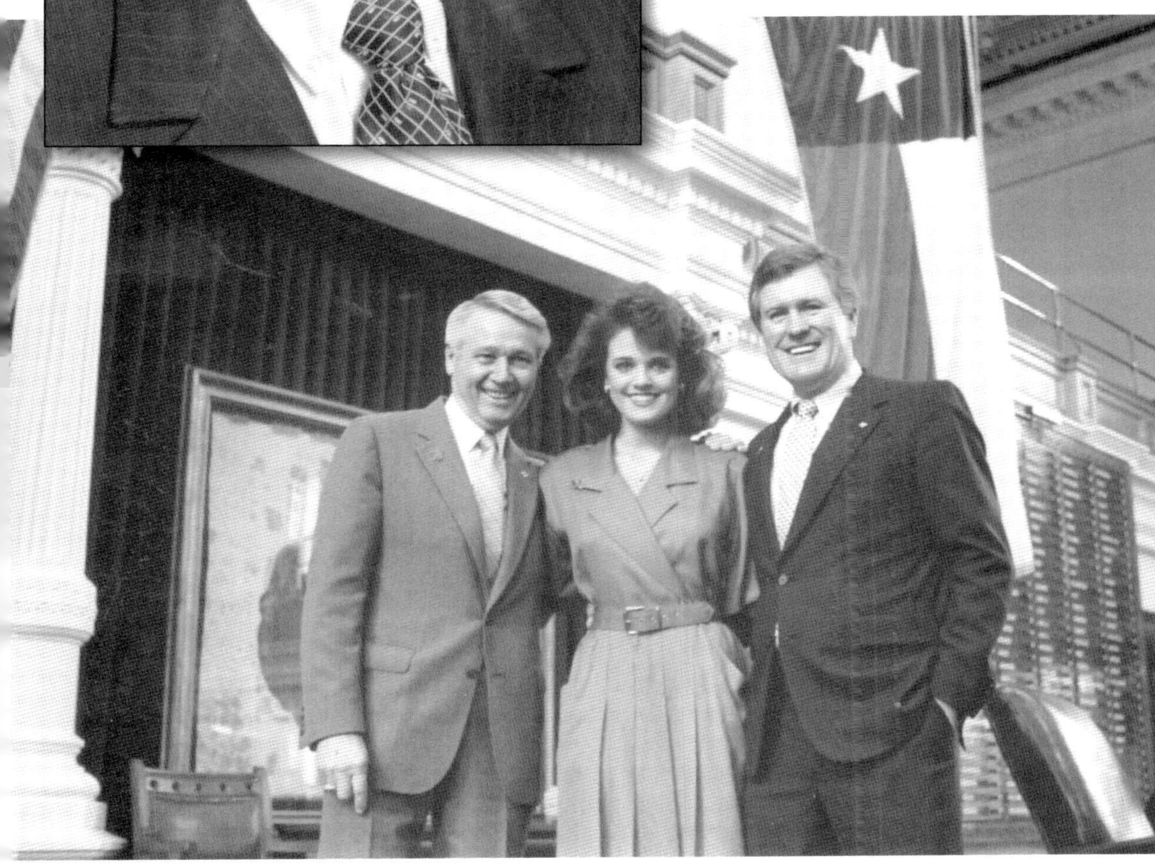

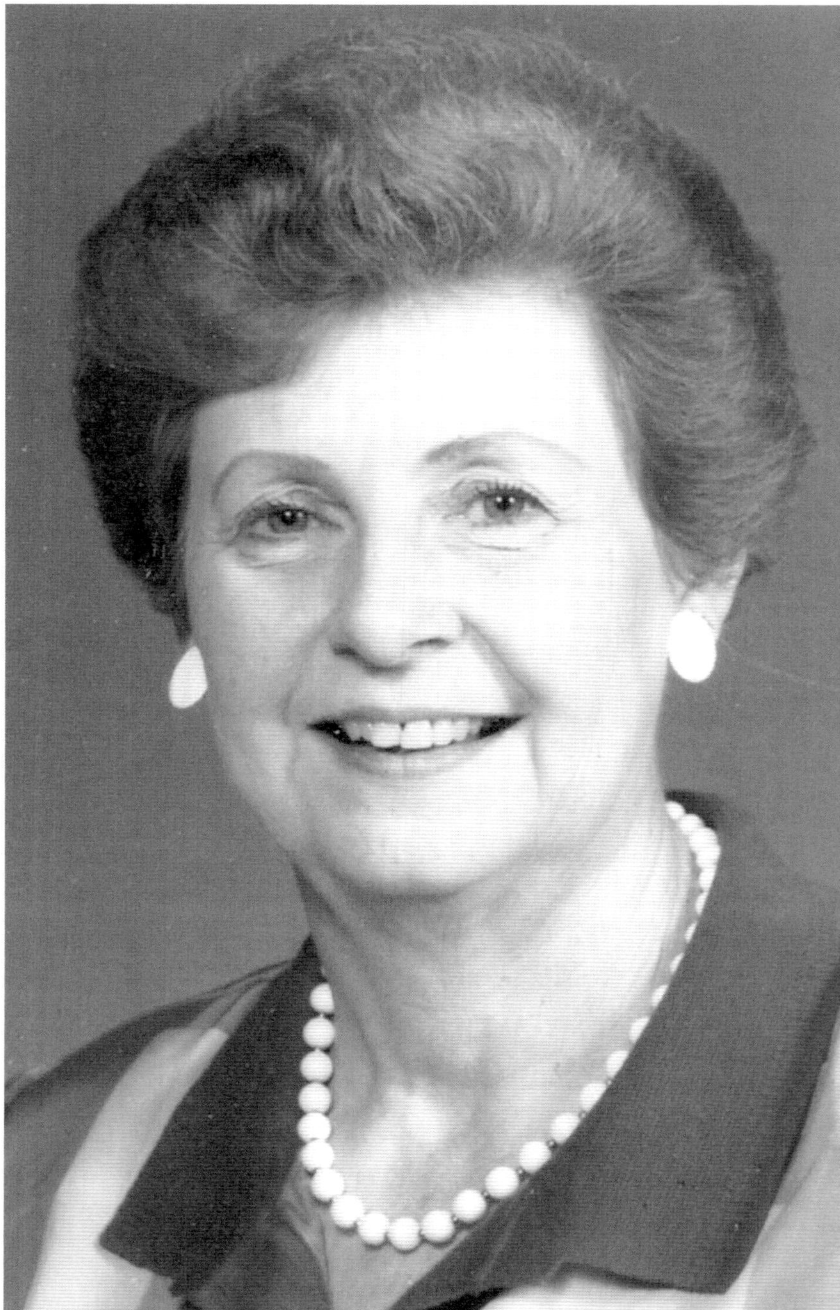

Ann Burton

Burton was a teacher who cared about her students, and this was evident as she poured herself into improving their lives. Her dedication to education saw her promoted, becoming a principal in the Grand Prairie Independent School District. But her dedication did not stop there. She also cared enough to make a run for the school board, although it was unsuccessful. (CofC.)

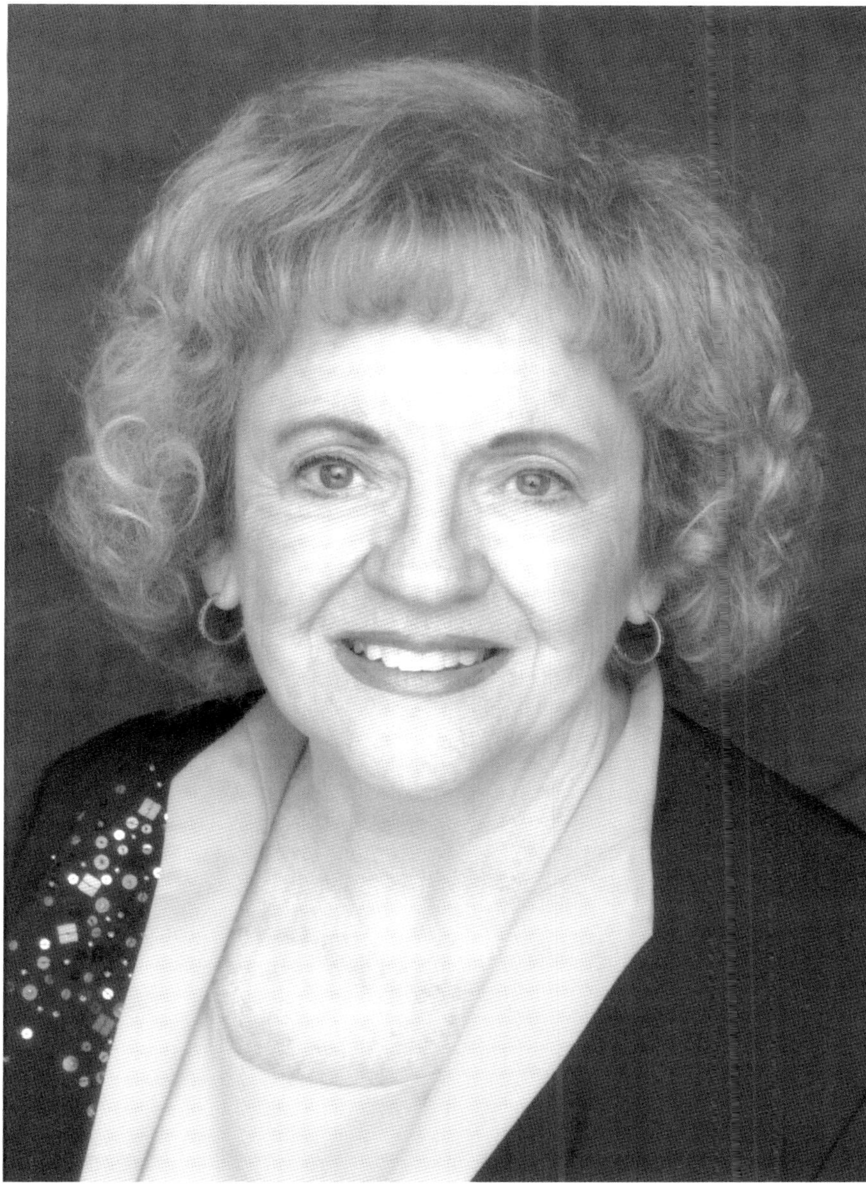

Bebe Bingham
Bingham's life has involved multitasking. After graduating with a bachelor's degree in business education from Delta State University, she worked as a flight attendant. She overlapped jobs as an accountant, co-owner of Grand Prairie Insurance Company, and as a tax consultant. Bingham then began her 20-year career with the Grand Prairie Independent School District while serving the community through a number of organizations. Her service was recognized by Epsilon Sigma Alpha with the Diana Award.

Bebe Bingham was clearly focused on leadership and education. Her education career began in 1979 as a typing and business-law teacher at South Grand Prairie High School. She was principal at Kennedy Middle School when she retired in 1998. But that did not end her service. It was not long before she was elected to the school board. (Courtesy of Doug Bryan Photography.)

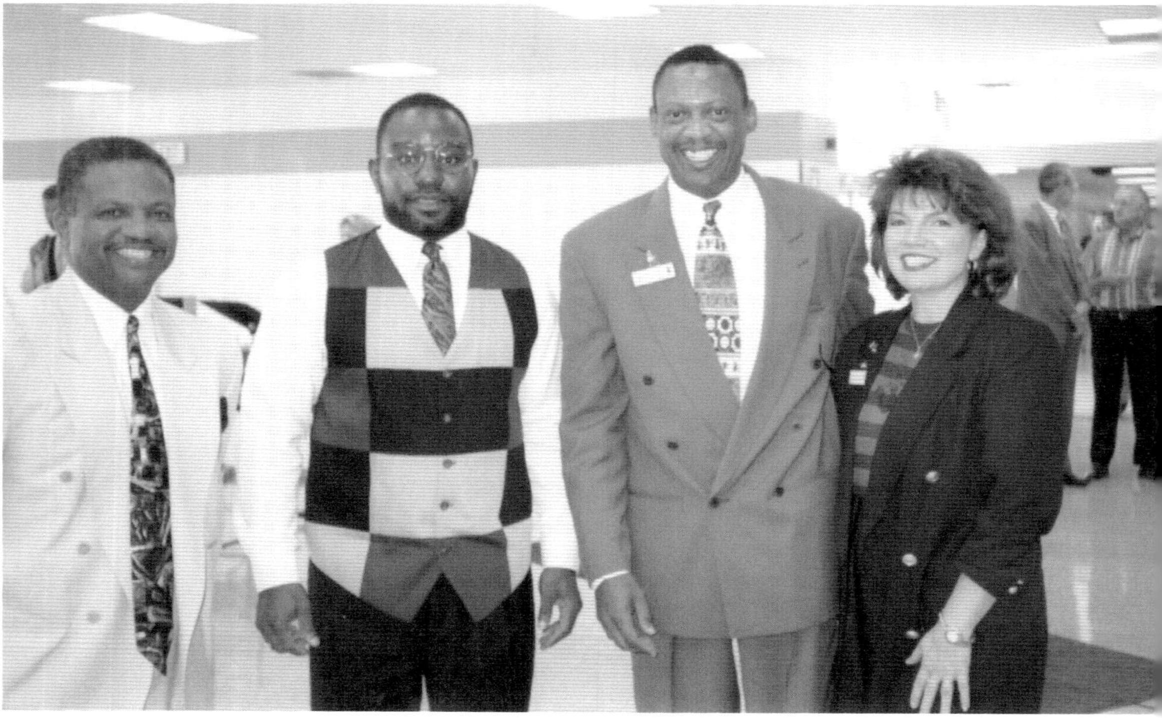

Vern Louis Alexander

Vern Alexander (far left) is the deputy superintendent of student services at Grand Prairie Independent School District. He has had a long and distinguished career with the district, but his private life has been just as distinguished. During his service in the Army, he was awarded the Bronze Star. He is pictured with, from left to right, Calvin Harris, Stretch Rideaux, and Karry Chapman. (GPML.)

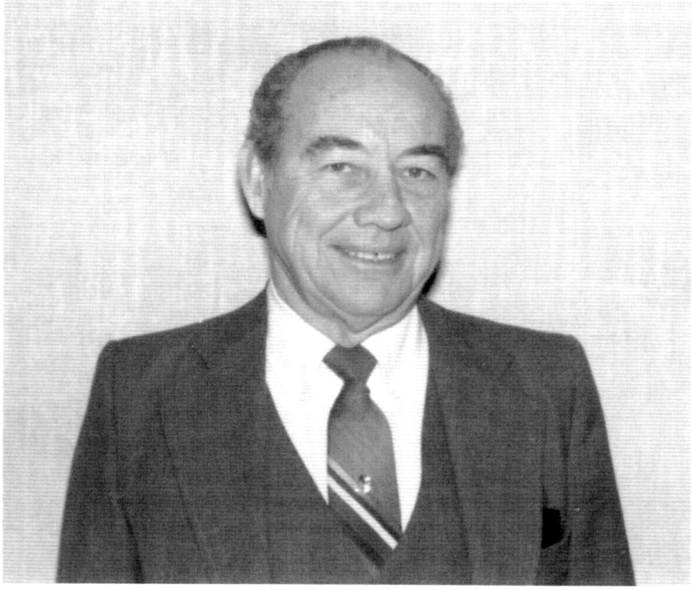

Hobbs Williams

Williams and his wife, Doris, came to town for positions with Grand Prairie schools. When he retired after 30 years with the district, he had obtained the position of superintendent. Williams earned his bachelor's degree from the University of Texas, where he attended on a baseball scholarship. He served as a bombardier in the 8th Air Force during World War II. (CofC.)

CHAPTER FOUR

Sports and Entertainment

Grand Prairie has produced many talented individuals. Coaches like Randolph Reed were professional players before producing talented athletes. Charley Taylor was one of those athletes. His accomplishments began when he was on the high school football team that went to the state playoffs. It was decades until his retirement as a professional player and coach. Others have passed along their talents, like Olympian Jennifer McFalls. She is now head coach for a women's fast-pitch softball team, the Dallas Charge. Others include Ashley Robinson, a professional basketball player; Kerry Wood, a major-league pitcher; and Wesley Duke and Robert Holt, professional football players.

Although the list of athletes from Grand Prairie reveals a great deal of talent, it is not the only field of expertise the town has seen through the years. There has been a long list of stars. Selena Gomez was discovered by Disney as a child. Dennis Burkley grew up and studied locally before going to Hollywood, where he had a long career in films. Billy Miller became a soap-opera star. Ben Capps, a novelist, was able to make his living through his writing. Al Howard shared his music throughout the area. These outstanding accomplishments should not overshadow the many individuals who have gained a high level of proficiency in their fields.

For many, talent does not just happen. Some people, of course, have a natural talent and, along with it, a great passion for their work. Others develop their talents through hard work. Some naturally posses a talent that drives them to write, paint, run, or jump. Others develop a passion as their performance improves. Passion, talent, dedication, and support are necessary, but encouragement from family and friends makes the difference in how long and how well someone will advance.

Talent is not confined within specific social, economic, or ethnic lines. The talent coming from Grand Prairie has crossed them all. Those who have taught upcoming stars from every type of background have given them what they needed. The professionals have grounded their charges in the basics, then pushed them beyond mere techniques to find each individual's avenue of expression. These mentors have been encouragers and role models. When others were not available, these teachers in sports, art, theater, and music shared their passions. Consequently, a great deal of talent has emerged from Grand Prairie.

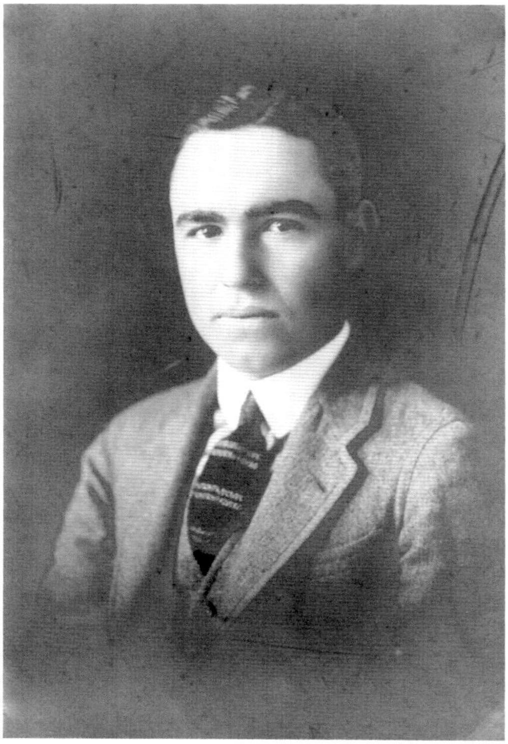

Benjamin Earl Grimes

Ben Grimes (left) joined the Grand Prairie High School faculty, where he taught several classes. He headed the first full-time football team in 1924 (below) and was the school's volunteer leader for all athletic teams. With a $200 budget, the football team went shopping and came back with what they could find—blue-and-white uniforms. The students approved, and, for the first time, wore uniform colors. Then, the team chose their mascot, the Gophers. It is also reported that Coach Grimes wanted this mascot in honor of his college, the University of Minnesota. He was credited with the cheer, "First 'n ten and Go-For-It-Again." (Both, courtesy of Ben Grimes.)

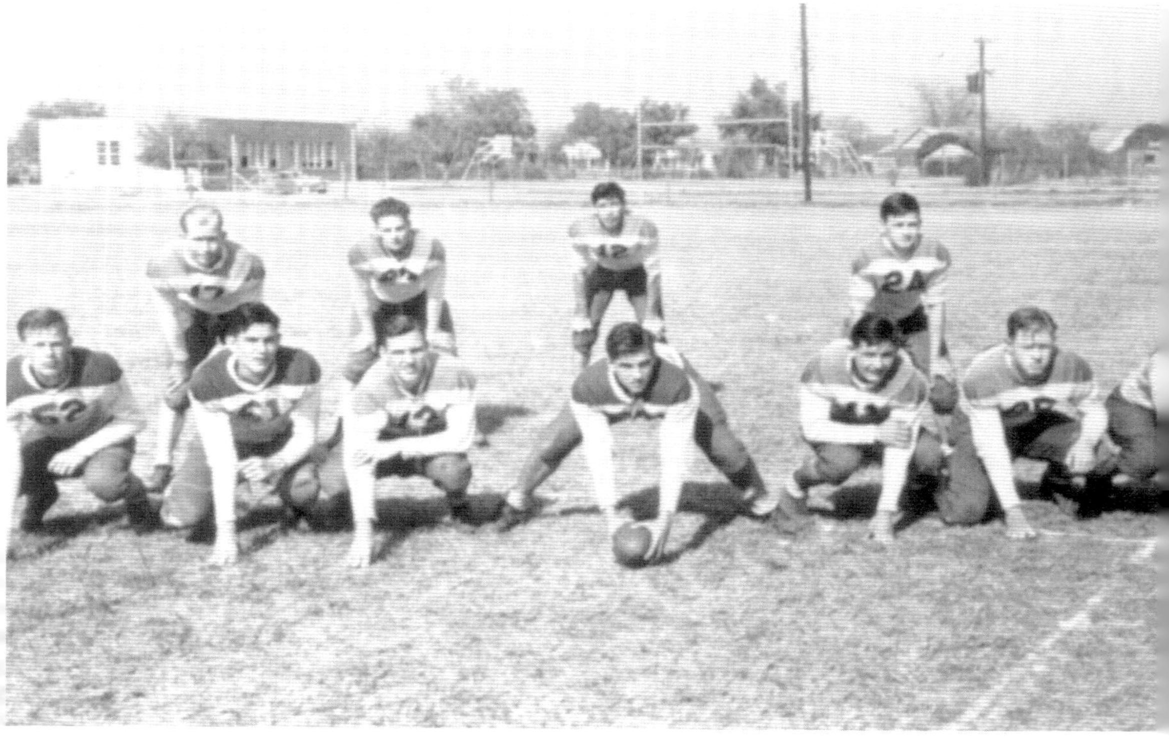

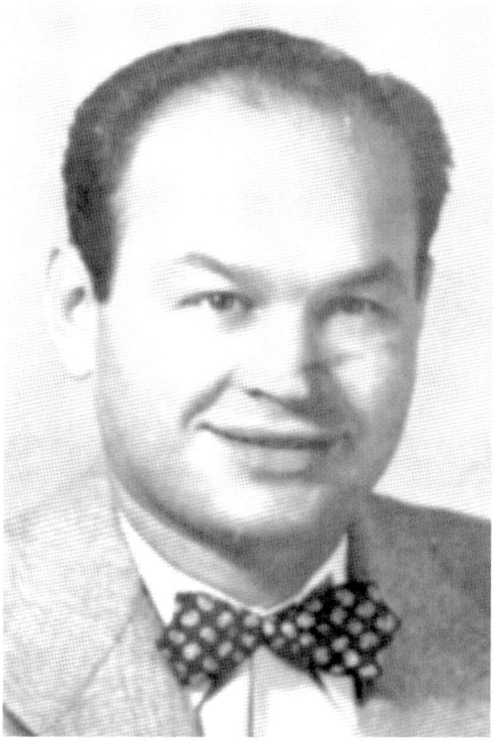

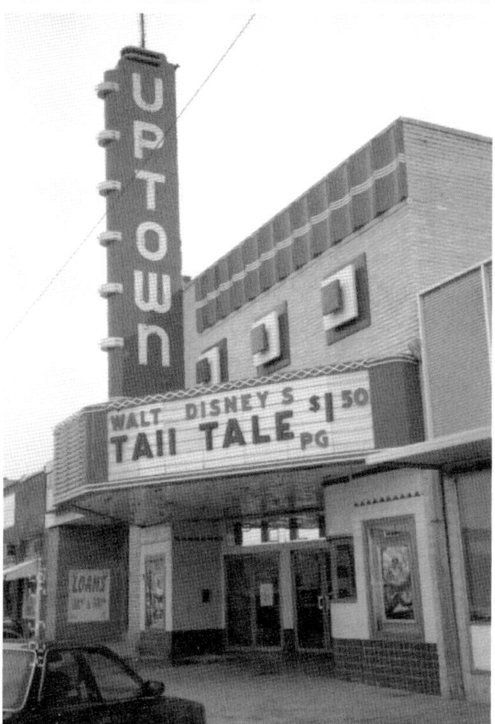

Sherman Silver and Donna Meager Easterling

Jerry and Sherman (pictured) Silver came from Minnesota to Grand Prairie in 1948. They purchased the Wings Theatre and leased the Texas Theatre, both located on Main Street. Already experienced theater businessmen, by 1950, they had planned and built the Uptown (below), their third venue in town. Besides first-run movies, the theater hosted a number of other events. The little stage saw beauty pageants, band battles, go-go contests, and even midnight viewings of *The Rocky Horror Picture Show* and other films for evening-shift workers.

Helen Fisher and her husband bought out the Silver brothers in 1959. The Fishers' daughter, Donna Meagher Easterling, was only 10 years old when she began working at the theater. She served as both an usher and a babysitter for the Saturday "kiddie" shows, which had children as young as five years old in attendance. By 1965, Donna was the owner of the theater. She was also a local attorney. She continued operations until the 1990s, when mega-theaters began to dominate the industry. This led to the closing of what was once a modern, state-of-the-art movie house. (Both, GPML.)

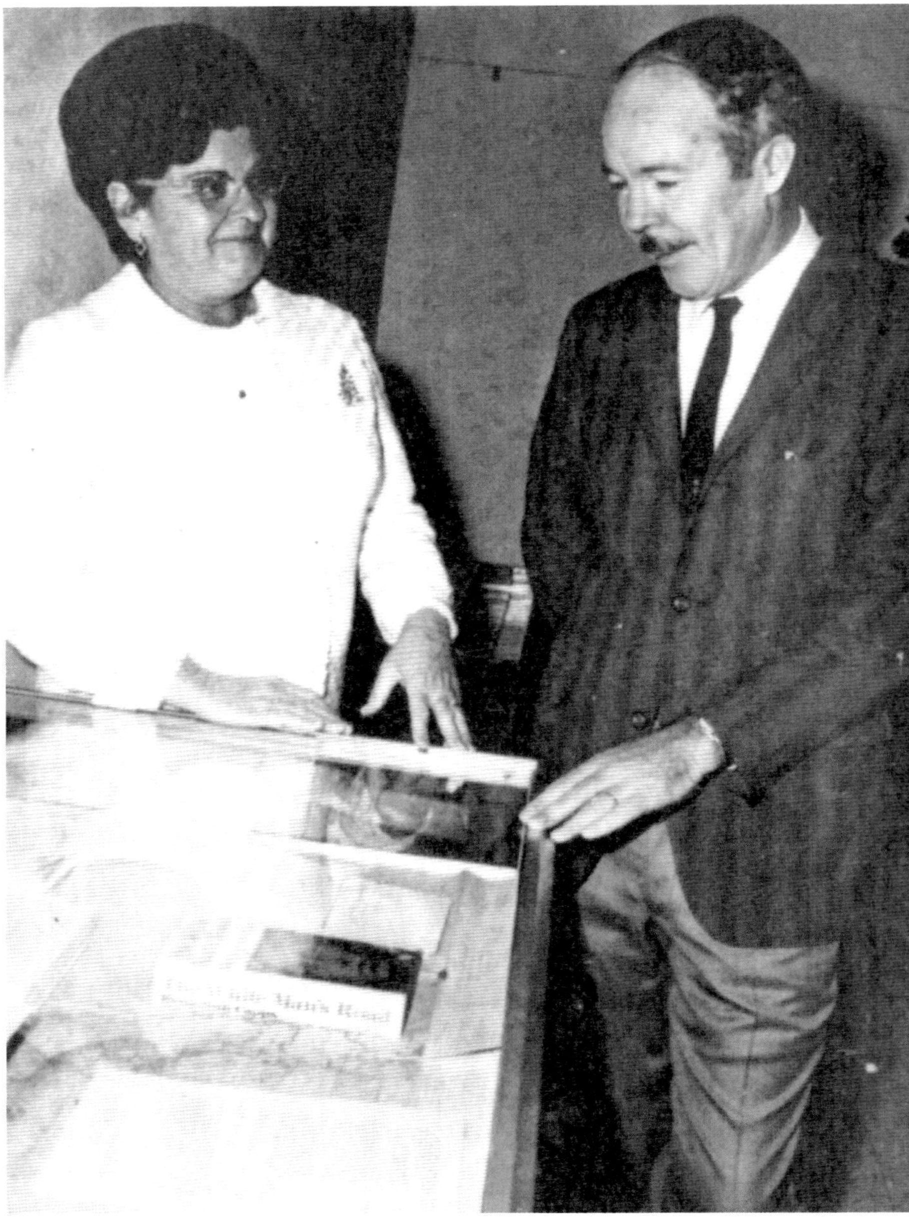

Ben Capps

Before becoming a writer, Ben Capps worked at Ling-Temco-Vought. By the 1960s, he was one of the few in the state of Texas able to make a living as an author. His work supported his wife and three children. Capps wrote Western-style novels that were well received. He gathered much of the information and background for his novels from Oklahoma, where he grew up. He twice received the Spur Award, the highest honor from the Western Writers of America.

Patti Lambright, head librarian, is pictured here with Ben Capps. His wife, Kathleen, supported him by handling many secretarial duties and reviewing his work. Working from home, he also wrote special-interest articles and wrote reviews for the Dallas newspaper. (GPML.)

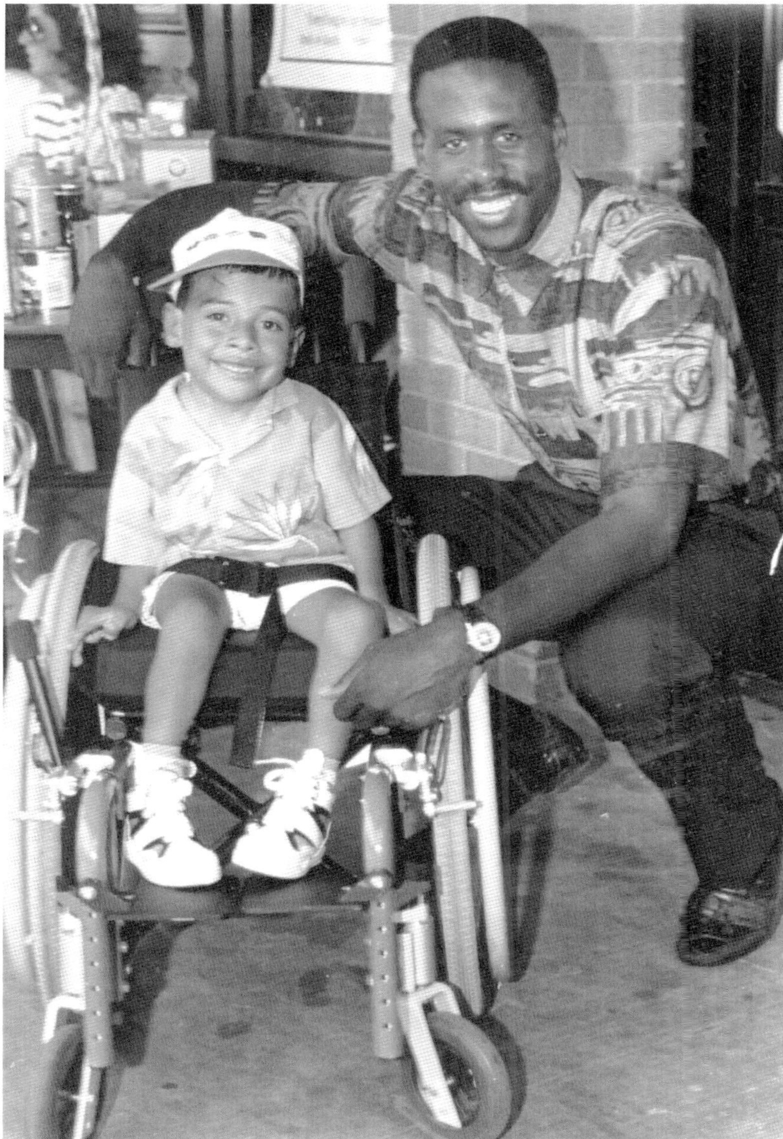

Charley Taylor

Taylor was born in Grand Prairie and, by eighth grade, was playing football, baseball, and basketball and participating in track. He attended the segregated Dalworth High School before it integrated with Grand Prairie High School. He was named All-State in both football and track while in high school. At Arizona State University, Taylor was an All-American and was inducted as a charter member of the Arizona State Sports Hall of Fame.

Taylor was drafted by the Washington Redskins and named NFC Rookie of the Year. He is listed among the top 100 all-time Redskins players. He played both as a running back and a wide receiver. He was a Redskins scout and receiver's coach after retiring from playing in 1977. Playing in a Super Bowl and being a Ring of Honor member are among his accomplishments. Grand Prairie's Charley Taylor Recreation Center is only one of his many recognitions. (GPHO.)

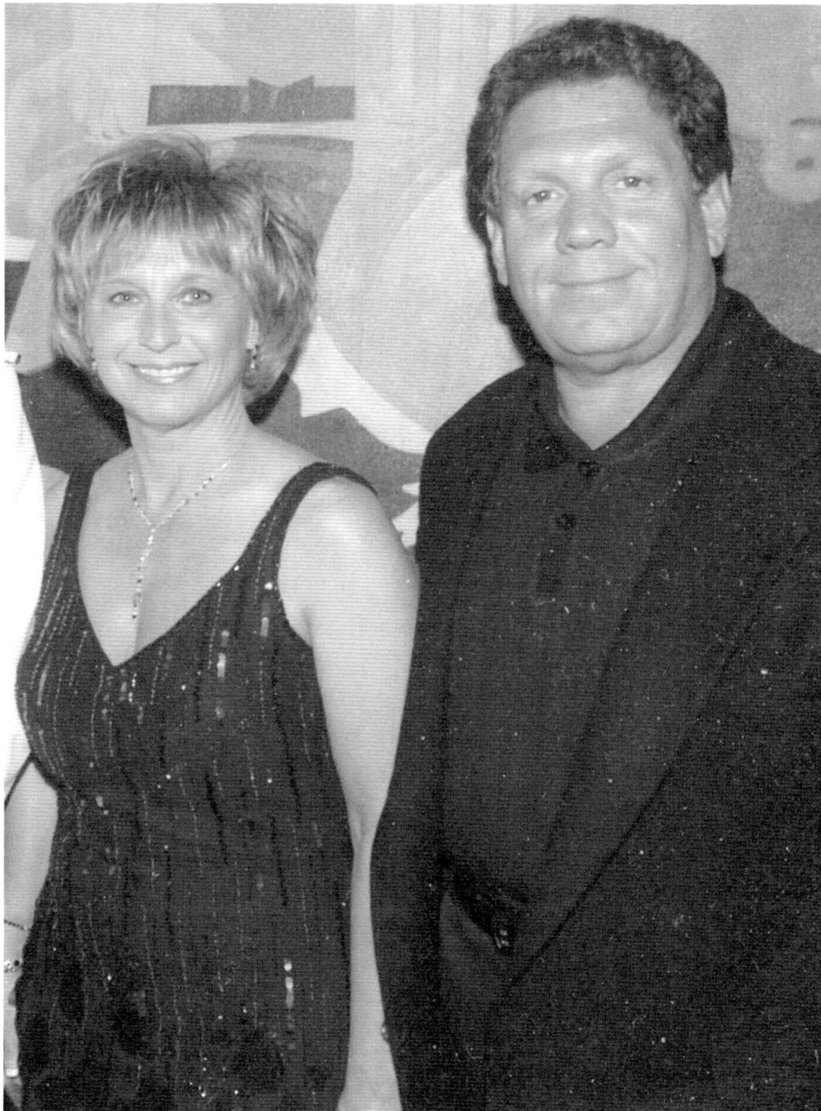

Vernetta and Kyle Turner

Vernetta Turner has lived in Grand Prairie all of her life. Kyle Turner managed the gym where he met Vernetta. She wrote the book on water aerobics. Asked by Harriette Algood to create some exercises that could be done in the water, Turner created an entire routine, used family members to test her concept, and launched Wetworks in 1983. Certified by the Aerobic Exercise Association, Aquatic Exercise Association, and the Arthritis Foundation, her program was first taught in fitness centers managed by the Turners and as a college credit course. It has been endorsed by Dr. Neil Dishon, chief of staff of UTA Student Health Services.

Vernetta Turner considers Wetworks her ministry, and says that the routines and her locations have all been part of "a God thing." She started Wetworks at the Natatorium. For over 25 years, she has seen people of all ages and fitness levels participate. Turner was inducted into the City of Grand Prairie Parks and Recreation Hall of Fame in 2008. (Courtesy of Vernetta Turner family.)

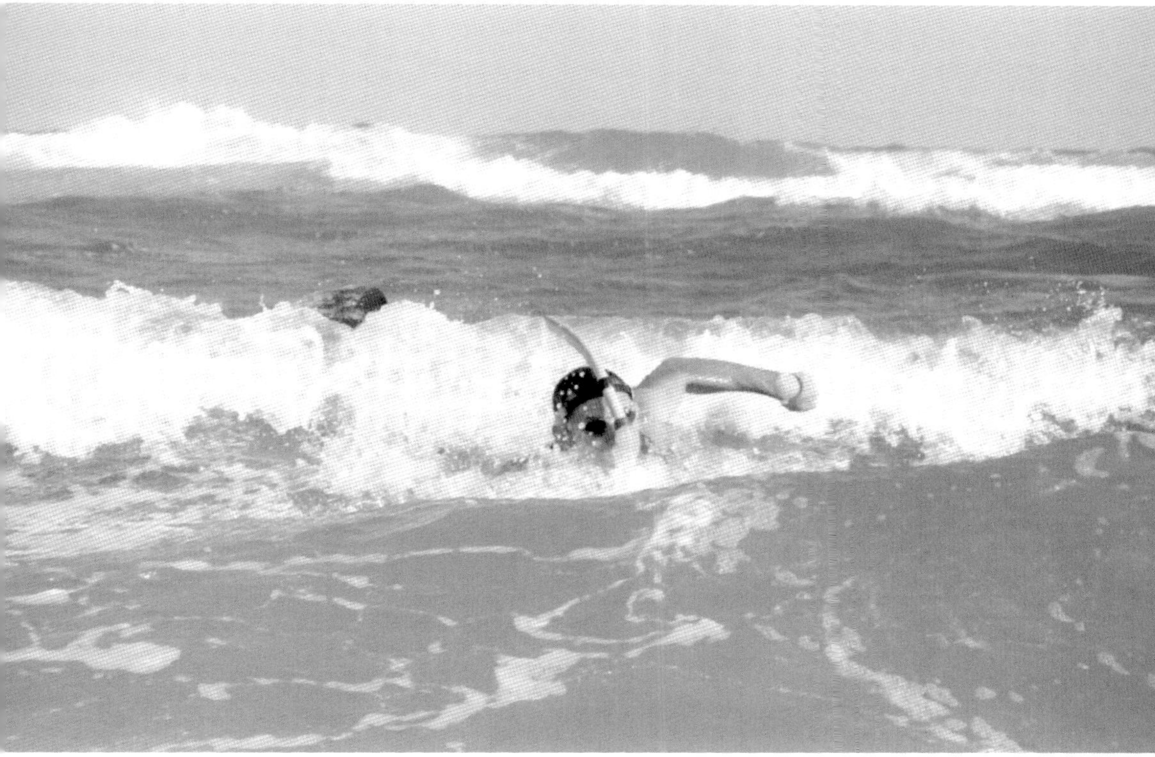

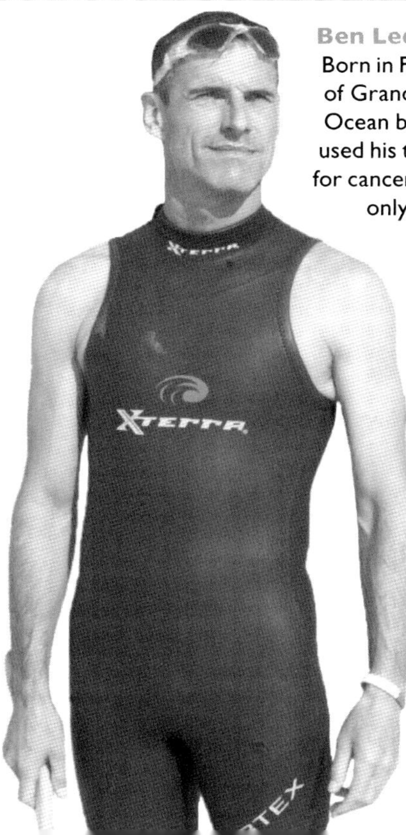

Ben Lecomte

Born in France and now a citizen of the United States and a resident of Grand Prairie, Ben Lecomte was taught to swim in the Atlantic Ocean by his father, who passed away in 1991 of colon cancer. Ben used his talent as a swimmer to honor his father and to raise money for cancer by swimming across the Atlantic Ocean in 1998. He is the only person to have swum the 3,700 miles across the ocean. Lecomte's next plan is to swim the Pacific Ocean, a greater endeavor. It is approximately 5,400 miles from Tokyo to San Francisco. Joe Pool Lake is his training ground for the planned six-month swim. (Both photographs by Gino Kallanoglu.)

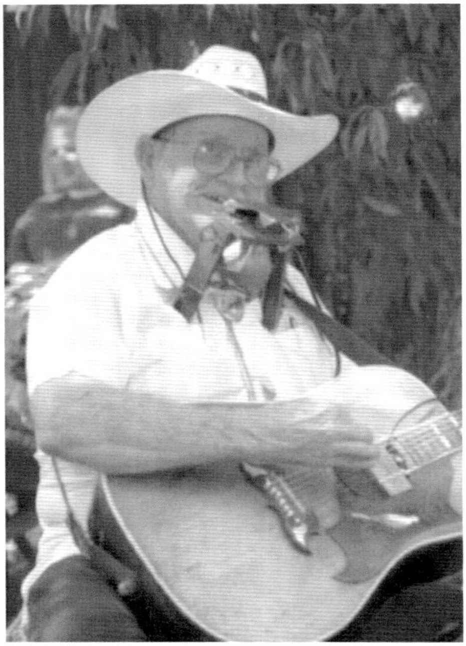

Allen Cline Howard

Al Howard loved music and wanted to share it with others. Born in Arkansas, he served in World War II and was present in Tokyo during the Japanese surrender. After the war, he worked in three different states before settling in Grand Prairie and working as a security guard at the cement plant. Howard's passion for music drove him to play at every opportunity. He played Panther Hall and Big D Jamboree with people like Willie Nelson and Waylon Jennings. Glen Campbell was the lead singer for the Howard Band in the early years. In later years, Howard discovered that he could play drums while performing, thus expanding his abilities. He eventually became a one-man band. Al Howard shared his music with patrons at Trader's Village and in front of Don Juan's and Jimmy's Catfish on Main Street in downtown Grand Prairie. He played not for fame or fortune, but for the love of it. (Both, courtesy of Allen Howard family.)

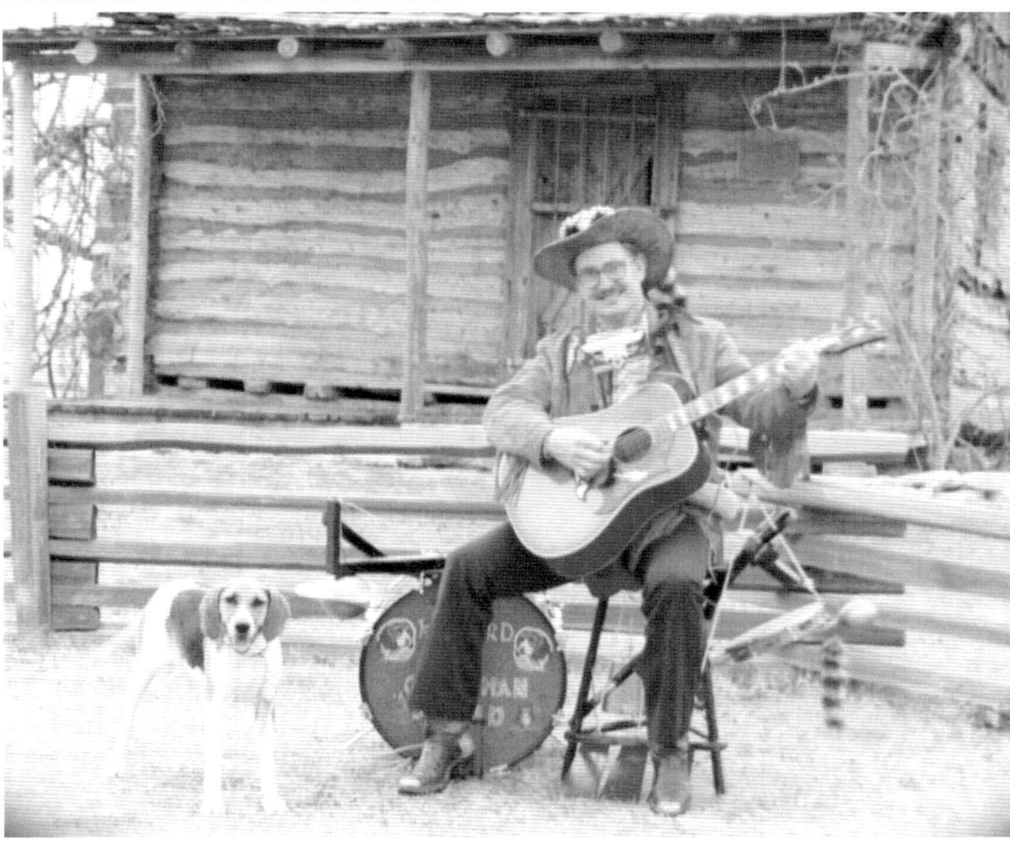

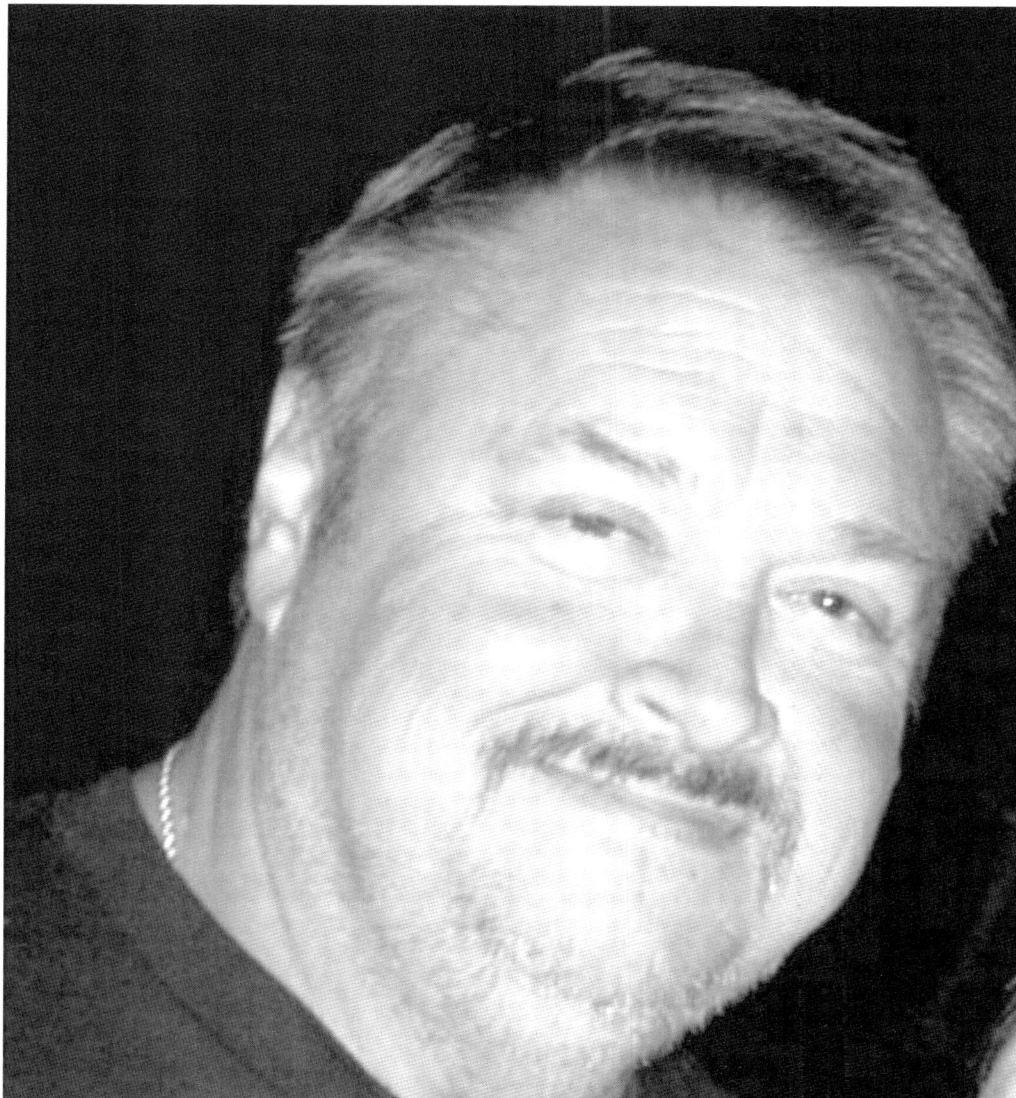

Dennis Buckley
Born in Van Nuys, California, Buckley was raised in Grand Prairie and graduated from Texas Christian University in Fort Worth with a master's degree in theater. He moved to Los Angeles to pursue an acting career. While working on becoming an actor, he cleaned swimming pools which is where he was discovered. One of the pools he cleaned was for the director Bob Rafelson, who cast him and another little-known actor, Arnold Schwarzenegger, in *Stay Hungry*.

Buckley worked in television and film from the 1970s until his death in 2013. His Southern charm led him through an impressive career, working in over 60 films and an untold number of television shows, including *Maude* and *Starsky and Hutch* as well as voice work in *King of the Hill*. (Courtesy of Bonnie Cockrum.)

Lonnie Hannah

A tragic accident left Lonnie Hannah paralyzed from the waist down at the age of 20, robbing him of his lifelong dream of speed skating. Lonnie, who had been on the ice since he was 16 months old, was a world champion. Being a champion speed skater spurred him on to learn more about disability sports, and in this field he again achieved great success. He is a multiple Paralympics sled hockey medalist and now teaches the sport. Hannah said in an article on the al.com website: "Just because my life changed doesn't mean I can't be active, that I can't do anything that I want to do. I just have to do it in a little bit different way." Inspiring others, with and without disabilities, to not give up and encouraging them to believe in themselves and achieve their best is the message he sends. (CofC.)

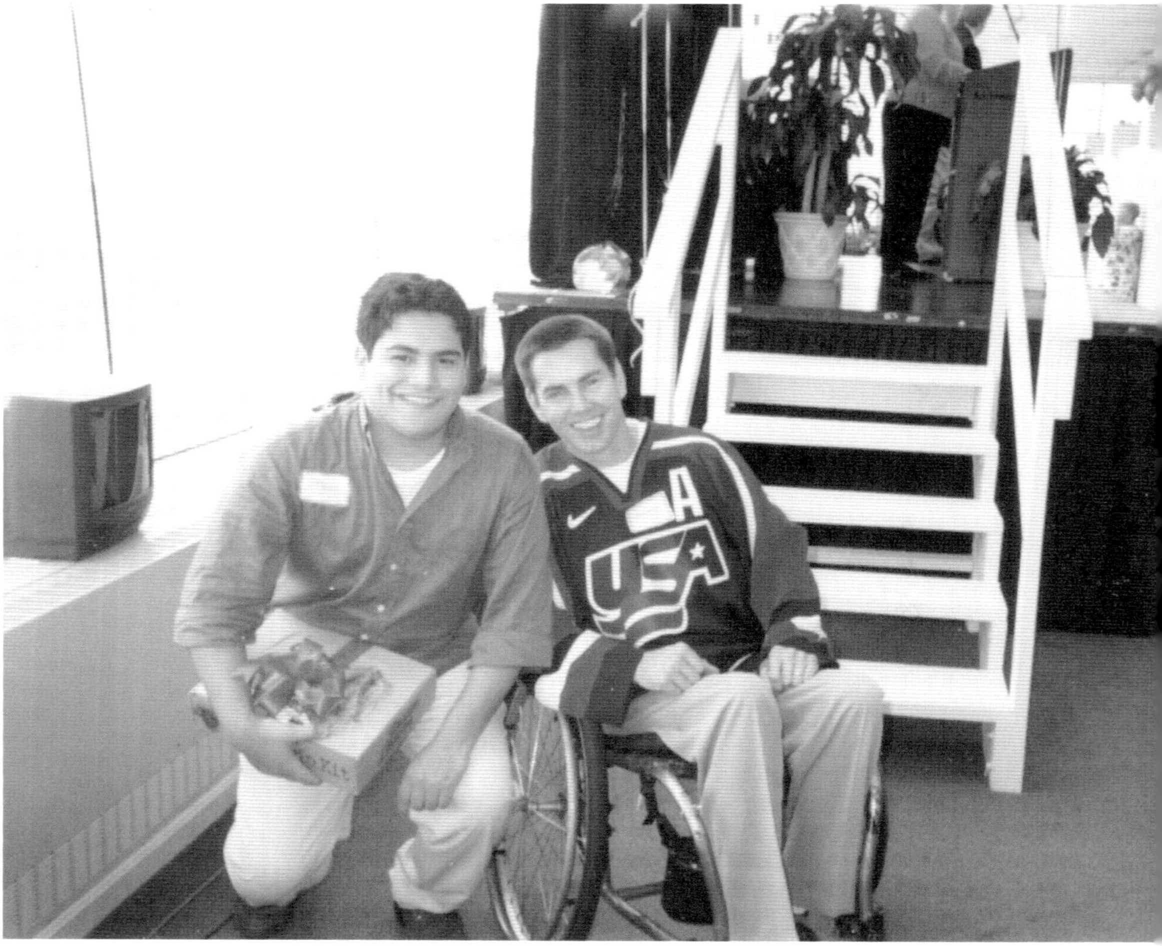

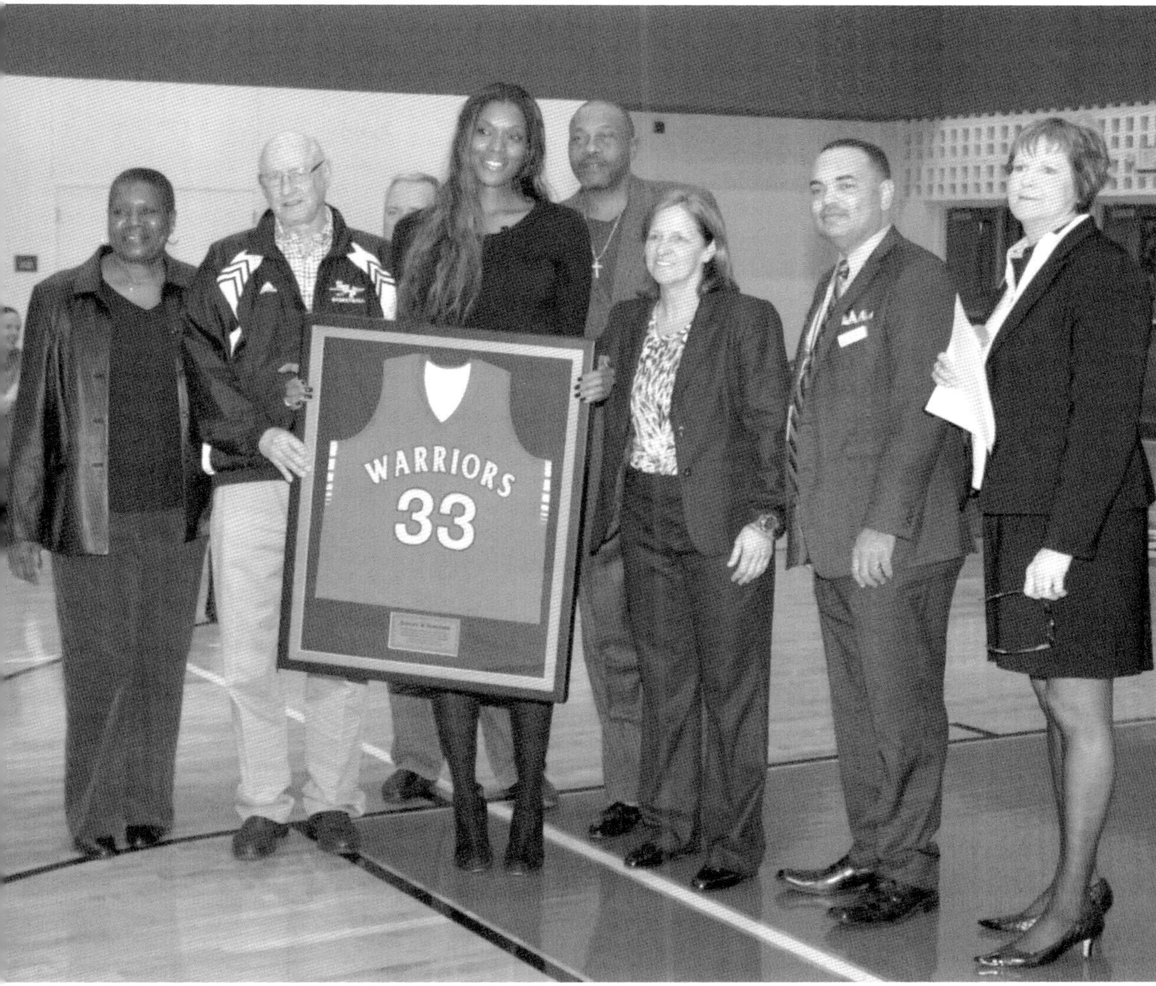

Ashley Robinson

Before Ashley Robinson's career with the Seattle Storm, she played for South Grand Prairie High School and the University of Tennessee. Considered one of the best female high school basketball players in the state, she was an all-around athlete, participating in volleyball, baseball, and track. South Grand Prairie High retired her jersey number in February 2015. (Photograph by Bob Fitch, *Grand Prairie Reporter.*)

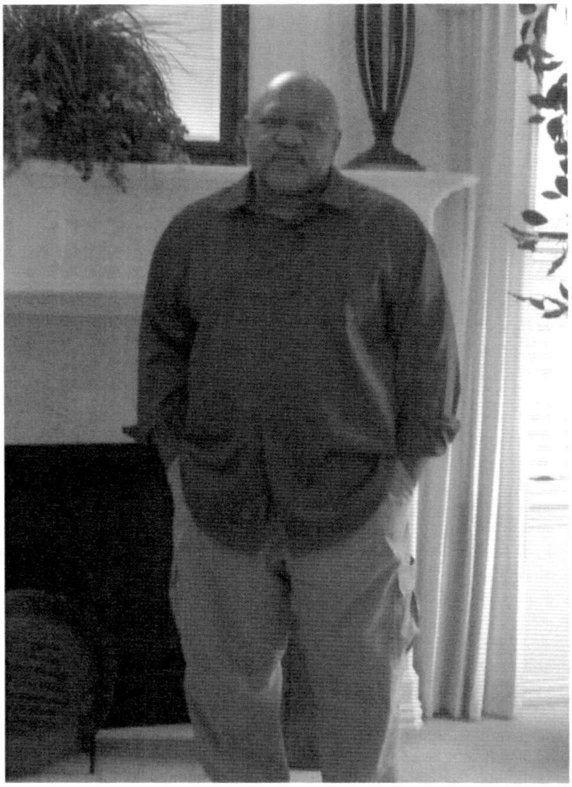

Larry Dell Alexander

Larry Alexander is an artist and author. Born and raised in Arkansas, he began drawing at about the age of four. His notoriety skyrocketed when he painted a Clinton family portrait and sent it to the White House. He was inspired by a group of his friends, who said that if anyone from Arkansas ever became president, they would paint him.

Inspired by life and surroundings, Alexander sees his talents and art as his role in life, developed and directed by God. Alexander believes that one has to leave a legacy of faith based on a personal relationship with Jesus, and that, until then, one is not fulfilling their purpose.

From 1996 to 2006, Alexander made an annual trip to give back to children in Arkansas, conducting a weeklong tour and putting on exhibits. His first book, *African-American History at a Glance*, has been used as a supplemental text for schools in Irving, Texas. Alexander also has written seven Bible studies and commentaries and does a weekly Bible study online. His legacy is being left through his community service, his art, and his writing. (Both, author photographs.)

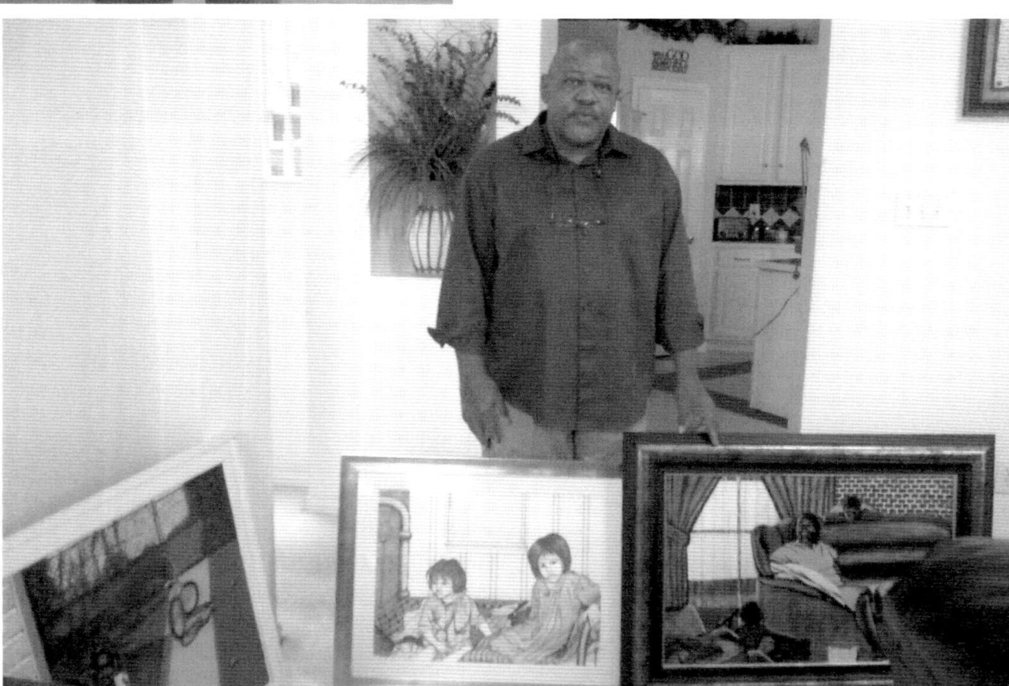

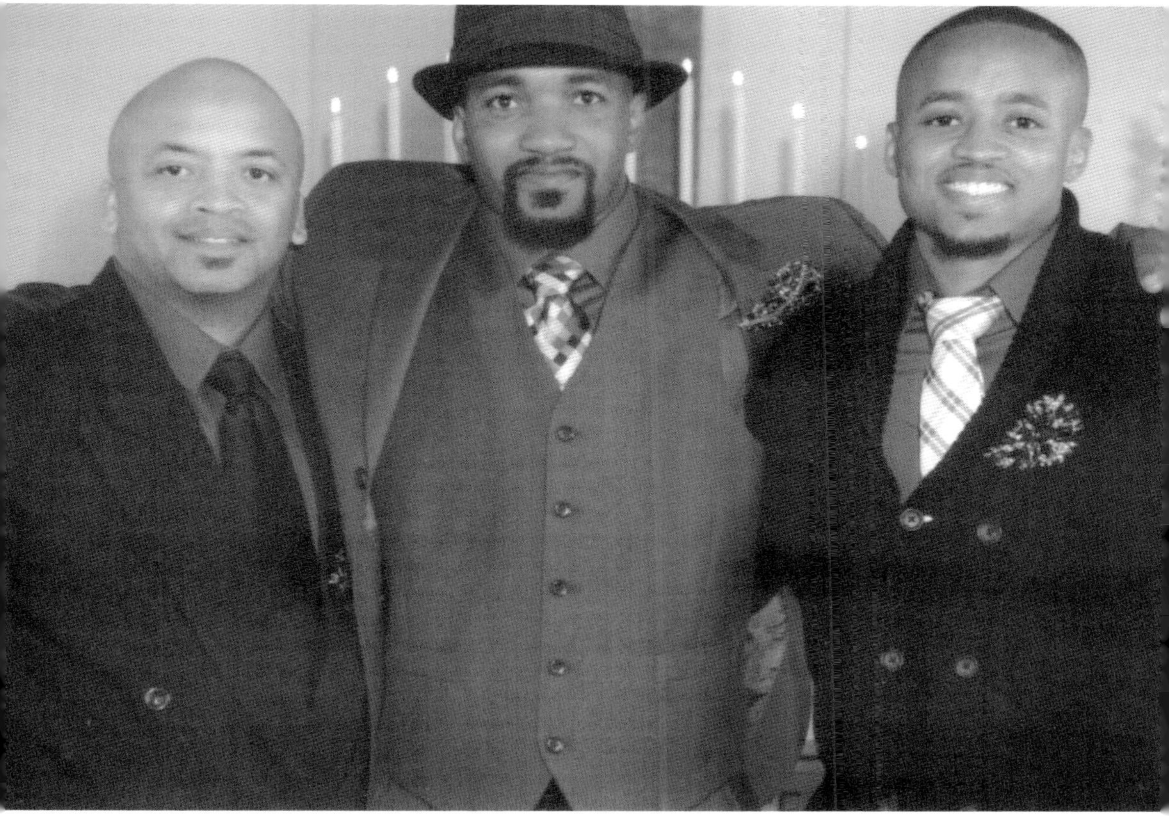

Charley Burks

Charles Anthony Burks graduated from East Central College and received his master's degree in sports administration in 2011. His first coaching job was at East Central University in Ada, Oklahoma, as a defensive back coach. Under the Bill Walsh Fellowship Program, he was a defensive back coach for the Detroit Lions for the summer. He also served as defensive coach one season for West Texas A&M and for Texas A&M–Commerce. In 2014, Burks became the first black defensive coordinator in the history of Southeast Oklahoma State University.

Other than his mother, Cynthia, Burks credits his coaches at South Grand Prairie High School as a great influence in his life. He said they taught him how to be a man and were like fathers to many boys who did not have fathers. Charley Burks is pictured here at right with his brothers Kendrick (left) and Marcus (center). (Courtesy of Burks family.)

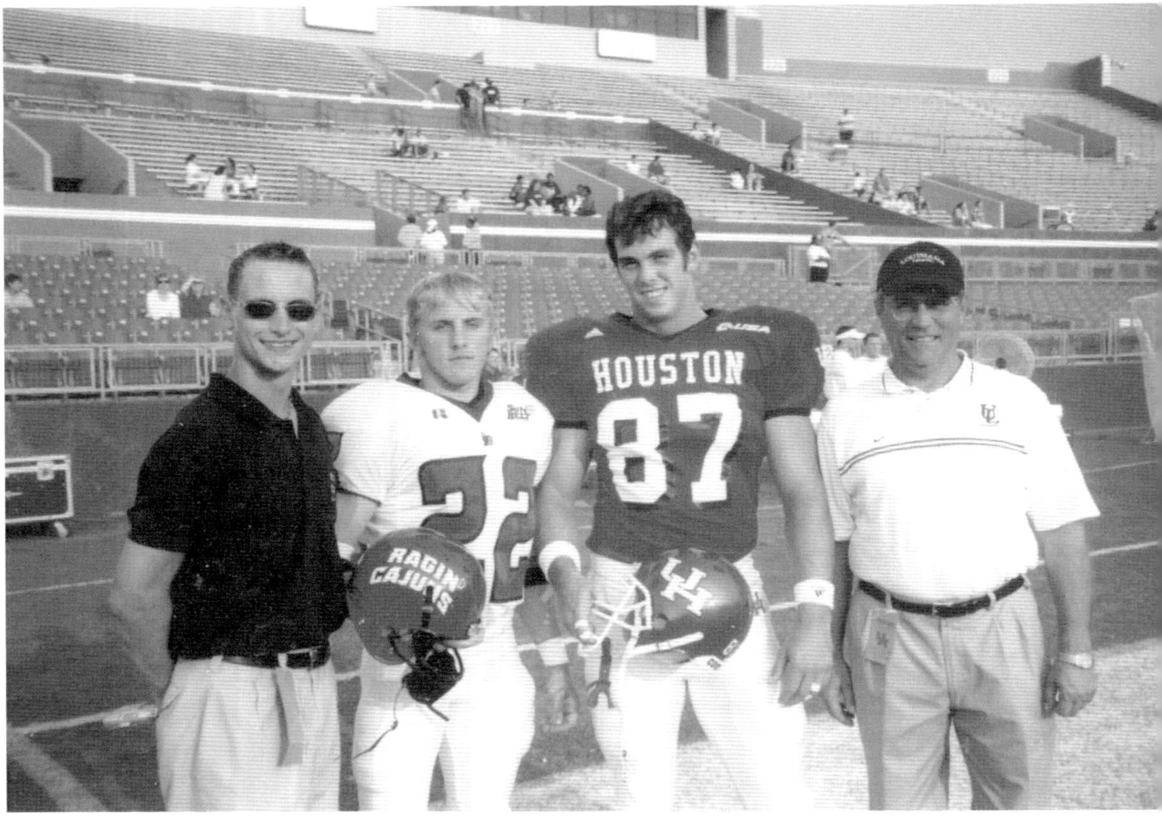

Gary Bartel

Bartel coached college football for 27 years before returning to his hometown to take a position as head coach for the Grand Prairie football team. During his college coaching days, he was lucky enough to have directed two of his sons, Eric at the University of Louisiana at Lafayette and Jonathan at the University of Houston. However, it must have been tough for Gary on the day that the two teams played each another. He was coach at Lafayette after having coached at Houston.

He has been the Grand Prairie High School coach for more than a decade, and his son Clint serves along with him. Gary Bartel assisted NFL player Jason Witten during one of his football camps. Pictured here from left to right are Clint Bartel, Eric Bartel, Jonathan Pritchett, and Gary Bartel. (Courtesy of Helen Bartel.)

CHAPTER FIVE

Civil Service and Politics

There can be no community without civil servants and politics. Even before incorporation, Grand Prairie enacted a system to deal with community issues. Before that, there were individuals willing to help one another. That ideal should be at the heart of every individual or politician serving the community. Unfortunately, that is not always the case.

Grand Prairie has seen many people with a love for the city help it develop and grow. Men like G.H. Turner, who spent many years as mayor and dealt with a town growing into a city, including during the Great Depression. Slowdowns did not stop his generosity or dedication to Grand Prairie. The city embraced innovation while other towns waited to see what side society would stand on. In 1960, when Natalie Minnie was hired as a meter maid, Grand Prairie became one of the first cities in North Texas to hire a woman to serve in its police department.

Besides being a city that is willing to try new things, Grand Prairie has included people dedicated to civic and political service. J.C. Swadley and his son both served the fire department for decades. Elmer Aamodt, Squat Cannon, and John Bement followed that example, also serving with the department. Many elected officials, including Ruthe Jackson, Roma Skinner, and Martin Frost, and civic leaders, such as Wendel Hulse, committed decades of service to the city, which grew and prospered as a result.

There are always a few individuals who are only motivated to seek power and prestige. In many cases, these citizens started out with high ideals. But those who are elected to higher office can sometimes forget their original visions and the honorable motives for which they were first elected. After years or decades in office, their attitudes can sour; the need for recognition becomes paramount, and they feel entitled. They lose sight of the very citizens who placed them in office.

However, dedication and commitment to seeing progress in Grand Prairie has been the norm for those who serve. Civil service was not limited to city government. Many men and women were actively involved in organizations like the Masons, Rotary, Boy Scouts and Girl Scouts, Kiwanis, the Women's Club, and the Lions Club. Through volunteers, these organizations better the lives of residents. Some people, though not active in organizations, quietly used their own positions, talents, and services to help others. The generosity was quietly given and accepted to avoid embarrassment to the giver or the receiver. Those who give are the individuals with the real heart of a servant.

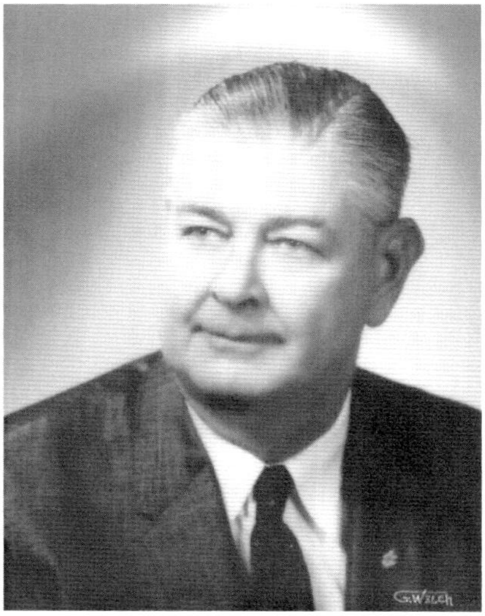

E. Caryle Smith

Mayor of Grand Prairie from 1949 to 1953, E. Carlyle Smith's fingerprints can be found all over Grand Prairie. He was a partner with Smith & Warder Architects and Engineers, responsible for a number of local buildings, including the Masonic lodge. A devoted Mason, Carlyle helped to raise money for the Sam Hamilton Masonic Lodge, and was instrumental in its design. Among other accomplishments, Carlyle was instrumental in the city setting up home rule. (GPML.)

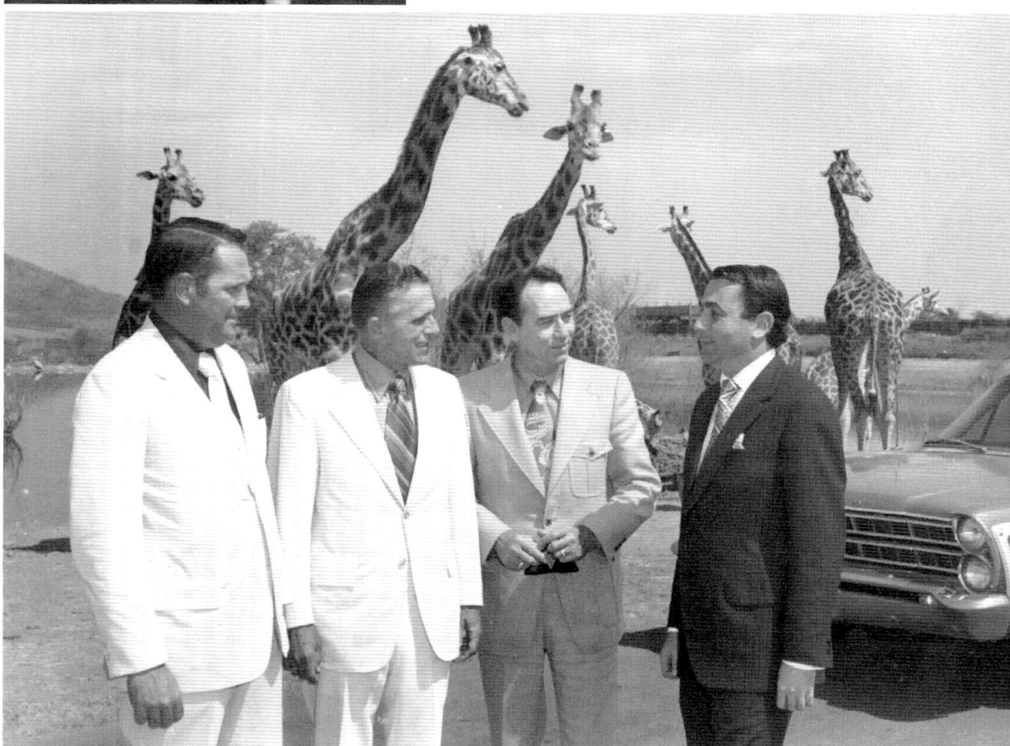

Lion Country Safari

In the early 1970s, when Joe Colwell and Bills Bowles were mayors of Grand Prairie, it was hailed as a tourist attraction. One of the things that brought so many to the city was the 485-acre Lion Country Safari. Unfortunately, the safari was plagued with scandal and other problems, and it finally closed after a flood destroyed the drive-through zoo, killing most of the wildlife and allowing other animals to escape. Could Mayor Colwell have understood what a tall order it was to maintain the park? Pictured here from left to right are Jerry Brownlow, Frank Cone, Mayor Joe Colwell, and unidentified. (CofC.)

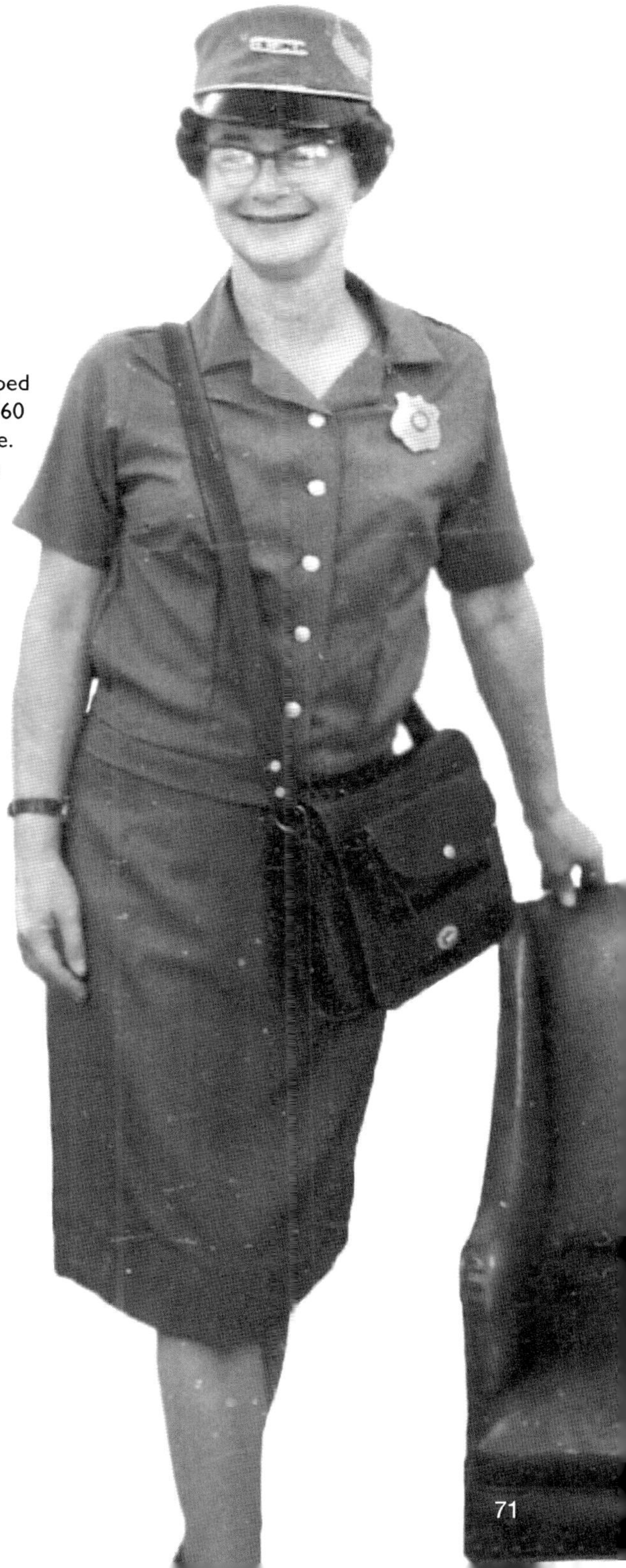

Natalie Minney

In 1948, Natalie Minney and her husband stopped over in Fort Worth. They ended up staying. By 1960 Natalie was divorced, with four children to raise. Grand Prairie was one of the first in North Texas hiring women to help with parking tickets and administrative duties. Affectionately known as "Minney the Meter Maid," Minney served 20 years and was Grand Prairie's only meter maid.

Minney kept a daily log of information she felt pertinent to her job. She carried transportation schedules and information, prepared to help residents. she considered her position a threefold ambassadorship: service to the city, to businesses, and to customers. She always maintained her sense of duty and a sense of humor. Her first ticket downtown went to the businessman's committee chairman. She once ticketed a horse, which promptly ate it. Her last duties were as a bailiff in the court. (Courtesy of Darlene Hubbard.)

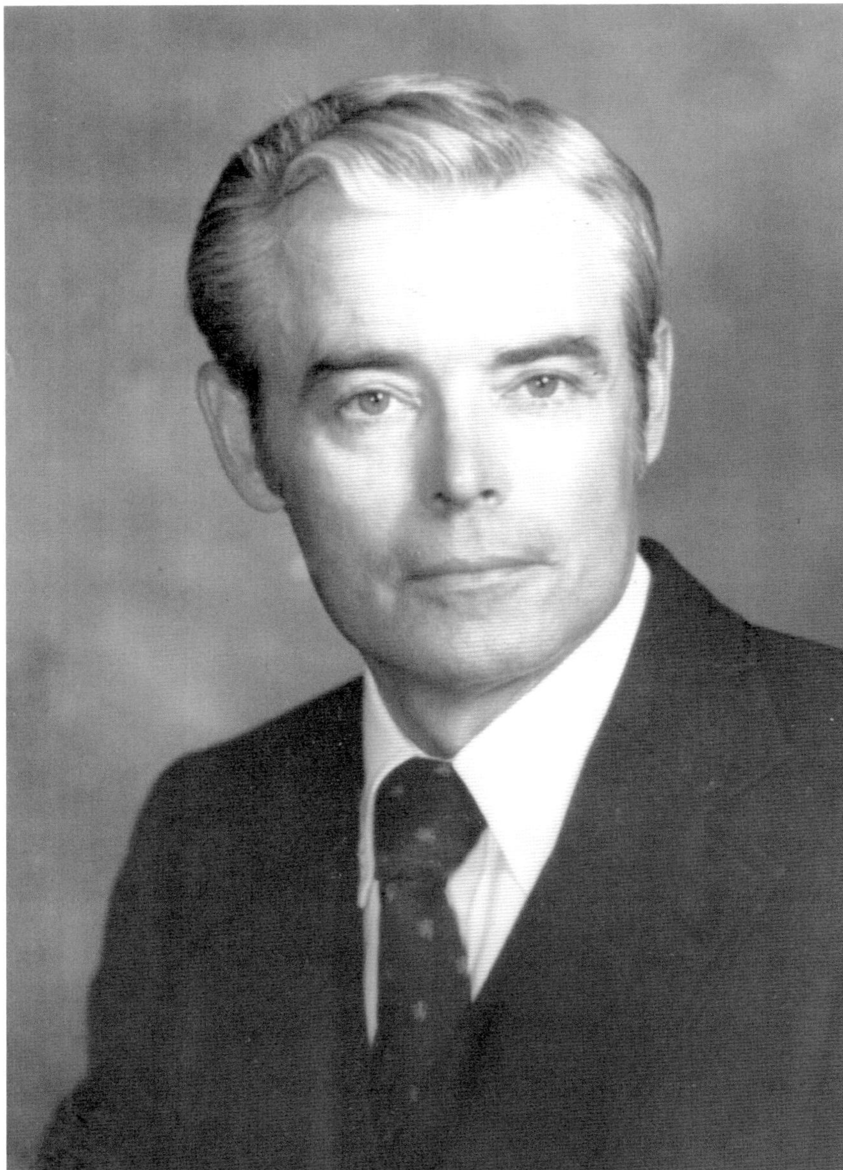

Ed Churchill

Churchill, a numbers guy, held many different positions. He was the manager for cost estimates at Collins Radio, budget control supervisor for the Vought Aeronautics Division at LTV, assistant to the president at Southwestern States Bankcard Association, and vice president of Boone-Hansen Productions Inc. He was the winner of the President's Award at LTV. These positions proved to be foundational for his work when he was elected to the city council in 1979. According to the *Grand Prairie News*, Churchill described himself as "an honorable man whose successful development business is built on sound judgment."

He participated in his community in other capacities. He spoke at the New Comers Club, he was the program chair for the PTA at Sam Houston Elementary, and he was named Outstanding Jaycee in Iowa and appointed to the city building board in 1977. (GPML.)

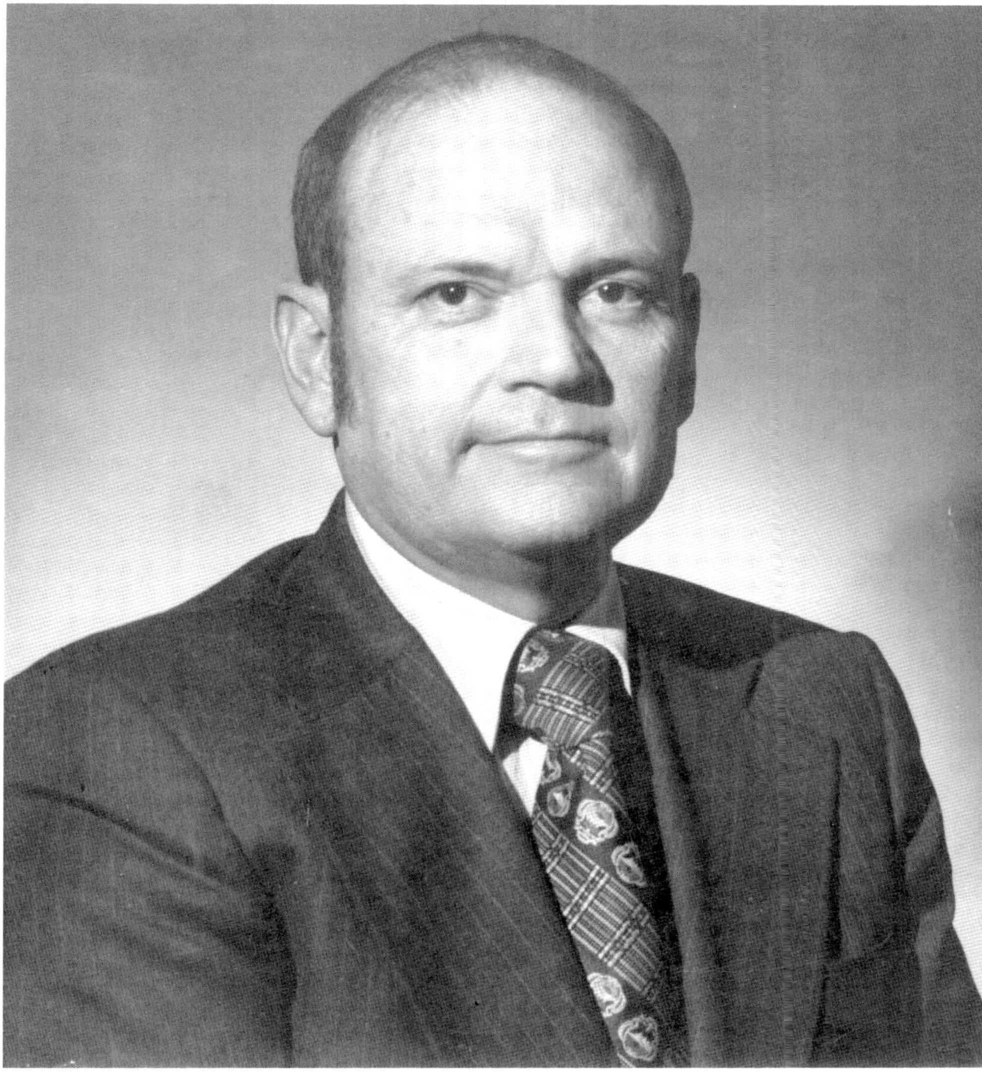

William Bowles

Bill Bowles has been a licensed attorney in Texas since 1957. He was mayor from 1972 to 1976 and had a cornucopia of issues to deal with. The town was booming, and Grand Prairie considered building a major tourist attraction. Mayor Bowles coordinated with the surrounding cities as well as the local chamber of commerce to help with growth.

He worked with the City of Arlington for an Amtrak station while dealing with concerns from property owners on Jefferson Street. They were upset over parking spaces built and the lack of assessments for parking along Main Street. Real-estate development was expanding, especially to the south toward I-20. There were other concerns, too: issues with the Environmental Protection Agency on plans for a regional mall, development of a city-subsidized ambulance service, and the opening of Trader's Village. The city broke ground and built a new city hall, and computerization of city departments began. Planning for Joe Pool Lake began, and the Hospital Authority was established. The hospital opened in 1975.

In the short time he was mayor, Bowles was able to juggle many issues facing the city. Whether projects were successful or not, Mayor Boyles maintained a focus on getting the job done. (GPML.)

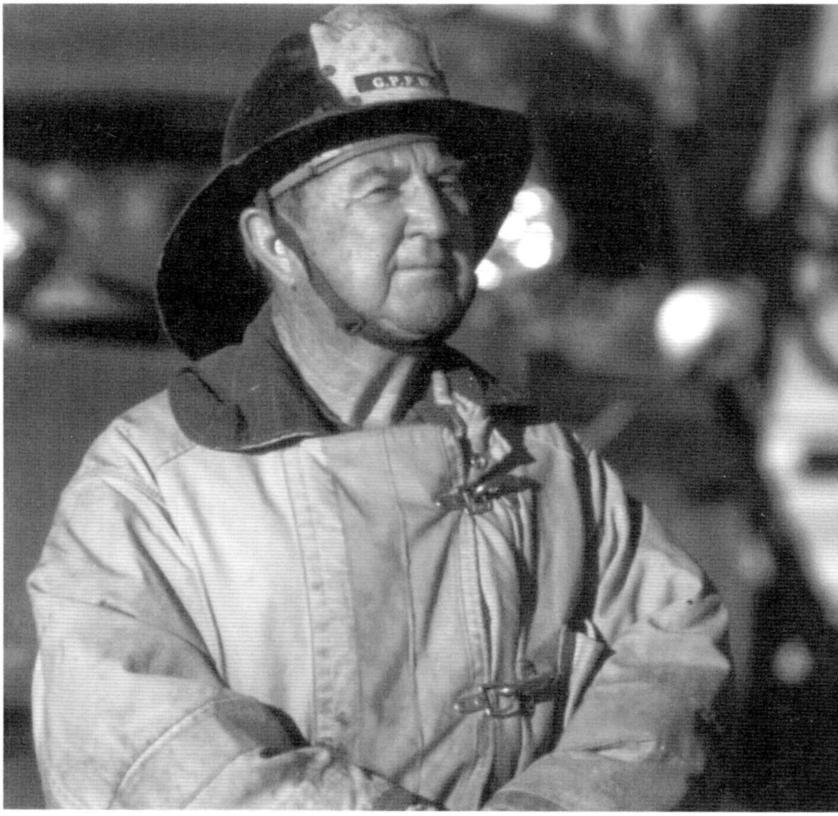

Lyndole Raymond Cannon

"Squat" Cannon was more than a fireman. With an entrepreneurial spirit, he invested in real estate, owned both residential and commercial properties around Grand Prairie, and was a co-owner with Billy Graves in GNC Mowing & Sales. Other firemen who tried to start mowing services ended up working for them.

Cannon was a multifaceted man. Many called him a character, but he also had character. When the fire department was involved in burning old structures to help with urban renewal, Cannon salvaged items for property repairs. Heading back to the station with a roll of fence or a toilet on the truck did not stop him from whistling at pretty girls. On one occasion, Cannon was pulling some wiring from the attic of a structure, and firemen were unaware of his activity before they set the fire.

He shared his entrepreneurial expertise with others, and possessed a generous heart. Whether greatly discounting the price of a car to preserve a man's dignity, or simply helping a family, his generosity was done quietly. He was known for giving away $2 bills, but he also bought barrels of work gloves at auction and gave them away. Cannon was well connected in Grand Prairie, but he was not much of a joiner. He was a lifetime member of the Grand Prairie Historical Organization and a member of First Congregational Methodist Church.

More than anything, Squat Cannon loved the fire department. He was once asked why he never made captain, and he responded that he liked being on the hose. The other firemen liked him being there, too. It has been said that there was none more trustworthy to go into a fire with, because men knew Squat Cannon would not leave them. When a close friend and fellow fireman and his wife were killed in a car accident, he insisted on going to the site of the incident. He took a cactus from the location and planted it at a building next to the old No. 1 station downtown. (Courtesy of Darcy Harris and L.R. Cannon family.)

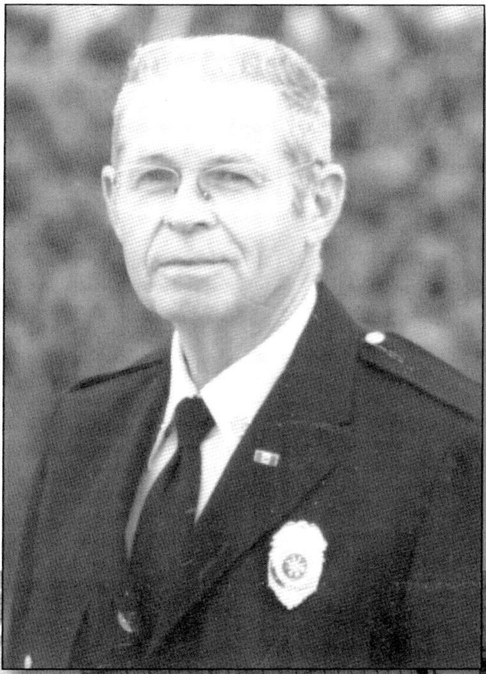

Elmer J. Aamodt

The silent memorial between two small buildings on Main Street adjacent to the old No. 1 Fire Station honors former fire marshal Elmer J. Aamodt and his wife, Mary L. Aamodt. They were killed in an automobile accident in June 2008. The small cactus found near the crash site was planted by L.O. Cannon, and has grown into a large plant. Though time can erase the memory of the 33 years Elmer spent with the Grand Prairie Fire Department and his 30 years as a reserve for the police department, as well as Mary's years at LTV, the small, unmarked memorial continues to honor this couple. They were married for 59 years. Active in the community where Elmer lived for 60 years and where Mary was a lifelong resident, it is obvious they had an impact. (GPHO.)

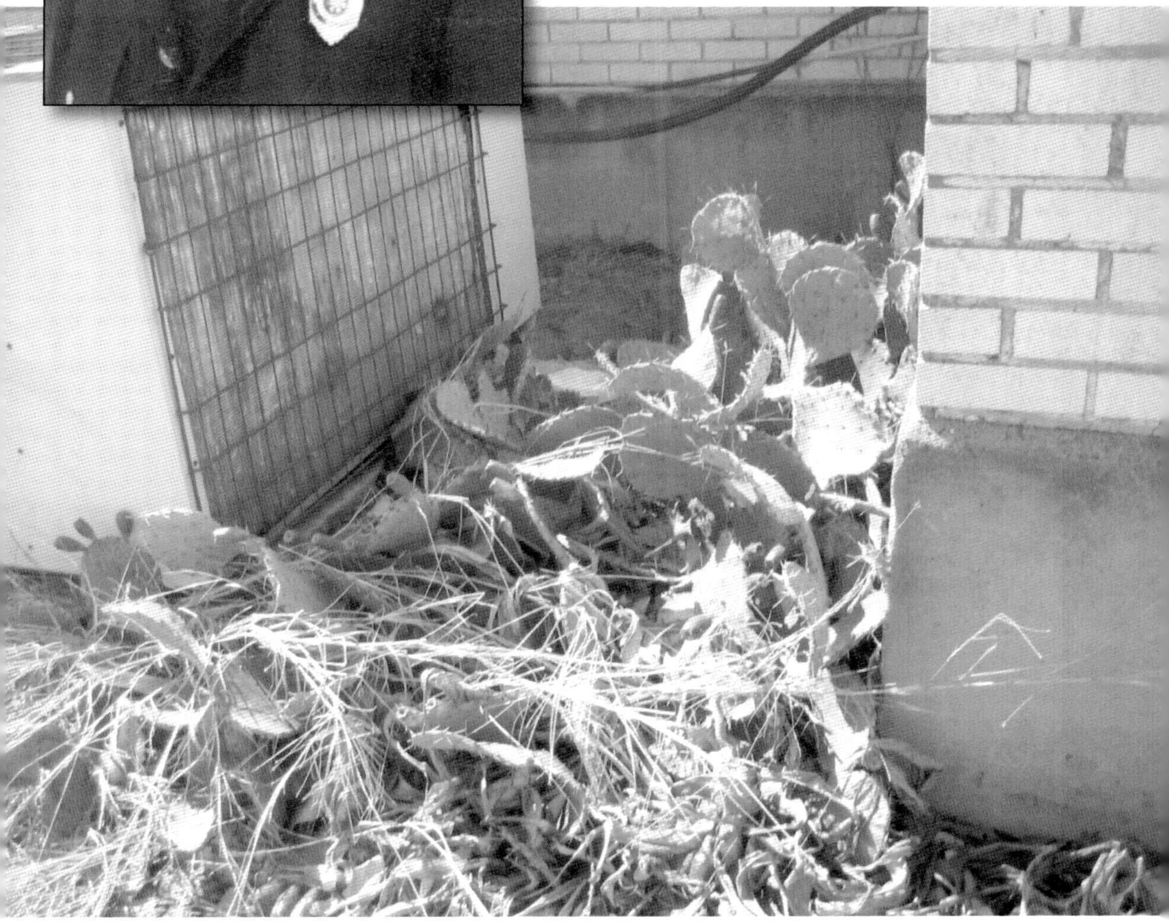

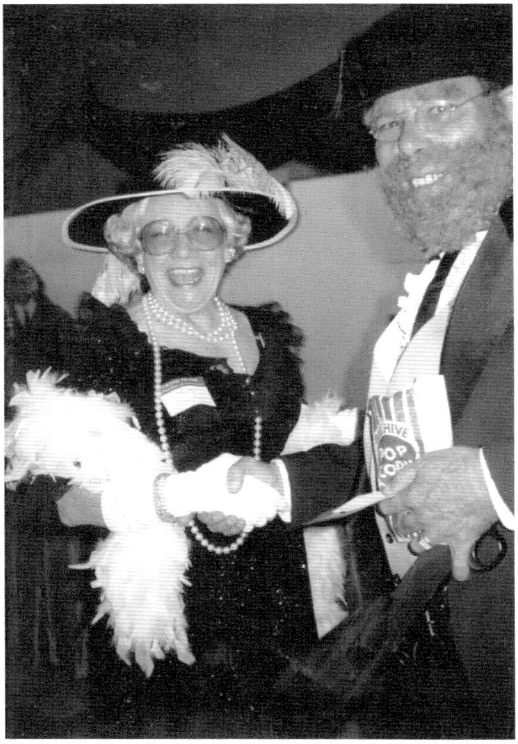

Anne Gresham

Spunky and fun-loving, Anne Gresham served on the city council for six years before running for mayor. She believed the citizens had been promised more and needed a voice. Her participation with the chamber of commerce in the Texas Municipal League and in the National League of Cities shows how deeply she cared about local government. She was very involved in her community. (GPHO.)

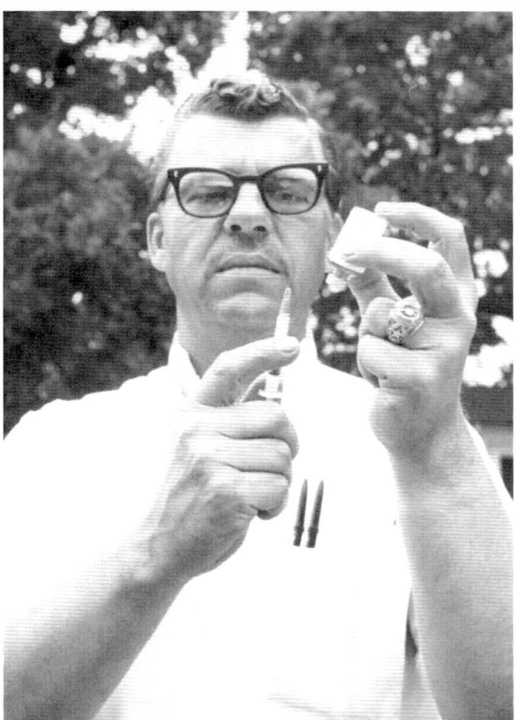

Dr. Robert Lovell Wilson

Bob Wilson served on the city council from 1971 to 1979. He retired from his veterinary practice at the Animal Clinic of Grand Prairie in 1999 after 40-plus years of service. His retirement came at the same time that he had to appear before the Texas State Department of Veterinary Medicine (DVM) Licensing Board for a complaint review. Felony and standard-of-care charges were leveled against him, as well as recordkeeping violations. According to the Texas Veterinary Records website, Wilson's license was suspended, and he received a fine. He was also required to submit reports and cooperate with the DVM board as part of the agreement. (GPML.)

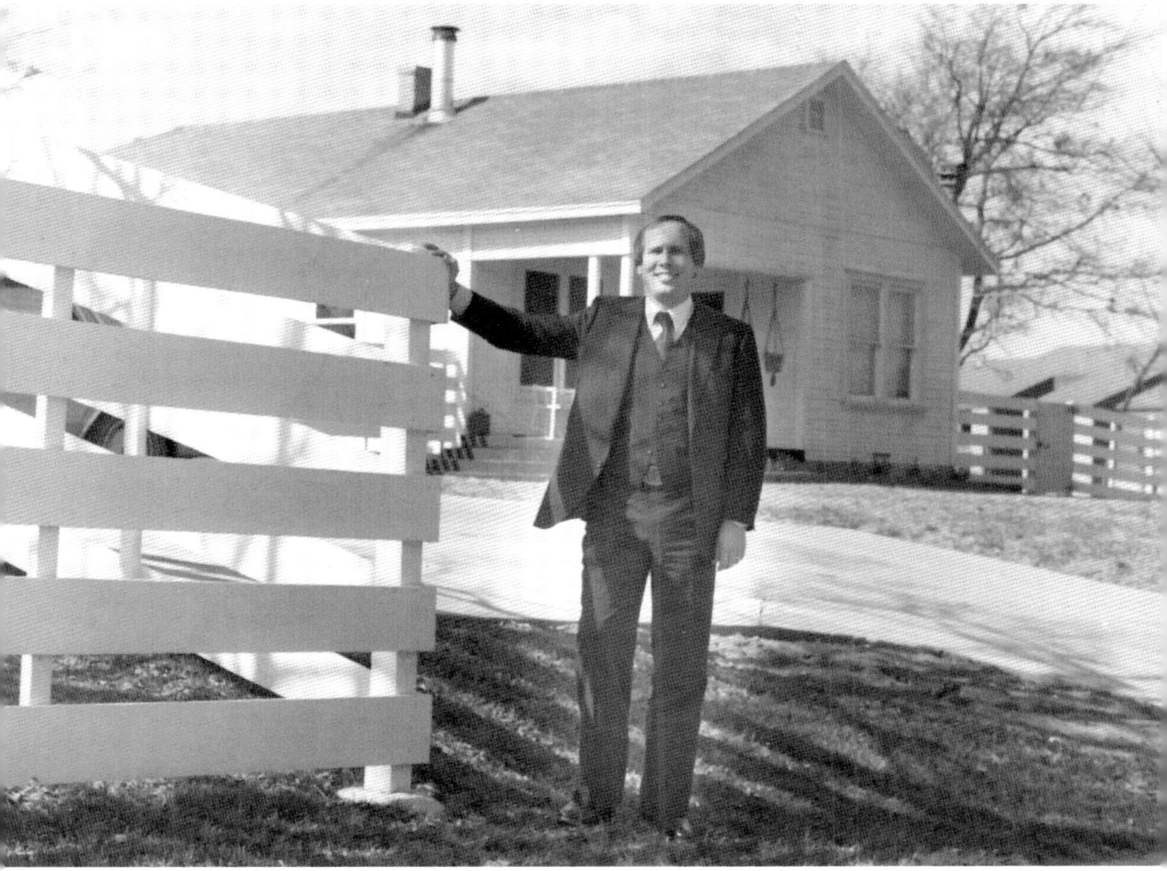

Cameron Gray

A criminal attorney with more than 30 years of experience, Cameron Gray is also an individual who fights for true justice. He is a member of local, state, and national associations and has been recognized for his outstanding service. Gray was given the Governor's Award for Exceptional & Distinguished Volunteer Service and Rotary International's Service Above Self Award. His dedication to others has been seen not only in his international volunteer efforts in El Salvador, Mexico, Honduras, Guatemala, and Haiti, but also in his service as an attorney and a judge. (CofC.)

Vernon Jackson

Married for 68 years, Vernon and Ruthe Jackson met at North American Aviation. Their devotion was threefold: to God, to one another, and to Grand Prairie. Vernon began his vending business with a small route of machines and grew into a company that reached throughout the southwestern United States. A community leader in his own right, Vernon served as president of the school board for several years. He was also chairman of the Urban Renewal Commission, a board member for Midway National Bank (later Republic Bank), an elder at church, and a member of both the Rotary and the Lions Club. (Courtesy of Jorja Clemson and Jackson family.)

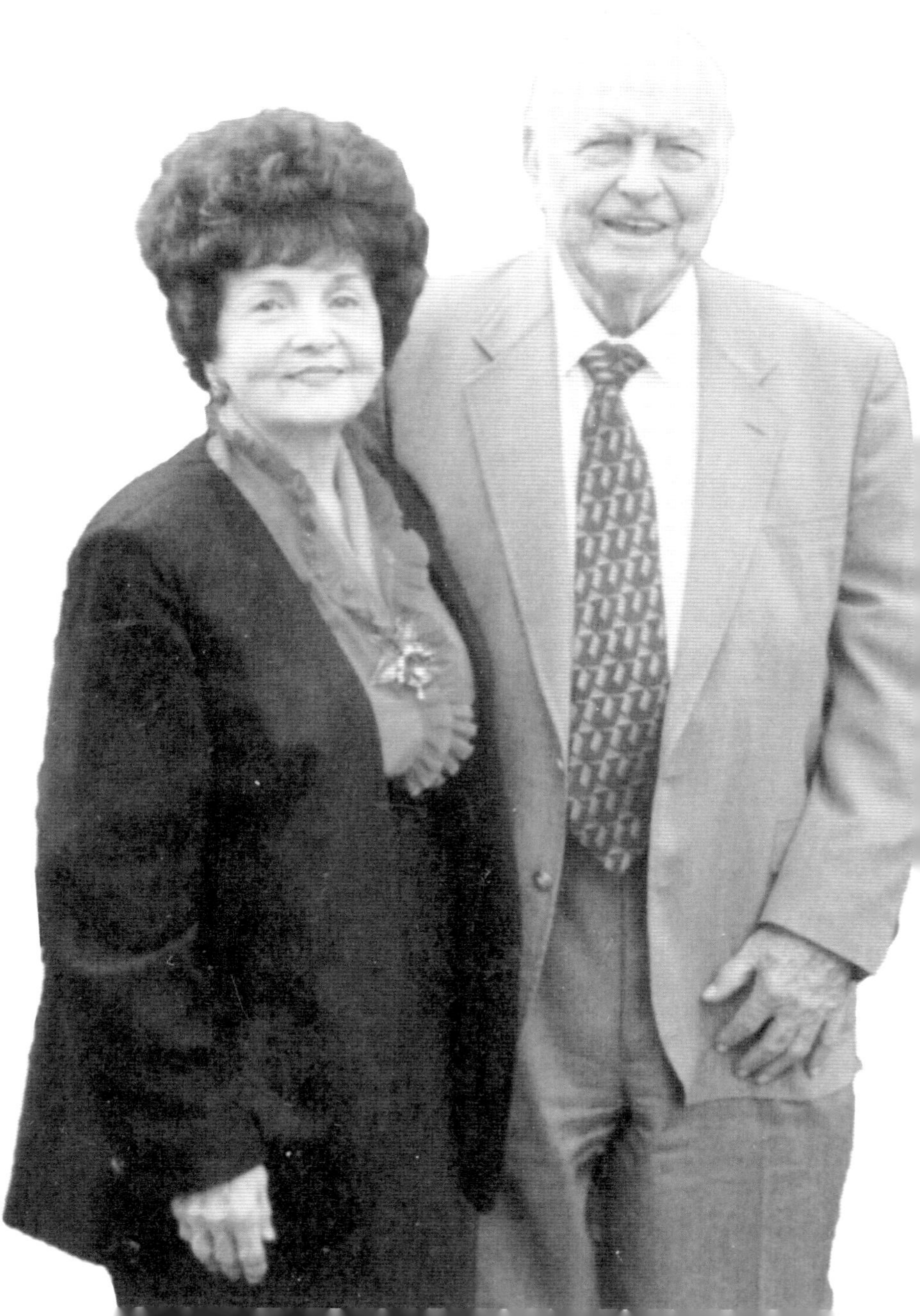

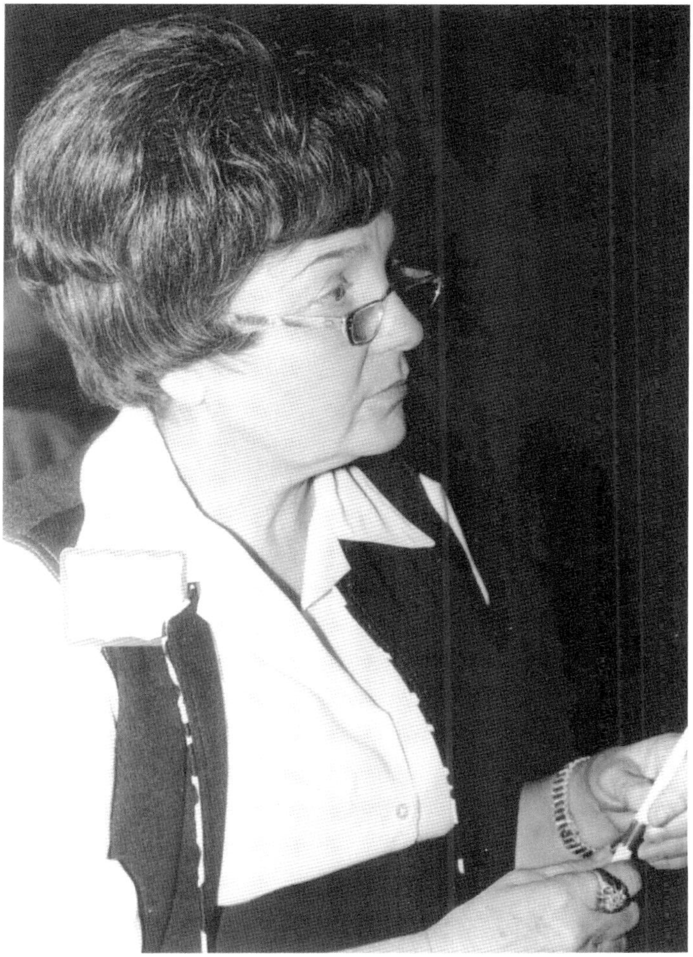

Ruthe Jackson

Vernon Jackson was a big supporter of his wife, Ruthe, and encouraged her in her community involvement. Afraid she might be asked to speak when she was first urged to be treasurer for the PTA, Ruthe overcame her apprehensions. She lived up to her saying, "You have to be braver than Dick Tracy." Ruthe served Grand Prairie as a councilwoman and mayor pro tem for many years. The local television station featured her talk show *What's Happening in Grand Prairie*, which spotlighted people and organizations around town. There was no organization in Grand Prairie in which she was not involved. She supported everything from nonprofits to chamber of commerce events. Jackson was a member, attended events, and made donations. The Jacksons' gumball-machine donation was always featured in silent auctions around town.

Ruthe Jackson's efforts were not only local. Her involvement extended to statewide programs. She was involved with the Texas State PTA and other programs, such as Keep Texas Beautiful. But, she above all loved Grand Prairie and its citizens. Once, when looking at the budget, she pointed out to the mayor that more money was being spent on dogs than on the senior citizens of the city. After that, the senior citizen center, The Summit, was planned and built. She was instrumental in having the old senior center dedicated to veterans.

Ruthe and Vernon's dedication to the city was expressed weekly in the prayer breakfast they sponsored for 25 years. Never missing a Saturday, they prayed for the city and for its citizens. (CofC.)

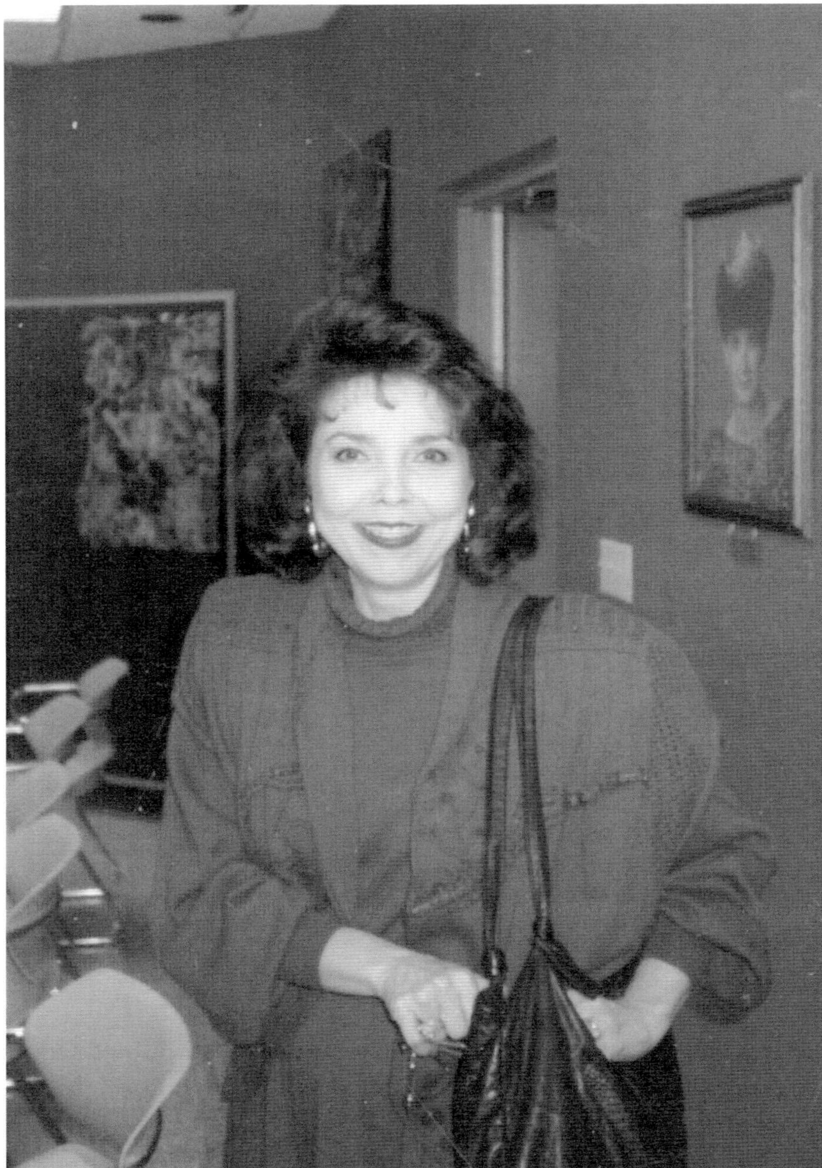

Jorja Jackson Clemson

A Grand Prairie girl all her life, Jorja Jackson went to college and met her husband, Dan, at UTA in Arlington. But, she says she got back to Grand Prairie as soon as possible. Her parents were great mentors, teaching her the importance of community service. She began at an early age, serving in Sunday school. Her many recognitions include being Miss Grand Prairie in her youth, to being named the chamber of commerce Woman of the Year in 2012.

Jorja Clemson serves her church on the worship team. She has also served as president of the PTA and the Women's Club. She was elected to city council. Her greatest passion is her family, and she was honored to be able to serve on the city council in 2013 with her mother, Ruthe Jackson, before Ruthe's death. (CofC.)

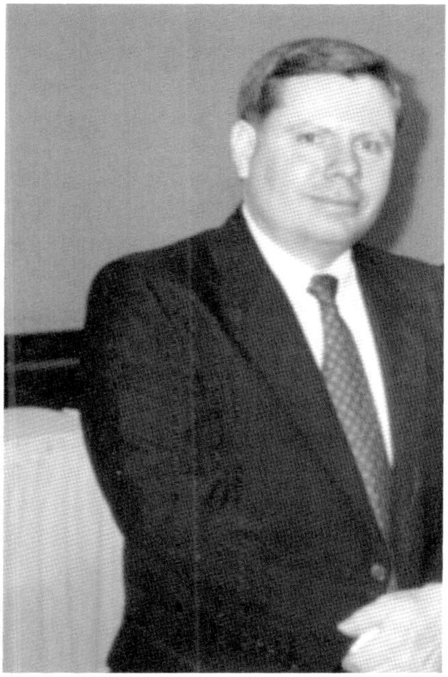

Roma Skinner

Roma Skinner began working as an electrician when he was only a teen. It was not long before he was selling a law-enforcement product line for Ithaca. Encouragement from a friend led him to the police academy and his long career as an officer. As a Dallas County constable, Skinner evicted individuals trying to set up a "Republic of Texas" headquarters at a house in Grand Prairie, where large numbers of weapons and ammunition were removed.

Always busy, he has sold for Sterling Limited out of England. Skinner was a partner with Ray Allen and an instructor for Grand Prairie's school for concealed handgun licensing from the 1990s into the early part of the 21st century. An avid pilot, he owns multiple airplanes. His Russian MiG (below) was painted pink during a fundraiser for breast cancer. (Both, CofC.)

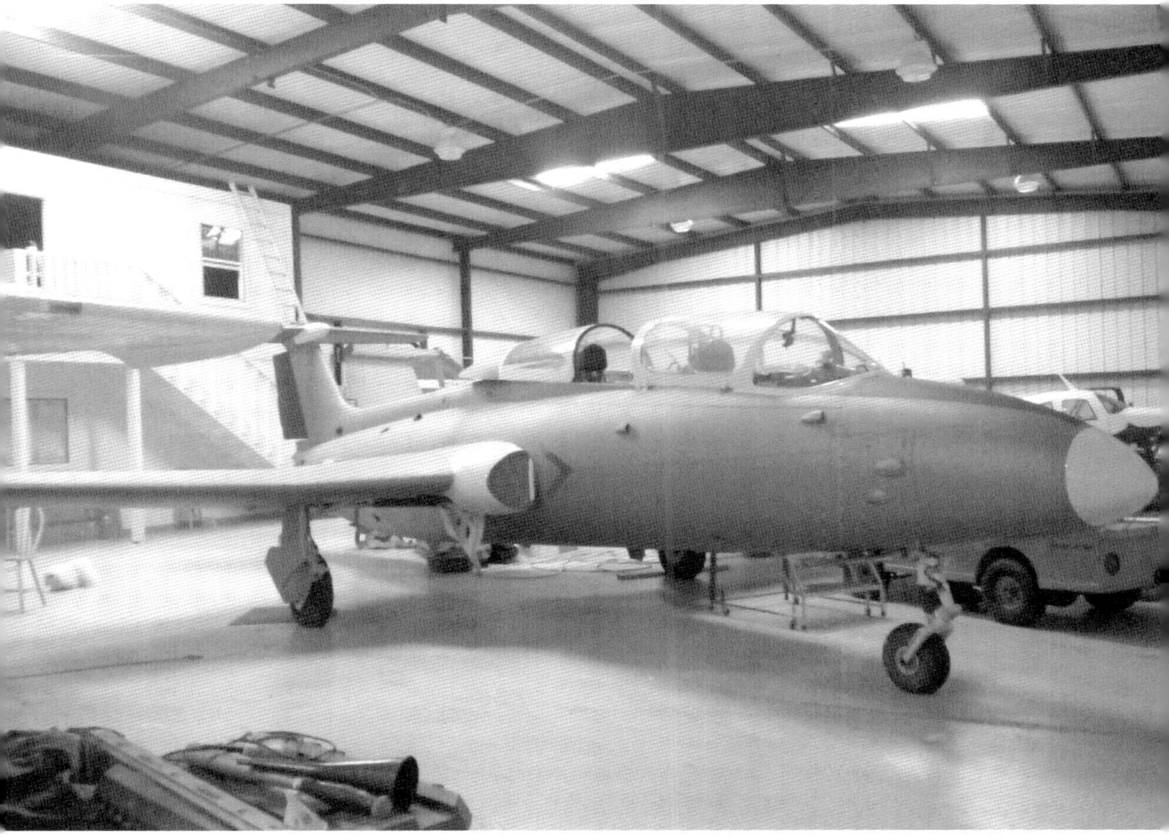

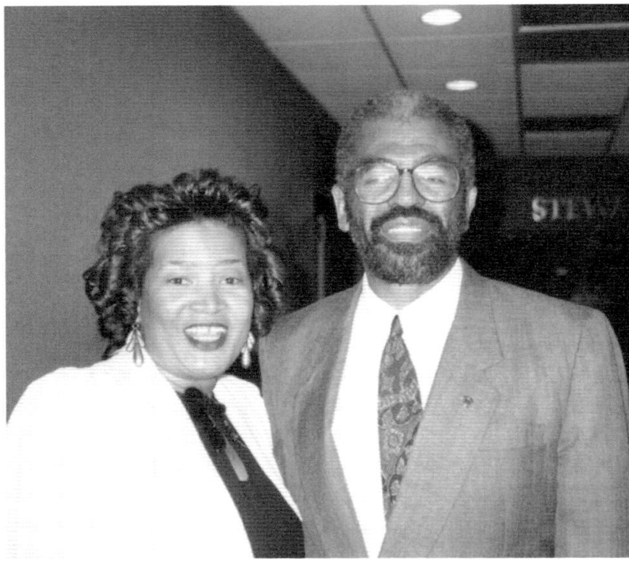

Lee Alcorn

Alcorn, a retired radiology manager, has been an interesting and controversial leader and activist. City council member, chamber of commerce board member, and city planning board nominee, Alcorn lost elections against incumbent mayor Charles England, Councilwoman Ruthe Jackson, and a run for the Grand Prairie School Board. Alcorn is pictured above with Marva Dixon.

The Black Dallas Chamber of Commerce awarded him the Willow Award for volunteer contributions, including developing a drug education center in Dalworth. He was founder and president of the Grand Prairie chapter of the NAACP and managed to have the use of the rebel flag by South Grand Prairie High School discontinued. In 2000, as president of the Dallas NAACP, Lee was suspended for a controversial statement about the US presidential race. He subsequently resigned, withdrew his membership, and started the Coalition for the Advancement of Civil Rights. (Above, GPML; below, CofC.)

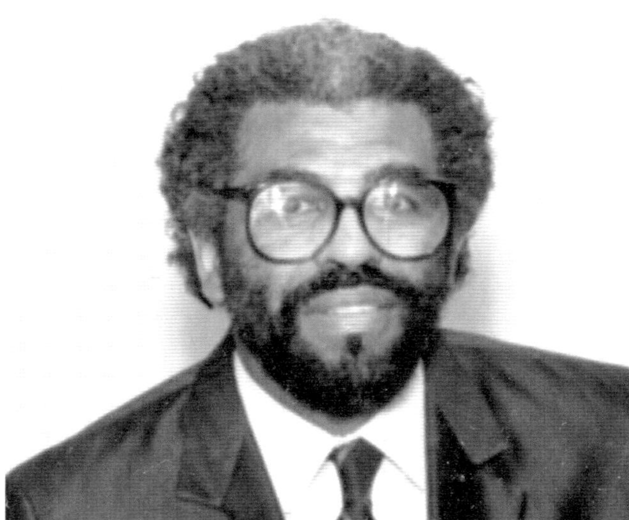

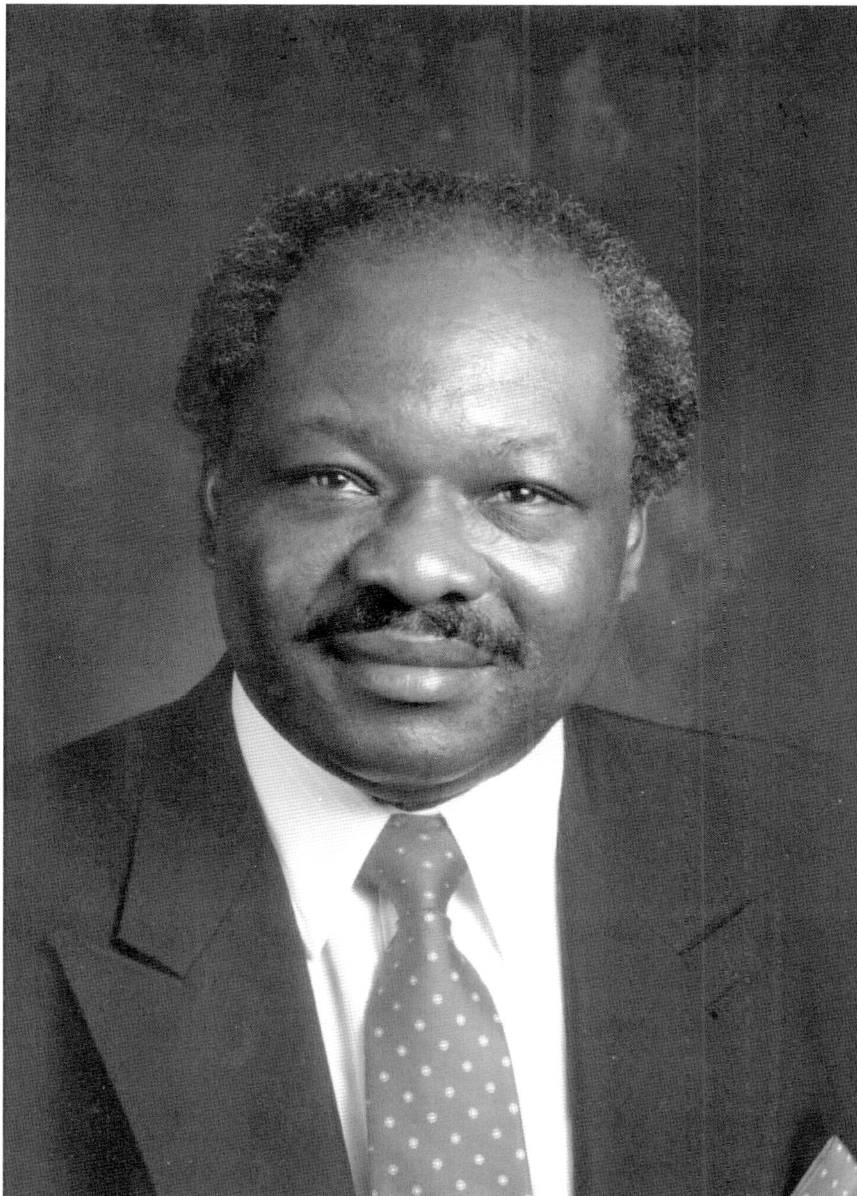

James Kellum
While most who serve the city, whether through business or civil service, are upstanding citizens with substantial character, there are some who fall short. Circumstances and opportunities can breed corruption. Such was the case with city council member James Kellum, who was caught in scandal and resigned. He was found guilty by a jury of 38 counts of fraud. Former general manager for Kellum's business, Dell Morgan, pled guilty to one count of filing a false statement. Alvin Johnson, the contract administrator, was acquitted. It appears that greed got the best of James Kellum, bringing him more than he anticipated. His company took shortcuts and used substandard materials in fulfilling contracts that ended up costing the government about $3 million. (GPHO.)

Wendel Thad Hulse

A man of ambition and integrity, Wendel Hulse graduated from Texas A&M in 1957 with a bachelor's degree in civil engineering. He later worked five nights a week for five years to obtain his law degree from SMU Law School. He served Grand Prairie as the city engineer, director of public works, interim city attorney, assistant city manager, and, finally, city manager. He resigned after 24 years of service when a dispute arose and he was asked to do something that was not legal. He now has his own law practice. (CofC.)

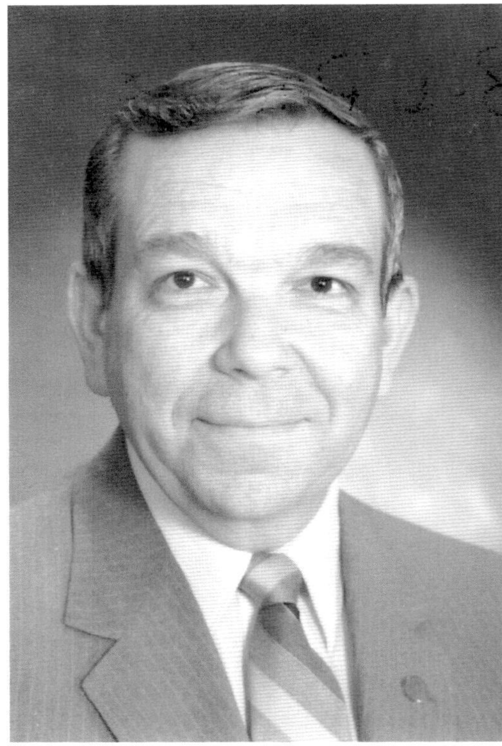

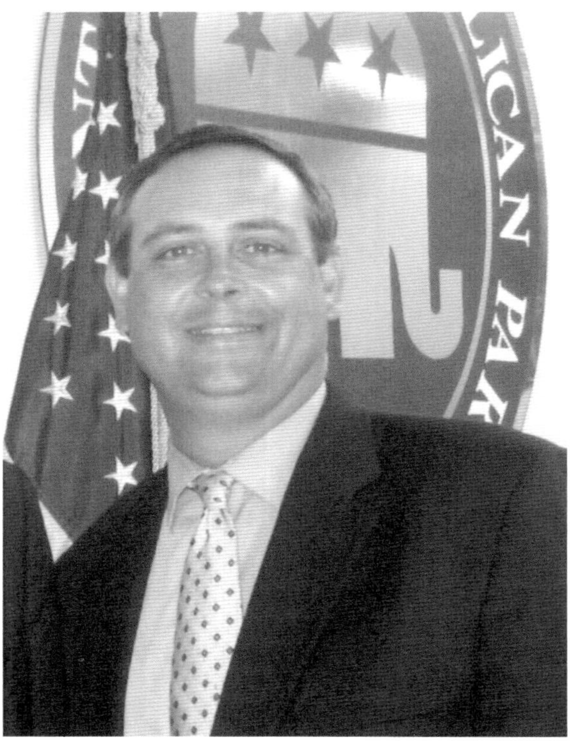

Rodney Anderson

Anderson fought an uphill battle to win his first seat in the Texas legislature, only to be redistricted out of a position. His next campaign was against longtime incumbent Linda Harper Brown of Irving, where most of the district was located. Again, he won the seat in Austin. He is the father of three, married to a local principal's daughter, and involved with Boy Scouts and the Rotary. In addition, Anderson is on the executive board for the chamber of commerce. He says that he is "About as boring a person as you would ever want to meet." (Courtesy of Rodney Anderson.)

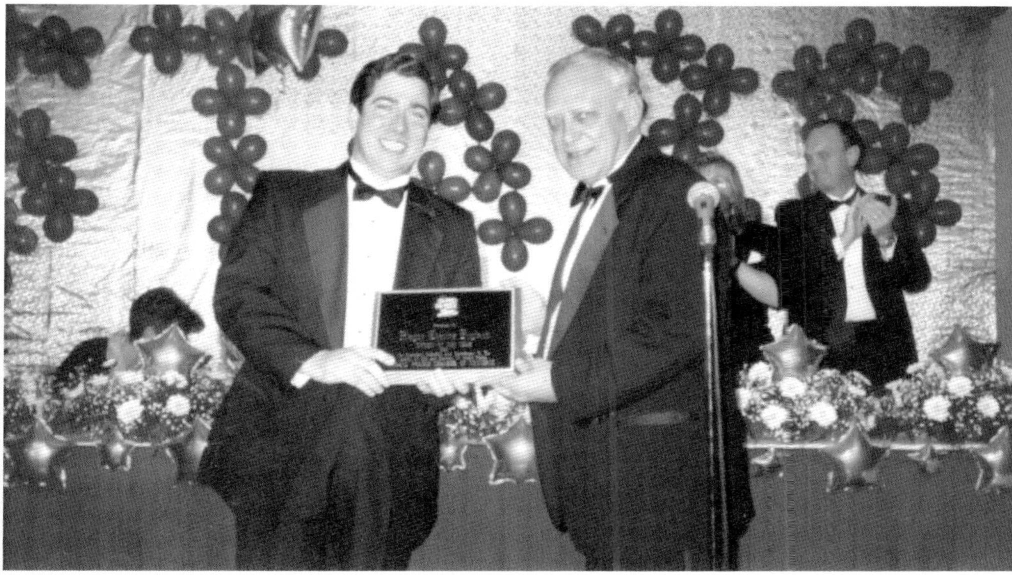

Charles England

England came to Grand Prairie as an eighth grader. He served three years on the Grand Prairie School Board and was president of the board in 1975. He was elected mayor in 1992 and served in that capacity until 2013. England married his high school girlfriend, Janice, and they settled in Grand Prairie, where he became an insurance agent. They have celebrated more than a half-century together.

England started college at A&M, but eventually graduated from North Texas with a business degree. He ran for mayor after the city voted to build Lone Star Park. His tenure focused on promoting Grand Prairie as a major tourist attraction again. While in office, the racetrack was completed, a major Metroplex concert theater was built, a minor-league ball team was brought in, and an outlet mall was built, among other developments. England is pictured above at right receiving the Citizen of the Year award from Marty Bragwynne. (CofC.)

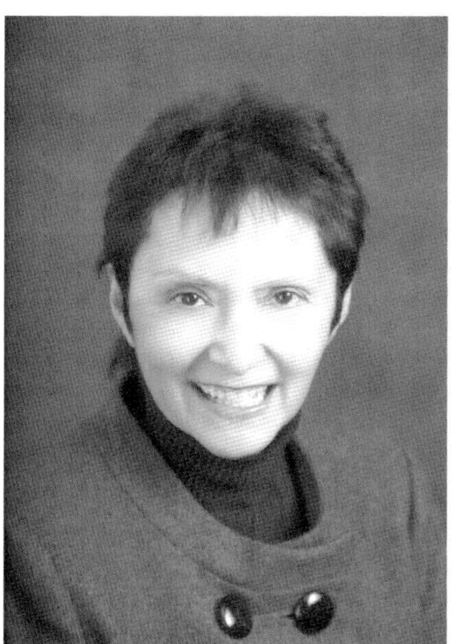

Anna Doll

Anna Doll has had a life as diverse as the city she has served since 1985. In 2002, she was recognized for her service by the Tarrant County Asian Chamber of Commerce. She has had many accomplishments, both personally and professionally. She has been an administrative assistant to the city manager, budget manager, and deputy city manager for Grand Prairie. She is a member of the International City, Texas City, and North Texas City Management Associations. On a personal level, she has been a Girl Scout leader as well as an active mom with soccer, volleyball, and orchestra. (GPML.)

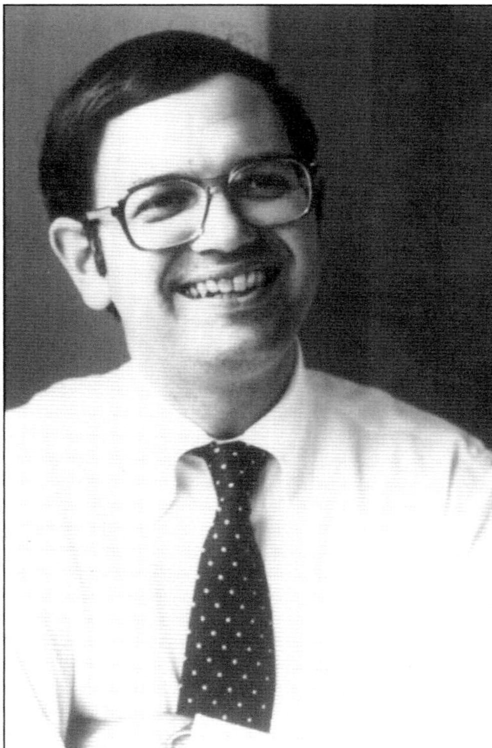

Martin Frost

The 24th Congressional district included parts of Grand Prairie. Martin Frost was a member of the US House of Representatives for this district from 1979 to 2005. A 1964 graduate of the University of Missouri, he later earned his law degree from the Georgetown University Law Center and worked as a law clerk for Sarah T. Hughes before starting private practice. Frost is pictured below at center with high school appointees to US military academies. (Both, CofC.)

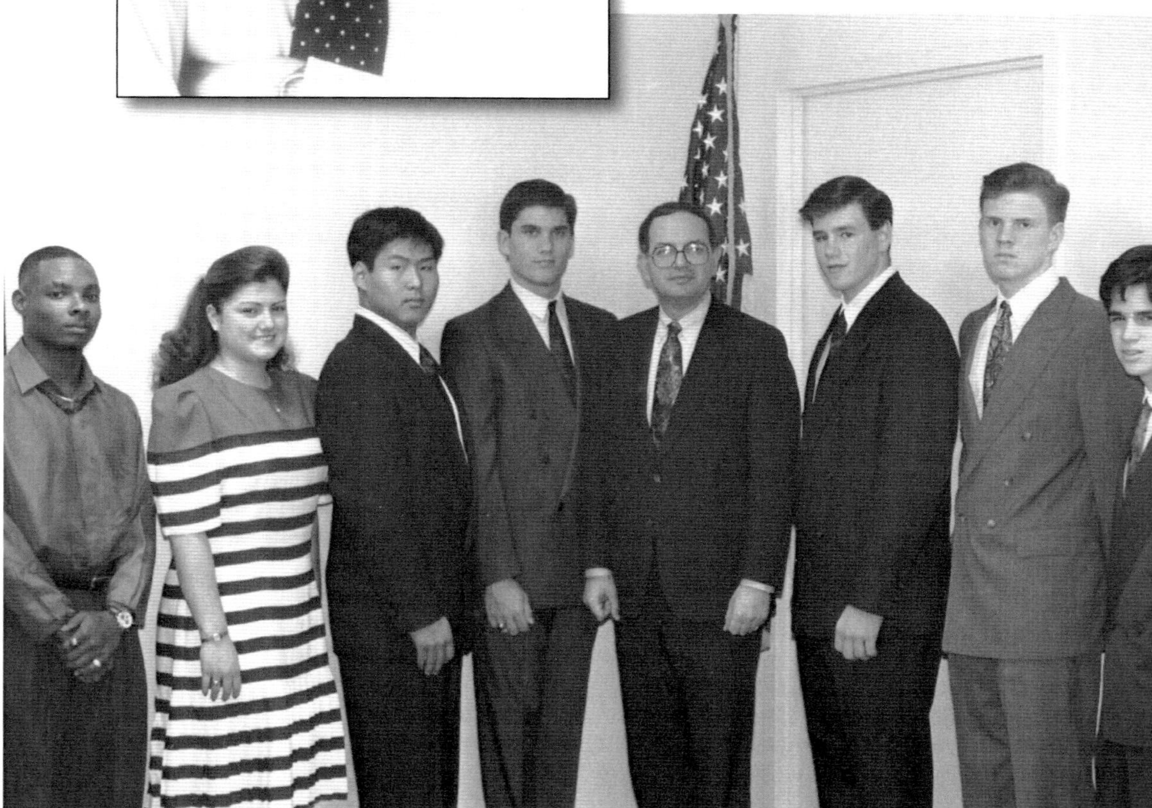

CHAPTER SIX

Community

Of course, everyone within Grand Prairie is part of the community. But there are a number of people and organizations that exist to serve others. The organizations are as many as they are varied. The Women's Club, for example, reaches out to the community in a number of ways and "seeks to provide educational and charitable benefits to the city."

Each club in the community has a specific vision for helping others. It can be as simple as members of the Grand Prairie Genealogical Society volunteering on a regular basis in the library to help people research their families. It might be people in the Historical Organization coordinating with the city's historical commission to preserve the town's rich history or gather information for a special project. Even the quilting club and garden club help to teach and retain skills that add to the community.

Some groups, such as the Pregnancy Resource Center, Brighter Tomorrows, and Lifeline Shelter, provide services for individuals in need. These organizations may have a core group of employees, but the bulk of their services come from volunteers, not paid staff. Free services, from pregnancy tests, to shelter, to life skills, are passed on by the volunteers.

Many individuals within the community participate beyond membership in an organization; they live as an example for others. For example, Beth Hill's long life earns the admiration of others, who learn from her example. Civic employees go above and beyond their job descriptions to ensure that others are served. Businesses liberally give to nonprofits and special projects. Many businessmen and businesswomen give their time and talents to promote individuals, the city, and more.

Often, exposure to these organizations or projects encourages people to serve in other capacities. The involvement of individuals throughout Grand Prairie is repeated again and again. Each leader, businessman, club, volunteer, church, and nonprofit providing help to others reflects positively on Grand Prairie. These efforts promote the image of a caring city. They also allow individuals to bond together.

The satisfaction that comes from helping others is something shared and multiplied. Leaders like Ruthe Jackson, who was involved in a great number of organizations across the city, are often imitated by others. The love and passion for a cause can be contagious. In this way, Grand Prairie has a rotating supply of volunteers and new ideas for the community.

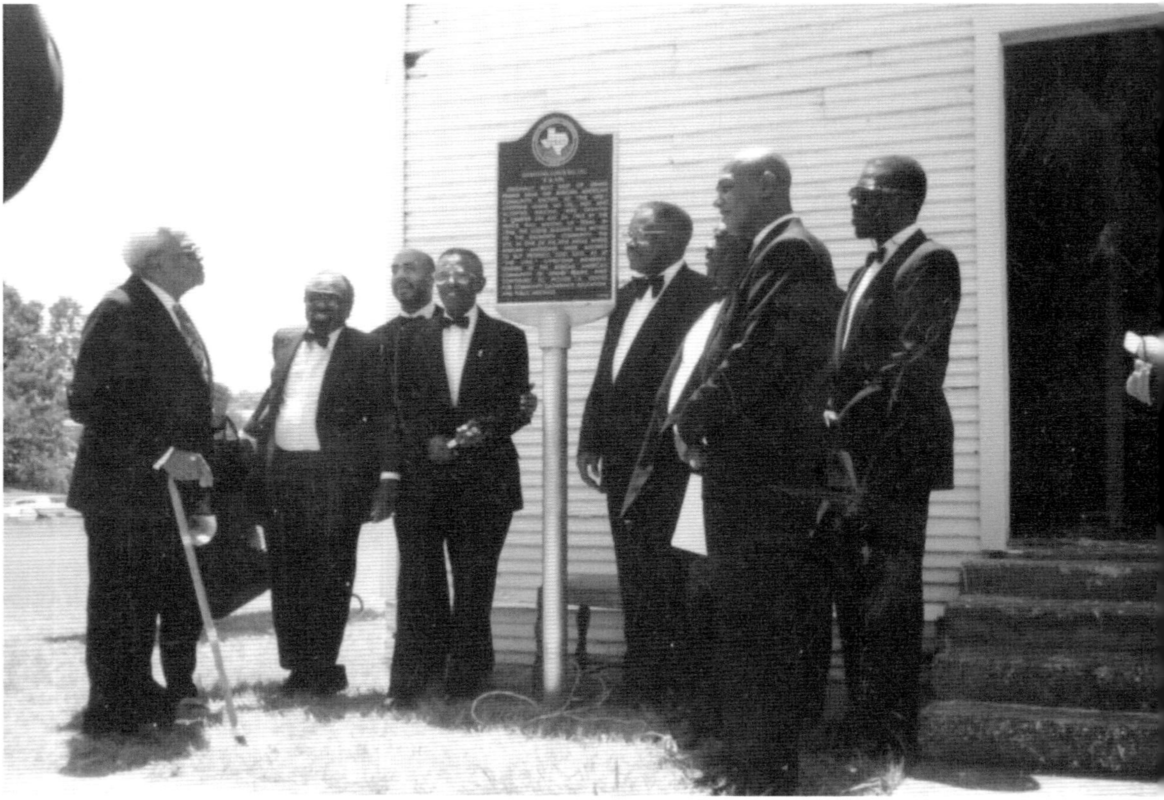

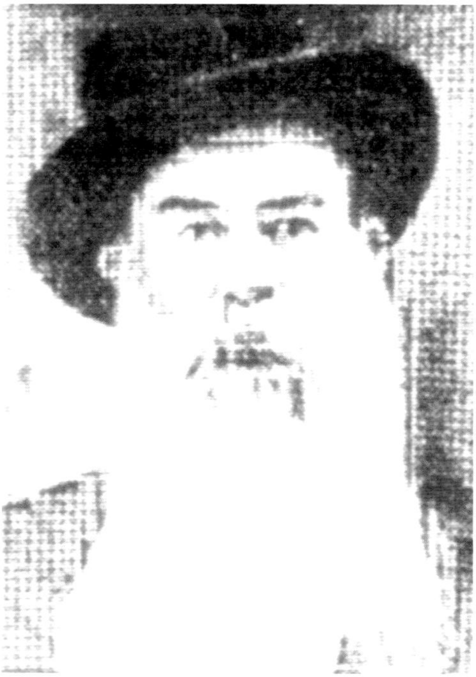

Livestone Lodge and Sam Hamilton Masonic Lodge

There are two Masonic lodges in Grand Prairie, and they have served for more than 100 years. The first lodge was founded and dedicated near "The Line" by freed slaves. Livestone Lodge was started in 1903 and received historical recognition in 1997 (above). It was a sad day when the old wooden building, neglected and beyond repair, was finally torn down.

The Sam Hamilton Masonic Lodge was designed by E. Carlyle Smith and named for the 1899 Texas grand master (left). Carlyle was also instrumental in raising funds for building the lodge in 1910. Located next to First Methodist Church, this is the spot where members met before the building was dedicated. It, too, has a historical designation.

Grand Prairie has a rich heritage of service from its resident Masons. They have served in all levels and capacities in the community. (Above, GPHO; left, GPML.)

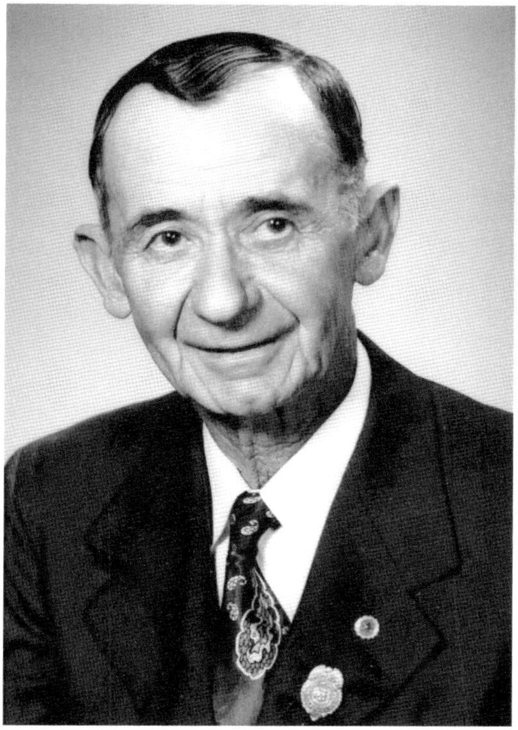

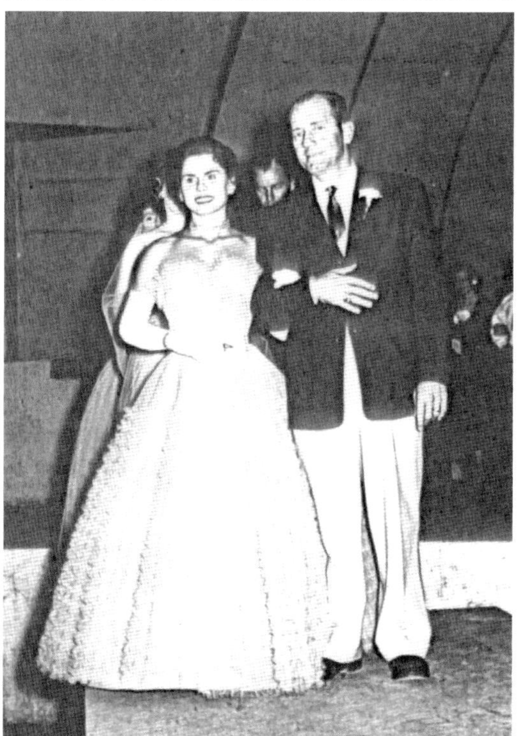

Jacob Swadley Sr. and Jacob Swadley Jr.

Jake Cleveland Swadley Sr. came to Grand Prairie before the turn of the 20th century. Along with John Stubbs and Jeff Small, he organized Grand Prairie's first fire department in 1917. Swadley (top) served as fire chief for 30 years, until his retirement in 1950. The fire department was not the only thing he was involved in founding. He was also a charter member of the Lions Club and First Methodist Church. He owned a garage, was a member of the chamber of commerce, and served as a city commissioner in the 1930s and 1940s.

Taking up where his father left off, Jacob Cleveland Swadley Jr. became fire chief in 1950. Beginning as a volunteer fireman, after 14 years, J.C. became the first paid firefighter, and later, the first paid fire chief. After retiring, he became the fire protection chief for Six Flags over Texas. In 1953, he was president of the State Firemen's and State Fire Marshals' Association of Texas. In the photograph at bottom, J.C. Swadley is seen escorting Miss Flame of Grand Prairie, Betty Ann Stephenson, at the State Fair of Texas. J.C.'s dedication was recognized when the Central Fire Station was named in his honor. (Both, GPML.)

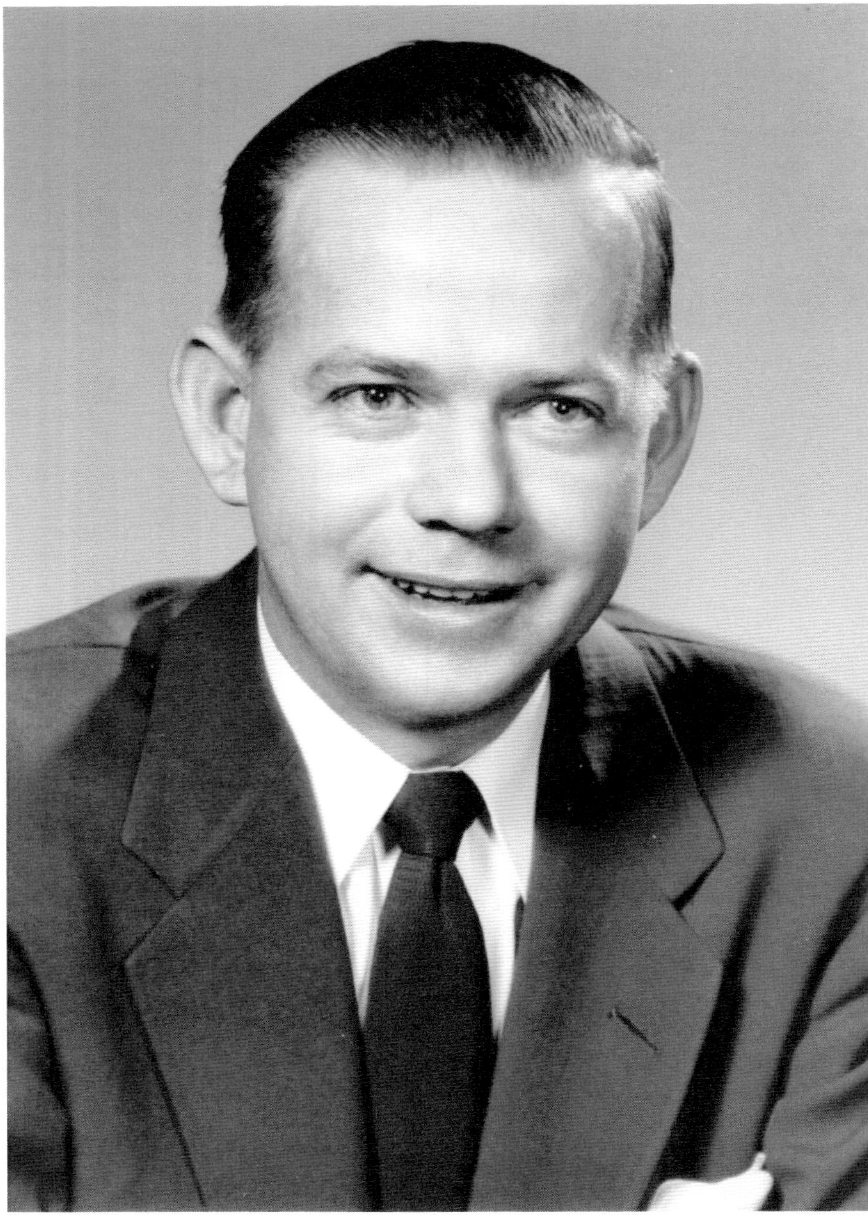

Charles William Powers

Bill Powers was born in Grand Prairie in 1925 and served as a first lieutenant in the Army during World War II, when he fought in Guam. When he retired, he was a senior vice president of the Bank of America.

His great passion for history led him to become a tour guide in the Dallas–Fort Worth area. Powers's membership in organizations included serving on the Dallas Fair Park Subcommittee and the Landmark Commission. He was a life member of the Grand Prairie High School Alumni and president of the Grand Prairie Historical Organization. Bill Powers married Nancy Jane Sanderlin, and they had three children. (GPML.)

Hallie Van Reekum

Hallie Virginia King Van Reekum was valedictorian of her high school class. She graduated from Grand Prairie High School with her twin sister, and they attended the University of Arkansas, where Hallie majored in English. She returned to Grand Prairie and was chairman of the library committee for the first Grand Prairie Study Club. As such, she spoke throughout the community to promote a Dallas County Library System. Van Reekum got the Dallas County commissions to start Grand Prairie Memorial Library as an experimental library. She also convinced the state library to loan books to Dallas, to be loaned to the new library. She read to children in her home and would bring a suitcase of books from Dallas for the children. Hallie Van Reekum was a member of the Daughters of the American Revolution, a genealogist, poet, book reviewer, and garden columnist. (GPML.)

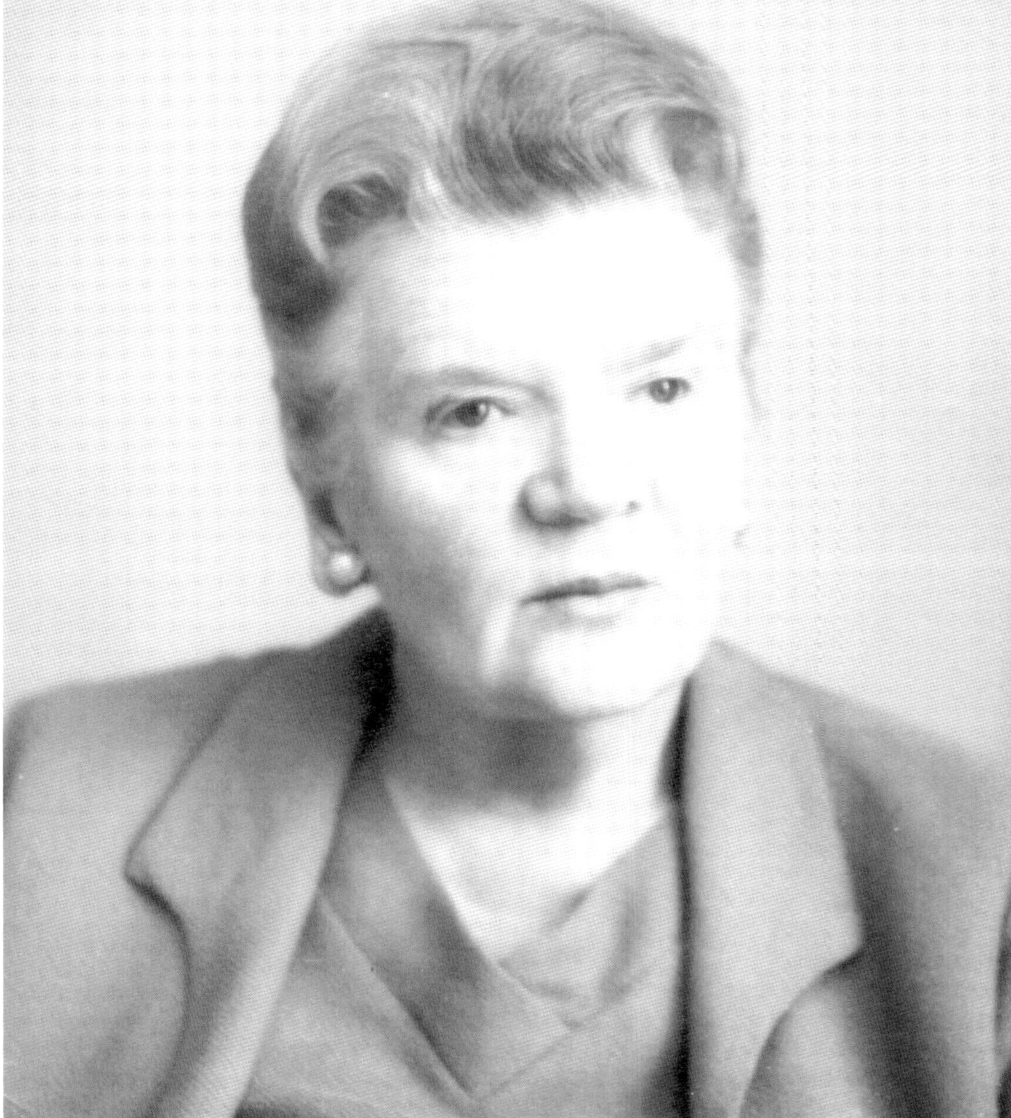

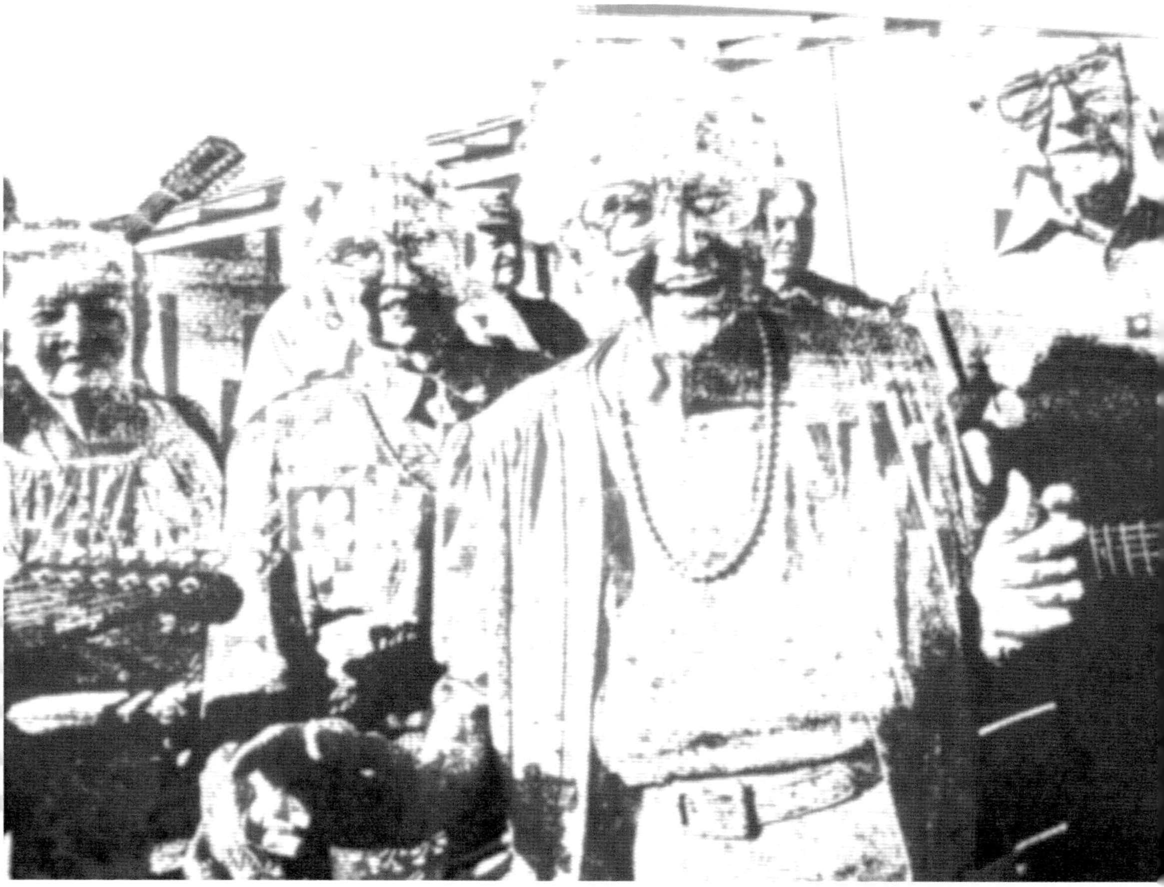

Mary Edith Stinson

Stinson's love for music is evident through her Sunshiners Band. She began directing this group of senior citizens in 1979. Speaking to a potential member, she asked not just their age, but wanted to know the amount of time they were willing to dedicate to performing. After she knew those things, she would assign the new member an instrument. The band could be found playing at the senior citizen center, at retirement parties, and in nursing homes. Starting with only six individuals, the band had as many as 25 members at one time. As the band's name implies, the performers bring a sunny disposition to any occasion. (GPML.)

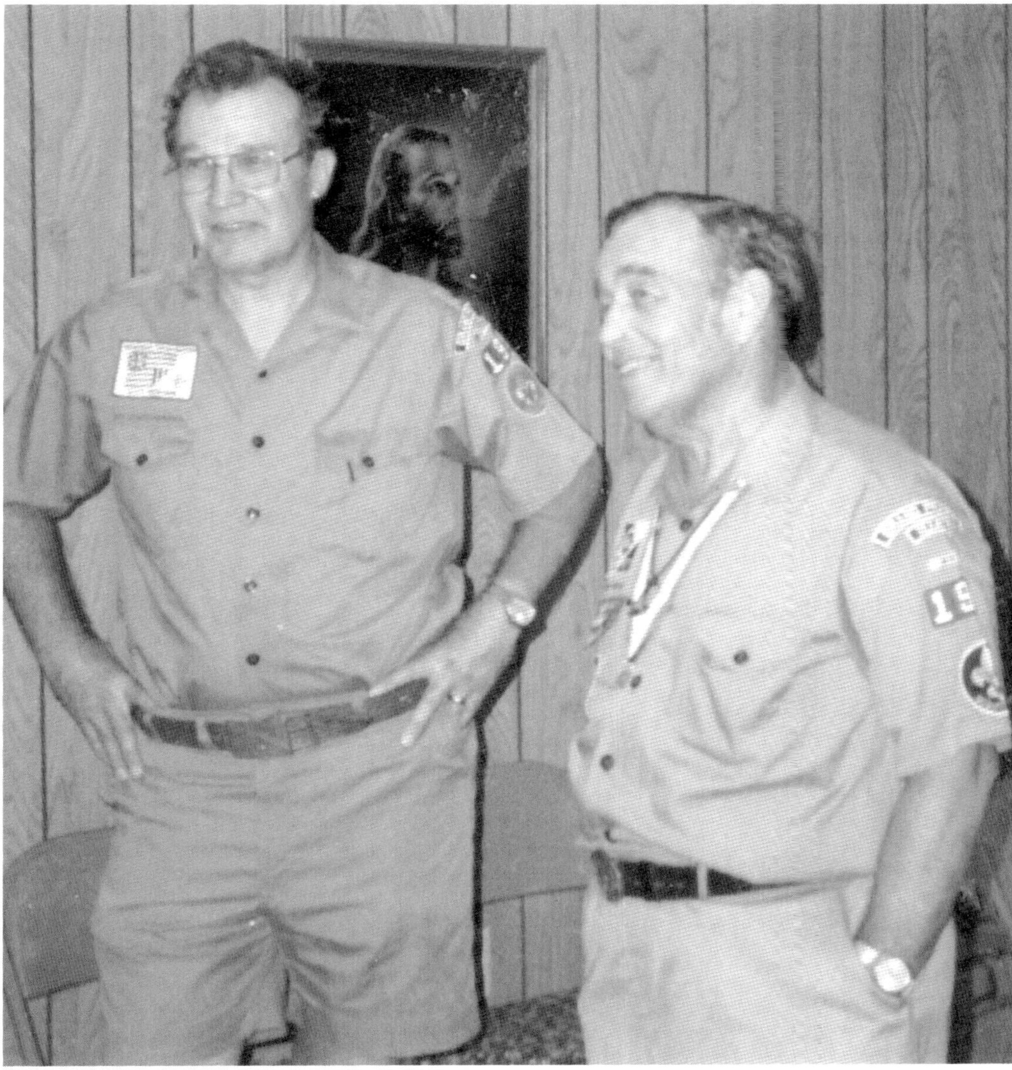

John Bement

Bement (right) had a distinguished career. He was 1962 president of the North Texas Fireman's and Fire Marshal's Association. He served as a Dallas County fire marshal after 14 years as the assistant fire marshal, and was a 32nd-degree Mason and member of the Scottish Rite.

Bement served as a trustee at First United Methodist Church, where he was deeply involved with the Boy Scouts. Focusing his efforts on area youth, he was recognized by the Boy Scouts of America for his dedication, and passed this Scouting legacy on to his sons. He began as a merit badge counselor and served in various capacities, all the way to chairman of a district operating committee. He was also a member of the Order of the Arrow. In 1975, John Bement was awarded the Silver Beaver award, the Boy Scouts' highest award. (Courtesy of First United Methodist Church.)

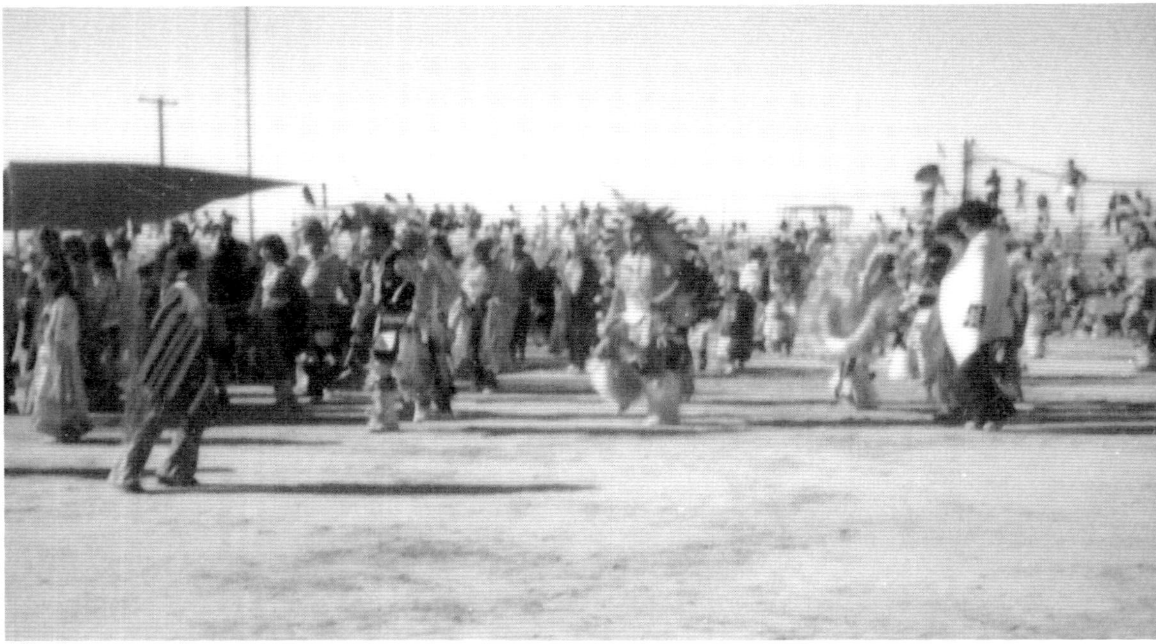

Henry Clayton

Clayton is a character. A 1995 *Dallas Observer* article by Ann Zimmerman describes all that was found out about him. Henry, his brother Gil, and two others made up the tribal government Native American Tribal Organization (Nato) Nation, headquartered in Grand Prairie. The nonprofit claimed membership of more than 5,000, including anyone of Indian descent, whether they know their heritage or not.

Clayton likes to be called "Judge," as he is the judicial branch of the self-appointed government. The Nato Nation is not recognized by the federal government, nor does it seem to stand in favor with recognized tribes. Clayton's motives, which are unclear, could be questioned. His daughter Rebeka does not trust them. Judge Henry tried to have an Idaho court turn over jurisdiction for custody of his grandchildren to the Nato Nation. Pictured here is the annual Indian powwow. (Courtesy of Nick and Irma Vega.)

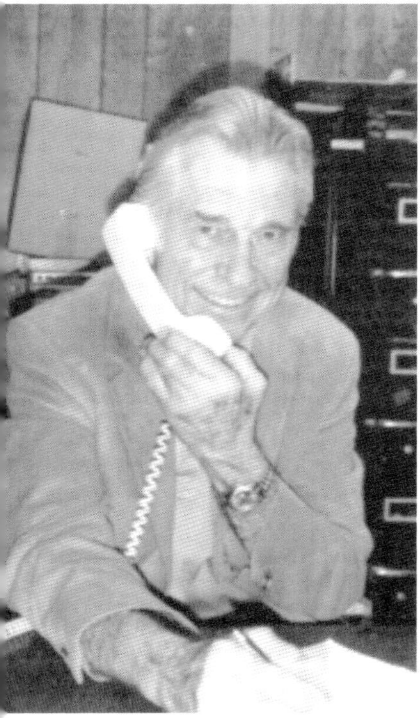

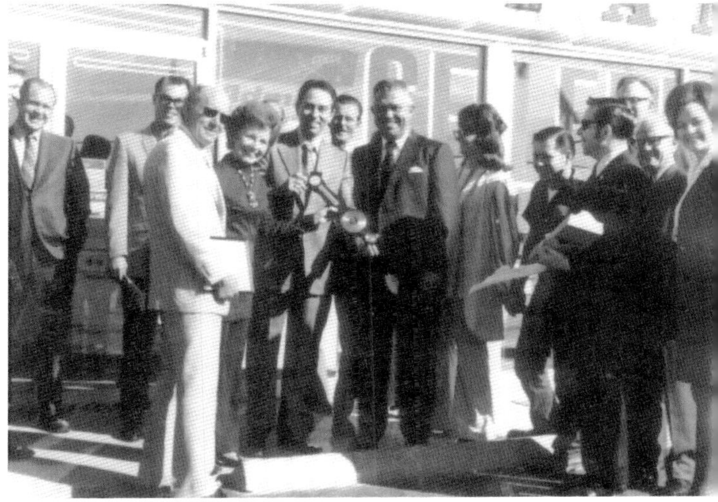

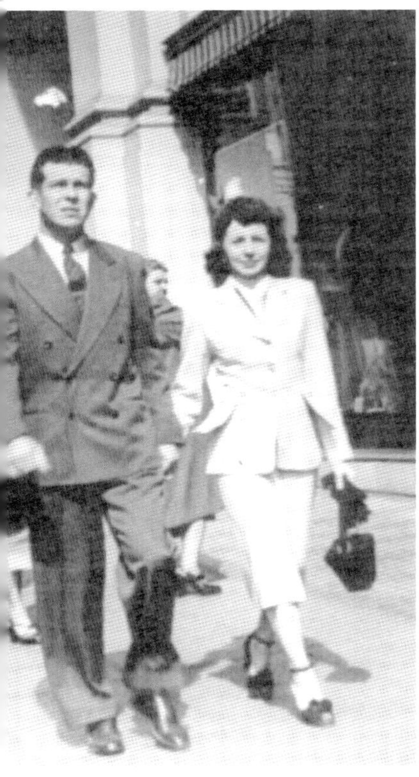

Walt and Gracie Minter

The grandson of German immigrants, Walt Minter spent over 10 years in the Air Force, serving in World War II and becoming missing in action during the Korean War. In 1954, he opened a business in Grand Prairie, and in the mid-1970s, served as president of the chamber of commerce for four years. Walt's Appliance was located downtown, next to the police department. Before moving into a larger location in 1972, it was fined monthly by the police for displaying appliances outside. Minter was a great salesman, and his wife, Gracie, took care of the business alongside her husband. When illness disabled Walt, Gracie took care of both the business and him. He died at the age of 85 in July 2007. Gracie still owns a major share of the store. Pictured above are members of the chamber of commerce at the ribbon cutting for the new store in 1972. (All, courtesy of Gracie Minter.)

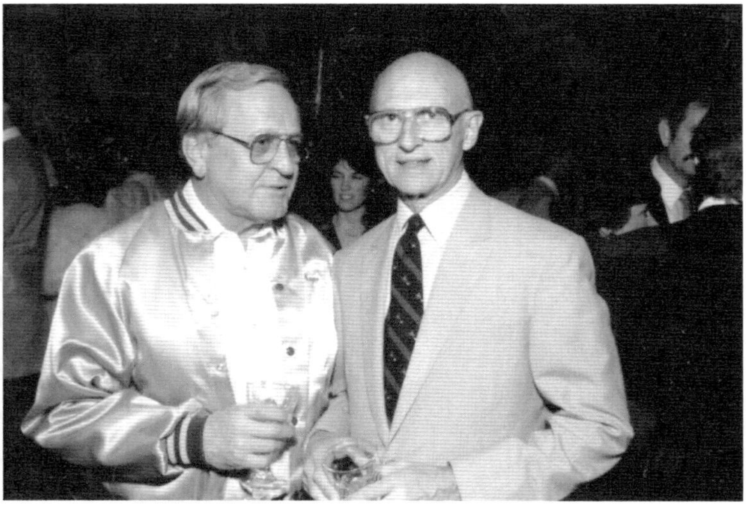

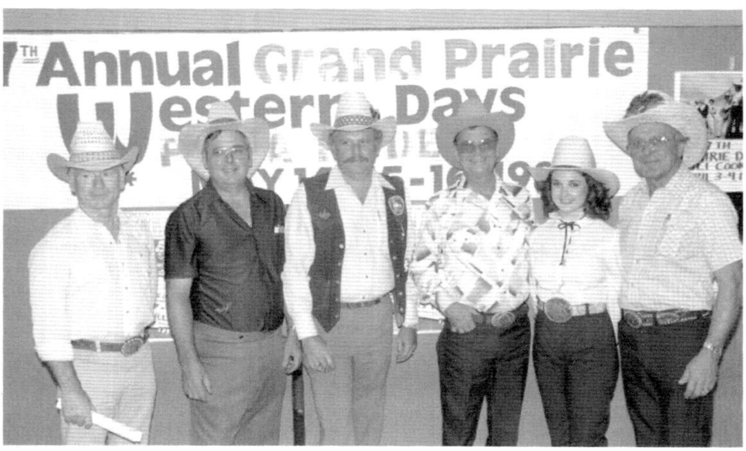

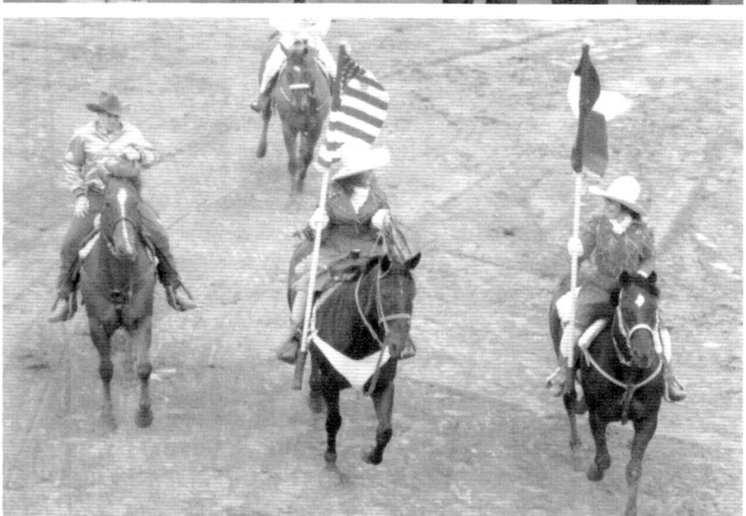

H. Wayne Hanks

Hanks was CEO of Control Products Corporation and an active member and volunteer in the community until his death in 2012. He participated in the foundation of Western Days in Grand Prairie. Hanks served on the boards of the chamber of commerce, YMCA, Rotary, the Rodeo Club, and the Medical Center. He also served in leadership positions for city committees, such as planning and zoning and the sports development corporation. Pictured at top are Wayne Hanks and Dr. Jim Matthews, at center is Hanks at far right, and at bottom is the Western Days Rodeo opening ceremony. (All, CofC.)

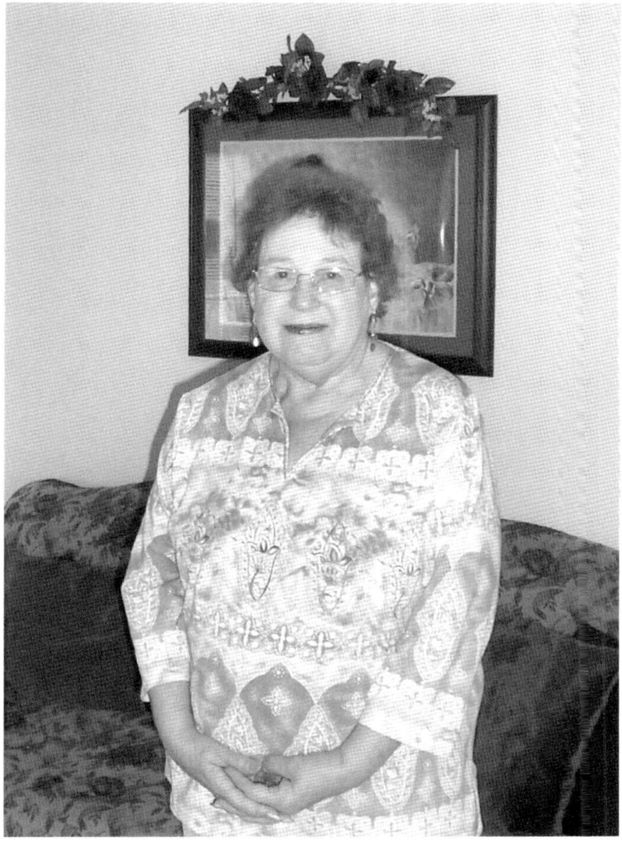

Helen Nelson

The Dechman home was where Helen Jolly Nelson decided to build her midwife business. She is a pioneer in her field. From a midwifery study group, Nelson helped to start the North Texas Midwife Association, and was involved in the formation of the Association of Texas Midwives. This energetic, dedicated woman was an important part of the formation of the Midwives Alliance of North America and played a part in helping the State of Texas develop standards for midwife licensing and writing the curriculum for the Department of Health's requirements for direct-entry midwives. As a midwife, teacher, and mentor, her involvement inside and outside of her business in Grand Prairie is a legacy that will forever impact her profession.

Approximately 80 midwives have completed training under Helen Nelson. Many of those have gone on to open their own facilities. When one of her students became a missionary, the student's veterinarian husband decided to take additional training to become an MD, and they served together in Africa. Still another student is director for Mercy House, providing housing for pregnant women.

Women have come from many places just to have their children here. Some children were difficult births. Some were quick, like the very first baby that was supposed to be born at the Birth Center. The labor and delivery went so quickly that the baby was born en route, on I-20. Every mother and baby are precious to Nelson. There was the father who was unsure about having a baby outside the hospital, until fate opened his eyes. Then there were the twins that she delivered, who, 22 years later, helped install a new roof on the Family Birth Service. Nelson has personally helped thousands of babies into this world. The largest baby she delivered was 16 pounds, 12 ounces, but it did not make the *Guinness Book of World Records*. In another instance, she delivered a baby 21 years to the day after she had delivered the mother. (Courtesy of Helen Nelson.)

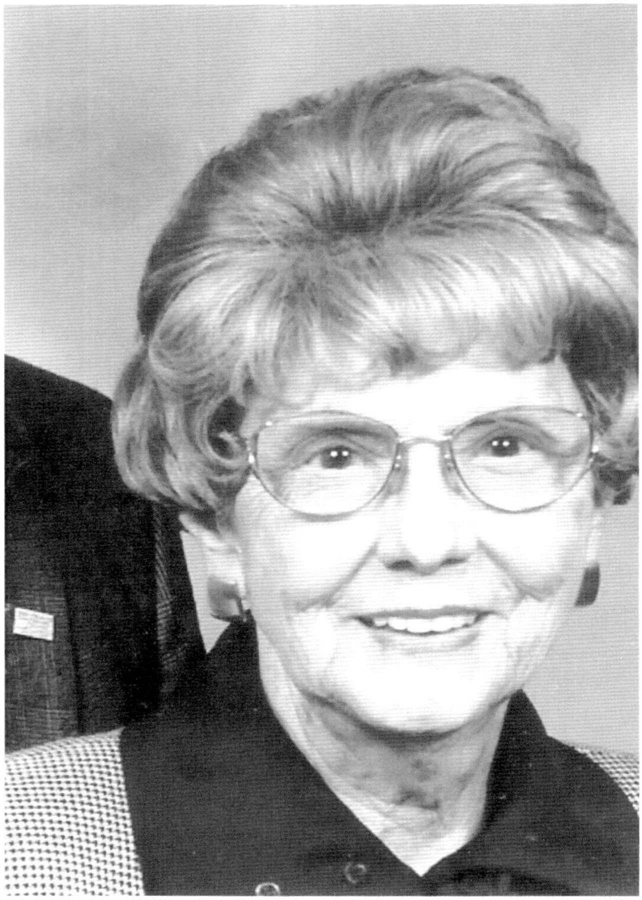

Doris Black

Doris Helsengren Black was a remarkable person. While working as a nurse, she graduated with degrees in English and biology. She joined the Army in 1944 and achieved the rank of captain. She ran a prisoner of war hospital in Italy during World War II and worked in a leprosy colony as a nurse in China.

Black's volunteer efforts dominated her service throughout her life. Beginning in New Jersey, she worked in a child health clinic, was PTA president, and was a Sunday school superintendent. After the family moved to Turkey, she taught English in Tarsus, lugged jugs of hot water to the hospital from 20 minutes away, and helped a young boy.

Doris Black served others for a long time. She helped the Peace Corps as it built a school; provided food, clothes, and shelter to strangers; headed the philanthropic committee of the American Women's Club; volunteered with the Rape Crisis Center; participated in the Texas Nursing Association; advocated through AARP for senior citizens; and was a board member and volunteer for Brighter Tomorrows, the battered women's shelter. She was recognized for her efforts with the following awards: Member of the Year from the Texas Nursing Association, Grand Prairie Senior Citizen of the Year, Outstanding Service to the Community, Texas State Leadership Council, and the AARP award for National Senior Volunteer. Doris Black is honored annually when Brighter Tomorrows names its Doris Black Volunteer of the Year.

Black's efforts are best summed up by a quote from a note her son found from the philanthropic committee she led: "In your philanthropic work, you have been an example to all of us. Some people give from the heart, others with their head, you Doris, give from your soul." (GPML.)

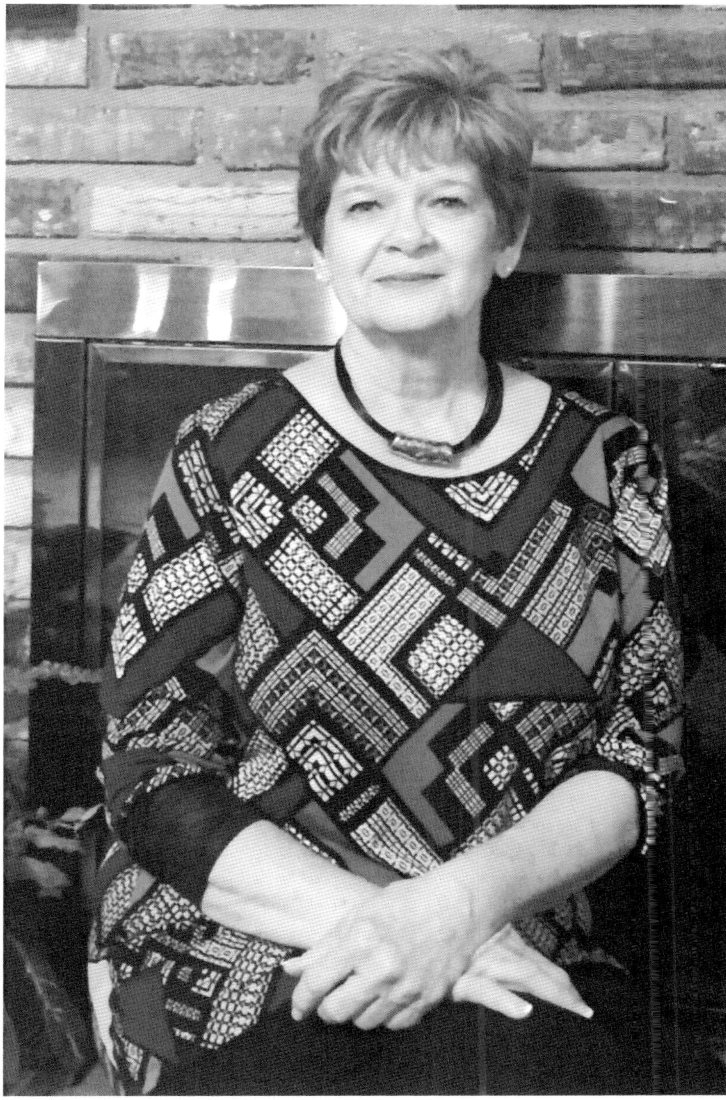

Jana Barker

Now retired, Grand Prairie native Jana Barker served the community while fulfilling her passion. She joined a steering committee of local leaders to help abused women, and before long, became committee president for Brighter Tomorrows and, later, the director.

Brighter Tomorrows opened its first house in 1989. Barker faced and conquered the challenges before her, including keeping utilities paid, moving the organization from a home to a trailer, purchasing a fourplex for transitional housing, developing facilities in surrounding areas, coordinating operations of a thrift store, and appropriating funding from the community, corporations, and state, federal, and grant sources.

Working with local authorities and hospitals, Barker helped start a rape crisis facility for Dallas County, which supported victims as they left the hospital to attend court to face their attacker. She served on nonprofit boards, including the Texas Association against Sexual Assault. She now pursues a lifelong dream and operates a tea room, Kupa Tea. (Courtesy of Jana Barker.)

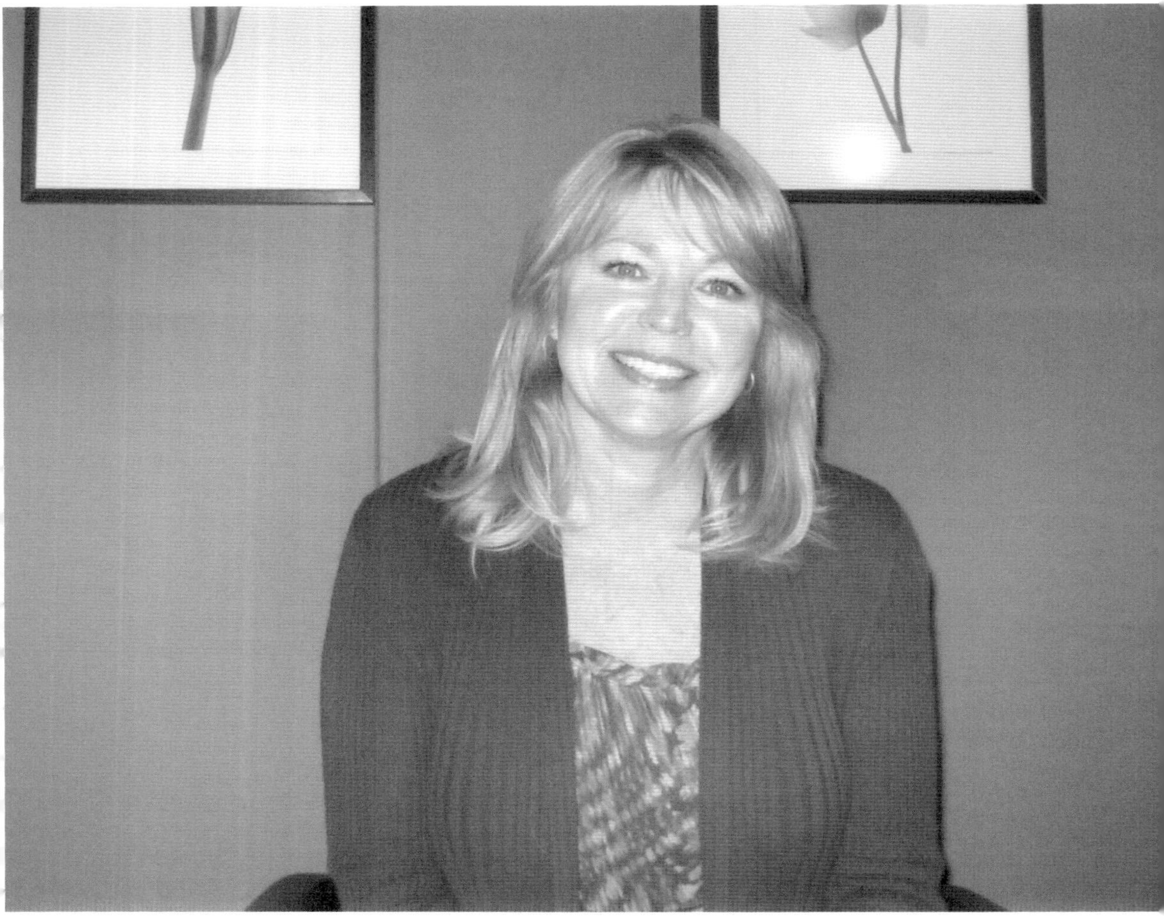

Tammy Williamson

Williamson was raised in a diverse but stable home. Growing up around pastors, evangelists, and bar owners, she learned to be comfortable around all people. She met her husband, Terry, through a friend. A downturn in the local economy brought them to Texas, where she worked at Mary Kay Cosmetics as a receptionist and advanced during her seven and a half years to head of media coverage for products and sales.

She heard about a vision for a crisis pregnancy center. Williamson served on the steering committee before becoming director. Her idea that everyone must leave knowing they are loved set the tone for the ministry. Williamson realized that her heritage is manifest through this ministry. She has served for more than 20 years, letting all who leave know they are loved. (Author photograph.)

Cynthia Burks

Burks was a first sergeant in the US Army and a single mother. During her tour in Saudi Arabia, where she served as a medic, her three boys were in Grand Prairie. The eldest son, Kendrick, took responsibility for his brothers Marcus and Charlie when he was only a teenager. Upon Cynthia's return, she became ill, which was eventually linked to exposure to Agent Orange. She received a medical discharge after more than eighteen years of service.

Burks fought hard for her family and veterans until she was killed by a drunk driver in 2013. A member of the Veterans of Foreign Wars and the Disabled American Veterans, she continually worked for veterans' rights. She could regularly be found at the VA hospital helping patients. She welcomed troops home at the airport, participated in the burials of the homeless, and was part of the Patriot Guard.

Cynthia, seen here with her son, Charlie, struggled with her illness and with post-traumatic stress disorder, but she made things as fun as possible for her boys, who have fond memories. She taught her sons ethics and to be thankful for what they had. Consequently, they excelled in their efforts and in their education. Kendrick works as a web manager in the broadcasting field for a well-known radio personality. Marcus became a network manager for a company working with hospitals. Charlie pursued his passion for football. (Courtesy of Burks family.)

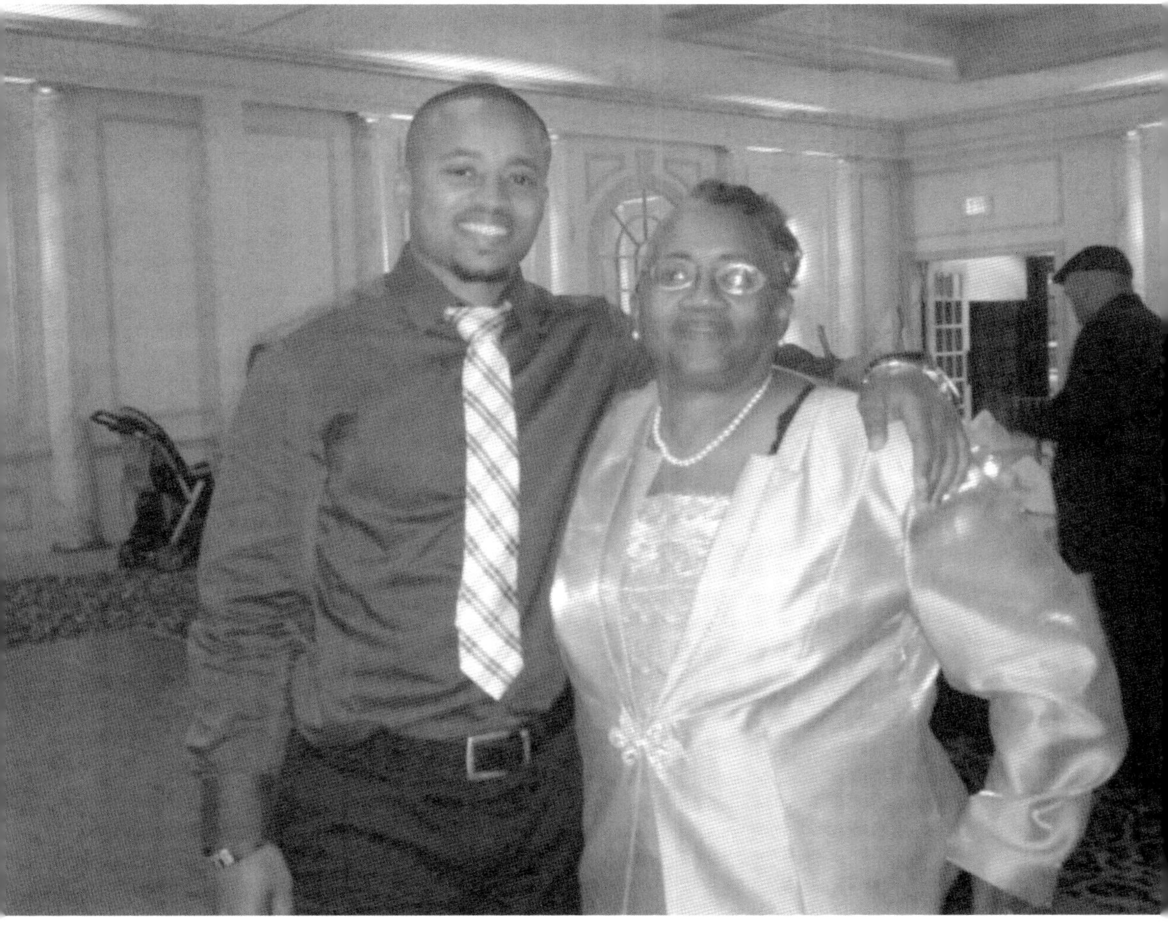

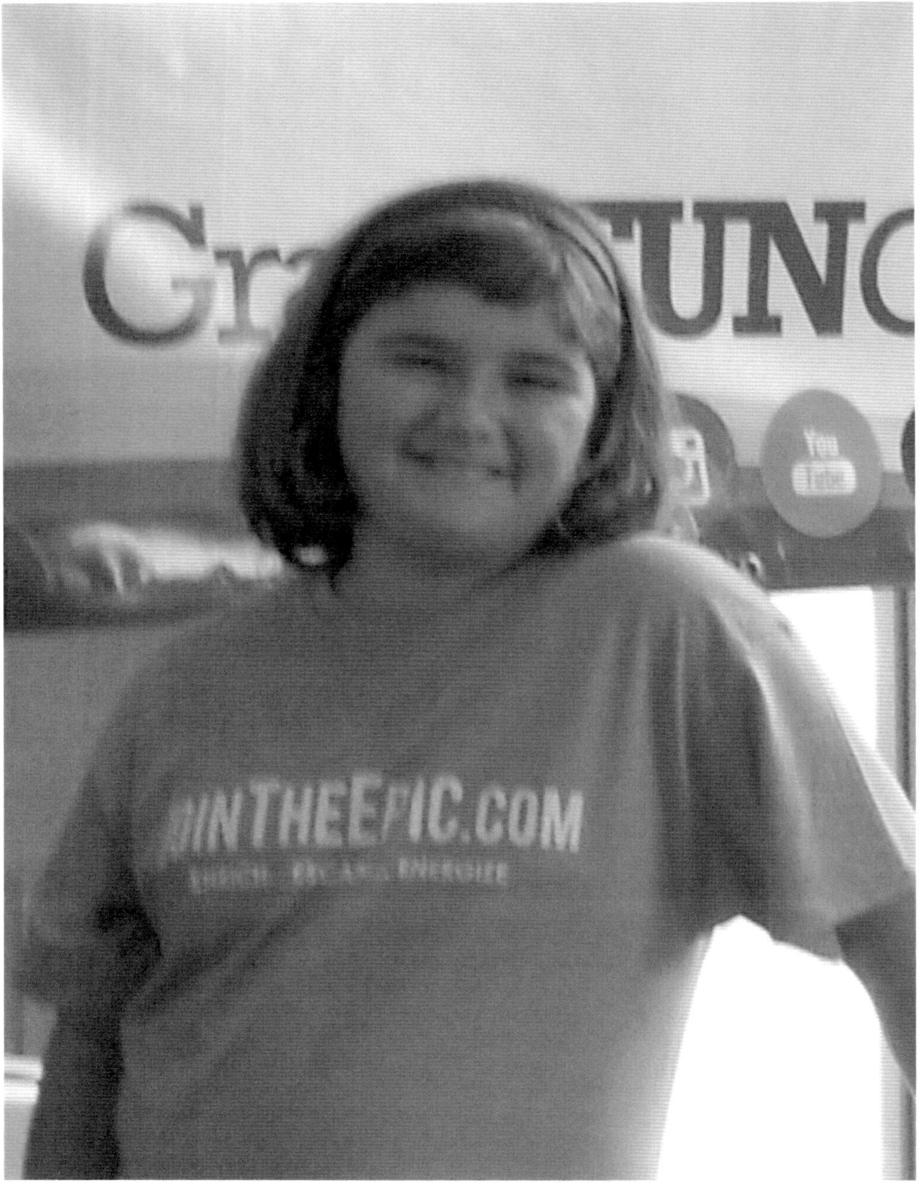

Jessica Stephens

Cooking runs in Jessica Stephens's family. She discovered a love for cooking at the age of six while watching her mother in the kitchen. She began helping by chopping vegetables. When she was nine, her mother suffered a stroke, and Jessica started cooking regularly for her family. She sometimes helps her great-grandmother at her taco stand in Fort Worth. She has also cooked for a teachers' luncheon at her school. Following in the footsteps of her grandmother, who earned "bunches of blue ribbons," Jessica earned her first blue ribbon at the State Fair of Texas in 2013.

As an 11-year-old sixth grader, in 2014, Jessica competed in the *MasterChef Junior* television show's second season. She earned the coveted master chef apron and ranked among the top 12 junior chefs. Jessica has a delicious life ahead. (Author photograph.)

CHAPTER SEVEN

Economic Development

The economy of any community is affected by outside forces, as well as by individuals within the community. Businesses, nonprofits, schools, churches, and city facilities are all part of the complicated equation of economic development. The vitality of a city depends on the ability of its citizens to survive, maintain, and grow within it. If they cannot, they move on to a place where they can make it.

Grand Prairie was fortunate from the beginning to have individuals who understood that their survival was not solely dependent upon themselves. The Jordans and Alexander Dechman knew the importance of transportation. Early mayors, like the Turners, understood the importance of developing businesses and a solid infrastructure. Women like Emmadean Berry were not deterred by social ideologies of the day. When most women married and stayed home, she had a career. Even in difficult circumstances, citizens have endured and found success.

Mayors and council members alike have understood that, as times change, so must the community. When one industry that has been central to the city's existence begins to fade it is necessary for another to develop. As the aviation industry slowly changed, so did the face of Grand Prairie. The city turned to entertainment, where there had already been success. This industry became diversified. Instead of depending on one large corporation, the city now has a multitude of entities. Mildred Walker and her family went from running a sporting-goods store to managing a marina and restaurant at Joe Pool Lake. Jeanie Hulsey built the Forum Bowl and hosted tournaments. She now passes her legacy along to her family.

Every business, be it an insurance agency, drive-in hamburger joint, bakery, or bank, is vital to the city's survival. If not for doctors like William Colip, Charles Cupp, and Horace Copeland, bankers like G.H. Turner and Durwood and Marshall Sutton, and industry leaders like Al Graff and Jeanie Hulsey, there was always a chance that Grand Prairie could fail. Fortunately, there have always been men and women of vision to move the community forward.

Although Lion Country Safari, a big part of the aviation industry, and Forum Mall have faded away, others establishments have sprung up in their place. Grand Prairie is proud to have longtime businesses like Theo's Drive Inn, Don Juan's Mexican restaurant, Louis Tussaud's Wax Museum, and Ripley's Believe It or Not!

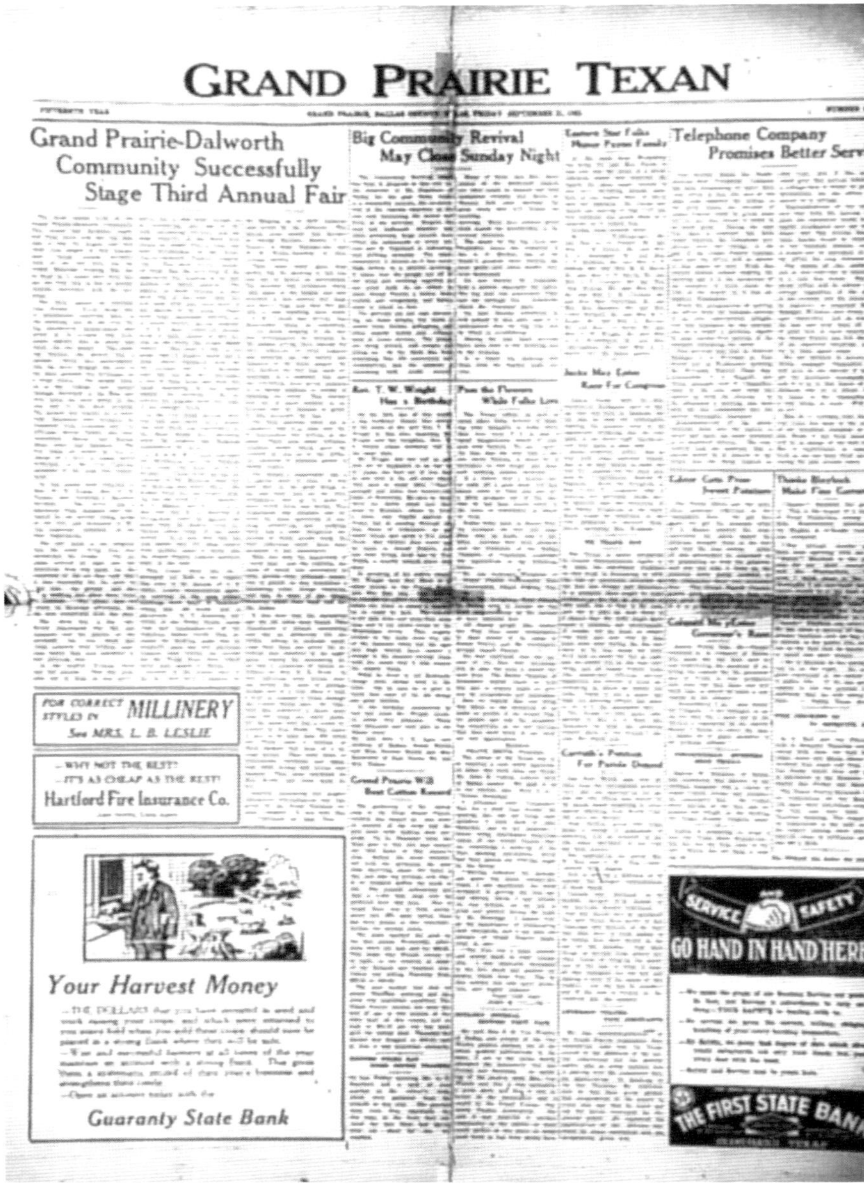

GRAND PRAIRIE TEXAN

Grand Prairie-Dalworth Community Successfully Stage Third Annual Fair

Big Community Revival May Close Sunday Night

Telephone Company Promises Better Servi

FOR CORRECT STYLES IN MILLINERY See MRS. L. B. LESLIE

Hartford Fire Insurance Co.

Your Harvest Money

Guaranty State Bank

SERVICE SAFETY GO HAND IN HAND HERE

THE FIRST STATE BANK

William Artie Brundage

The *Grand Prairie Texan* had William Brundage at the helm for 18 years. His service to the newspaper and as president of the chamber of commerce abruptly ended when he passed away preparing the paper for publication on a November morning. Having experienced poor health for about a year, he was actually feeling a little better. He had expressed on several occasions that he would like to be working and not suffering through a long illness when he died.

J.F. Bradford was the son of Arthur C. and Hannah Tinsley Bradford, early residents who moved to Grand Prairie in 1910. In November 1909, the *Grand Prairie Texan* started the second year of its publication. Due to an extended number of obligations, Ross Simpson leased the newspaper to J.F. Bradford, who continued publishing the newspaper as before. (Author photograph.)

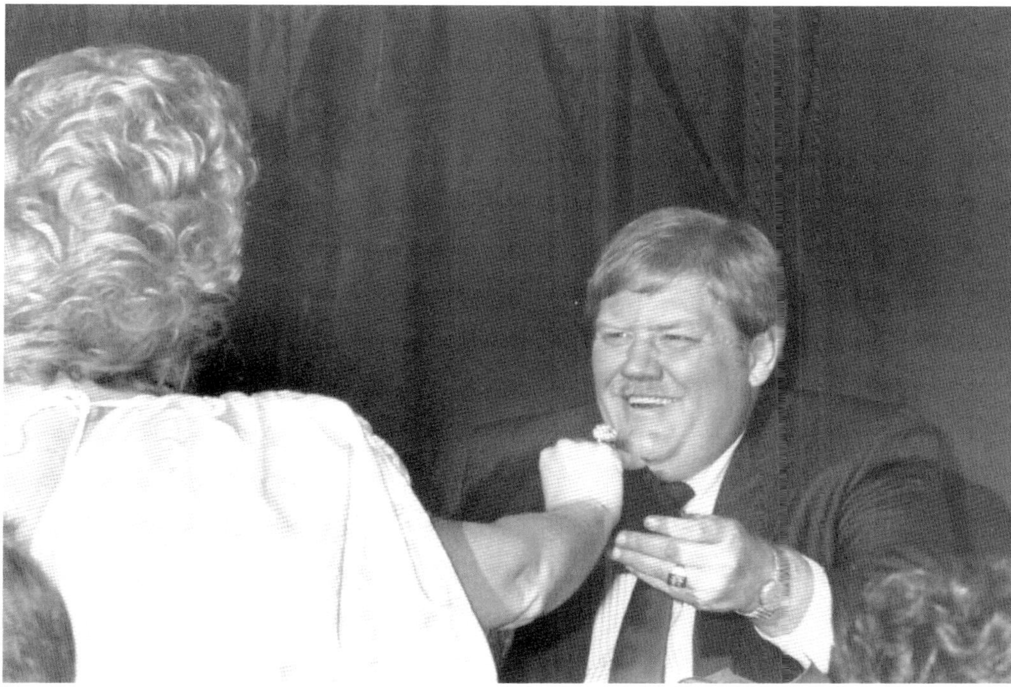

Mike Lewis

Mike Lewis Park, in north Grand Prairie near the Trinity River, was named after city councilman Mike Lewis. According to the December 10, 1984, issue of the *Gainesville Sun*, he "dumbfounded" some council members when he opposed naming a park after NFL veteran Charley Taylor, because he felt recreation facilities should be named for people more directly involved with parks in Grand Prairie. (CofC.)

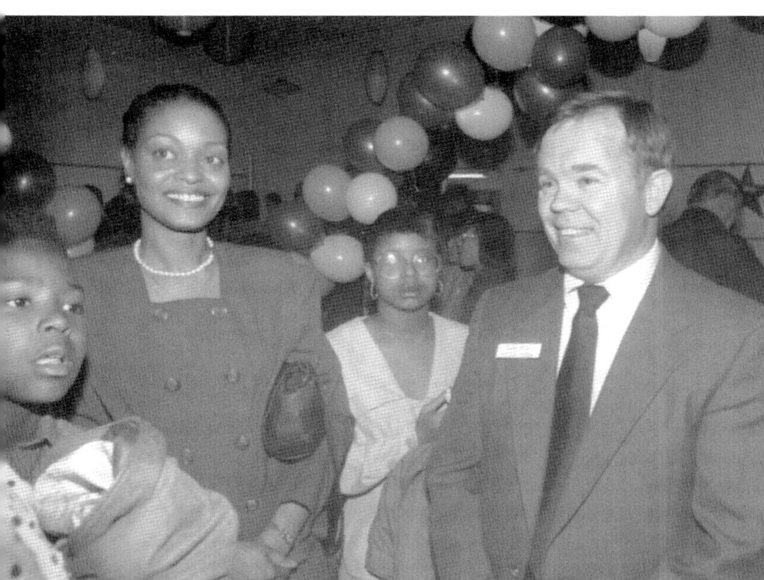

Ralph L. White

"Buddy" White and his wife, Judy, have been realtors and investors around Grand Prairie for many years. Buddy is pictured here with Selah Bynum at a chamber celebration. Buddy and Judy have been active in many endeavors, including the chamber of commerce. Judy is a past president of the Grand Prairie Genealogical Society. (CofC.)

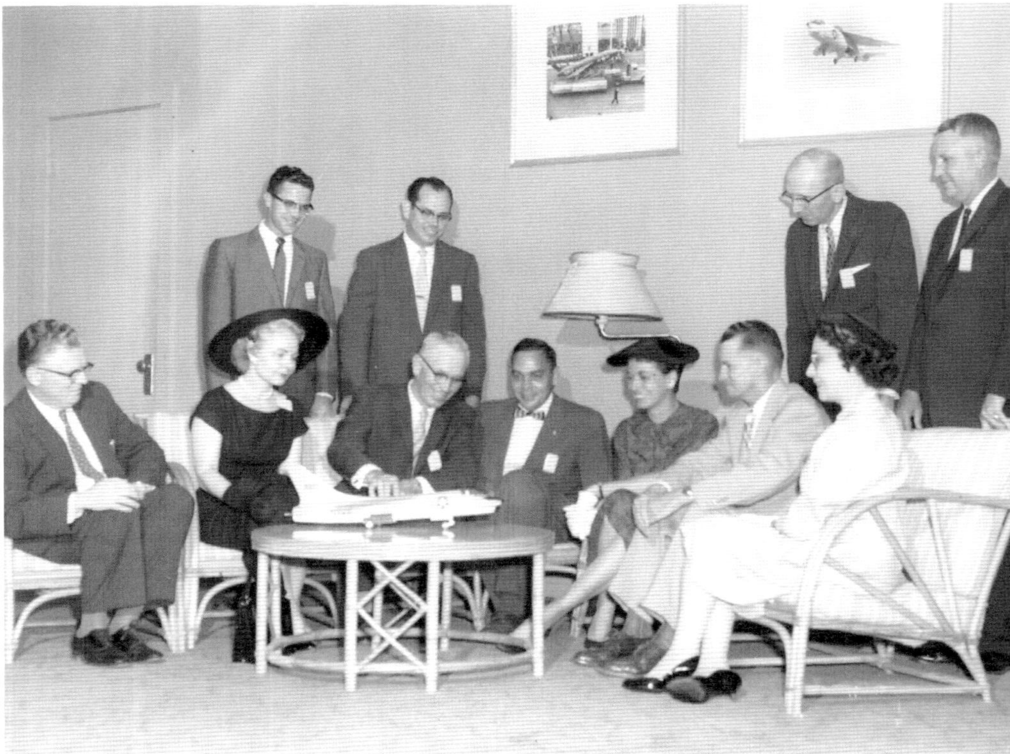

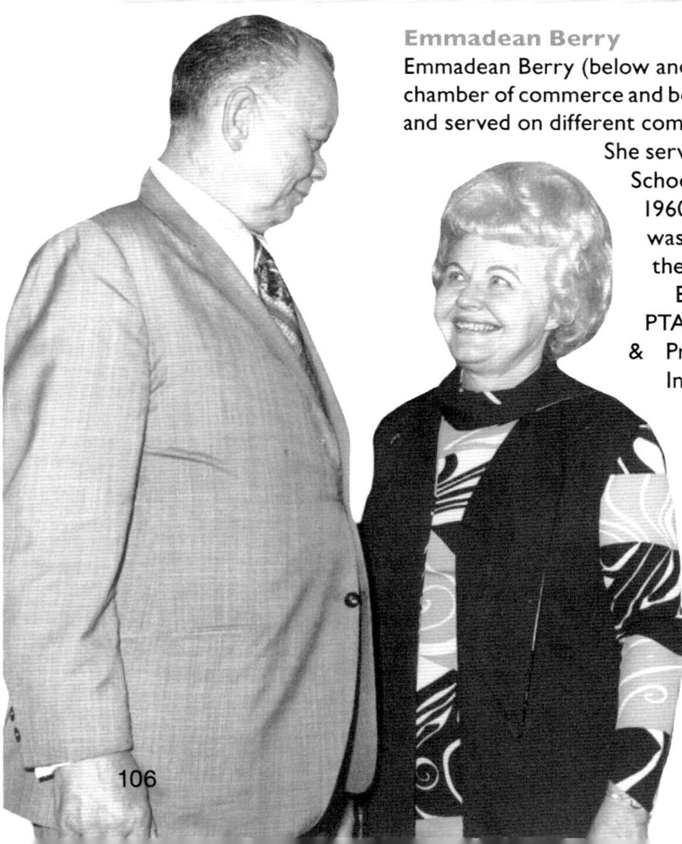

Emmadean Berry

Emmadean Berry (below and above, seated at left) helped to organize the chamber of commerce and became its first female manager. She held offices and served on different committees at the local, state, and national levels. She served as secretary to Grand Prairie Independent School District superintendent H.H. Chambers. In 1960, she founded Emmadean Berry Realty. She was awarded the Distinguished Service Award by the Texas Association of Realtors.

Berry served her community through the PTA, Federation of Women's Club, Business & Professional Women's Club, Toastmistress International, and Soroptomist International. She helped with United Charities, the Red Cross, and the March of Dimes. Berry organized a communitywide Easter-egg hunt, earning her a Distinguished Service Award.

Married to W.J. Berry for 67 years, she had three children, six grandchildren, and five great-grandchildren. She was a beautiful lady, devoted to her community, her faith, and her family. (Above, CofC; left, GPML.)

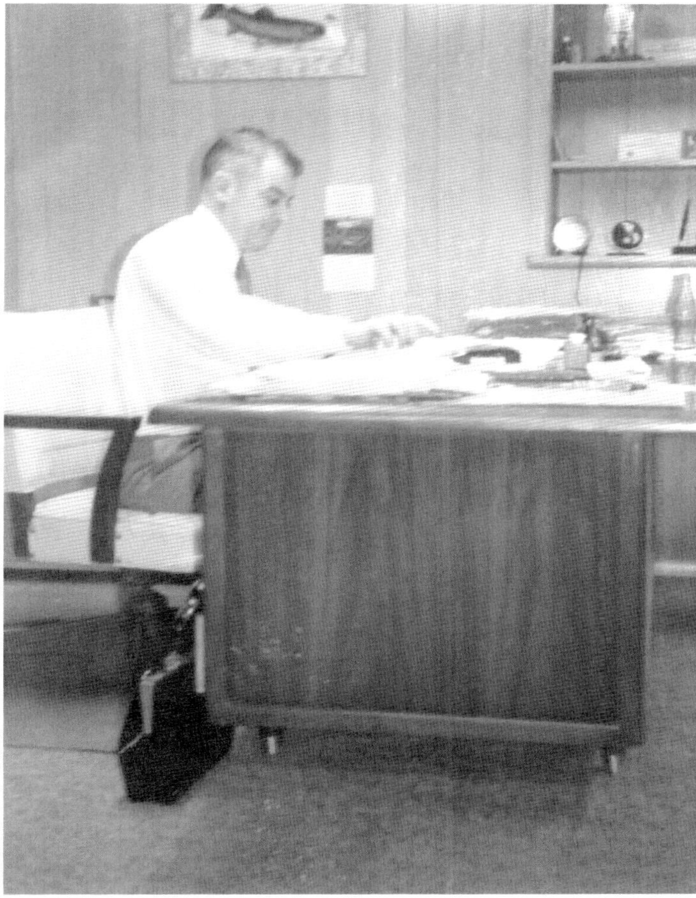

Al Graff

Al Graff began his career in aviation. When he was only about 10 years old, he was a caddy for William Boeing. By 17, with only a seventh- or eighth-grade education, Graff was working in the production department at North American Aviation and assisted in the first airplane built in the United States. When war broke out, he told his supervisor that he had enlisted as an Air Force pilot. His supervisor replied that the nation needed people to build aircraft and that he would be discharged by that evening. In fact, Graff was discharged by that afternoon.

In 1943, he came to Grand Prairie to assess production problems at the North American Aviation Company. He told his supervisors that the problem was they had hired the people he had fired in California. Not happy with his assignment, he nevertheless tackled the problems head-on. When faced with the shortcomings of the B-22 bomber, Graff gathered about a dozen engineers and told them they had to design a gun turret to prevent planes from being picked off by the Germans. By the end of the war, the Grand Prairie plant was more productive, with fewer employees and problems, than the plant in California.

Graff's career in aviation ended when he was fired by Robert McCullough, Tempco's president and one of his best friends. His family legacy began then. He helped finance the Stoltz Ford dealership, which stood on the corner of Main and Fourteenth Streets. By 1952, he was asked to be the Chevrolet dealer, and thus began Graff Chevrolet.

Along with the dealership, Al Graff passed on to his family a spirit of generosity. He said, "If you have something to give, give it to your employees. They are the ones that made it for you." (Courtesy of Graff Chevrolet.)

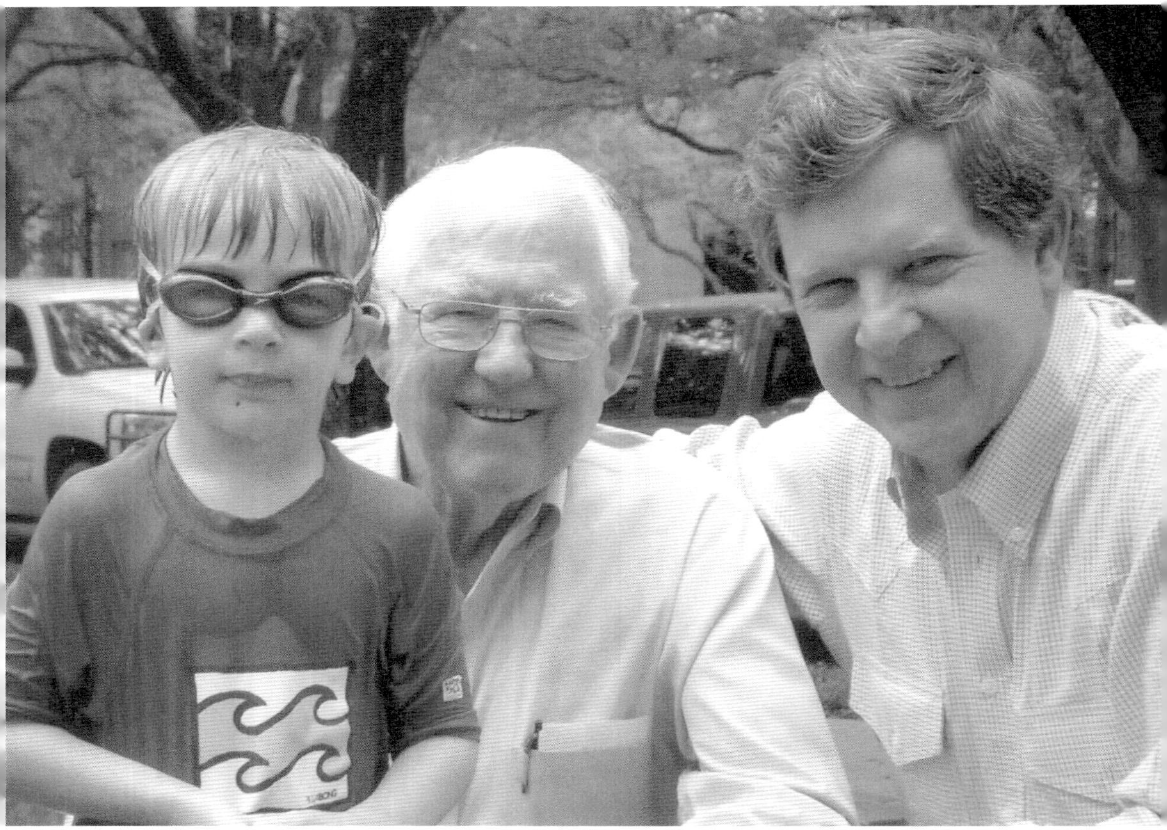

Stan Graff

In 1981, Stan Graff (right) moved from San Antonio to go into business with his dad, Al Graff (center). Stan has continued to be actively involved in real estate. When he purchased the property where Stoltz Ford once stood for Graff Chevrolet, it brought a grin to his dad's face. Graff Chevrolet has been in Grand Prairie for more than 60 years, standing now on three corners at Main and Fourteenth Streets. Stan Graff continues to expand the family business. He purchased a Chevy/Mazda dealership in McKinney.

The Graff family traditions will continue, as Stan's son (left) stands to inherit the legacy passed down by his father and grandfather. Graff Chevrolet and the generosity that has benefited so many in the community promises to be around for at least another generation. (Courtesy of Graff Chevrolet.)

Dr. Horace Victor Copeland

Horace Copeland arrived in Grand Prairie early in 1902. He hung his shingle in the local drugstore of S.S. Tullos and began practicing. Although he had worked for a year in Euless, he came back to where he had been raised. Dr. Copeland was the grandson of James R. Copeland, who was one of the early settlers and part of the Peters Colony in the mid-1800s. James Copeland fought in the war with Mexico in 1816. Dr. Horace Copeland kept a copy of James's commission to assistant commissary and the rank of captain, signed by Pres. James K. Polk and attested to by the secretary of war, W.E. Massey.

Dr. Copeland saw Grand Prairie grow from a small community to a town of more than 50,000 before his death. When he began his practice, he walked or rode in a buggy to treat his patients. In 1910, he was the first in town to own an automobile, a 1910 Hupmobile. As a doctor in the growing town, he saw all sorts of aches, pains, and diseases. On one occasion, a boy was found on the side of the road and brought to Dr. Copeland. The boy had set fire to a package he had found. Not realizing it was a package of powder, he was seriously burned about his face. During the flu epidemic in 1918, there were hundreds of people who died locally. However, Dr. Copeland managed to only lose three patients to the deadly influenza.

Dr. Copeland (center) delivered more than 3,500 babies during his practice. He was responsible for delivering as many as three generations of children in some families. After their marriage in 1917, Francis Watson Copeland compiled a journal for more than 51 years, recording the family's events. It is a treasure for generations of the Copeland family.

Dr. Copeland was active in his church and the community. Today, the Copeland home still stands as a historical landmark in the city. It is operated by the Grand Prairie Historical Organization, which conducts tours each March to honor Grand Prairie's birth. (GPHO.)

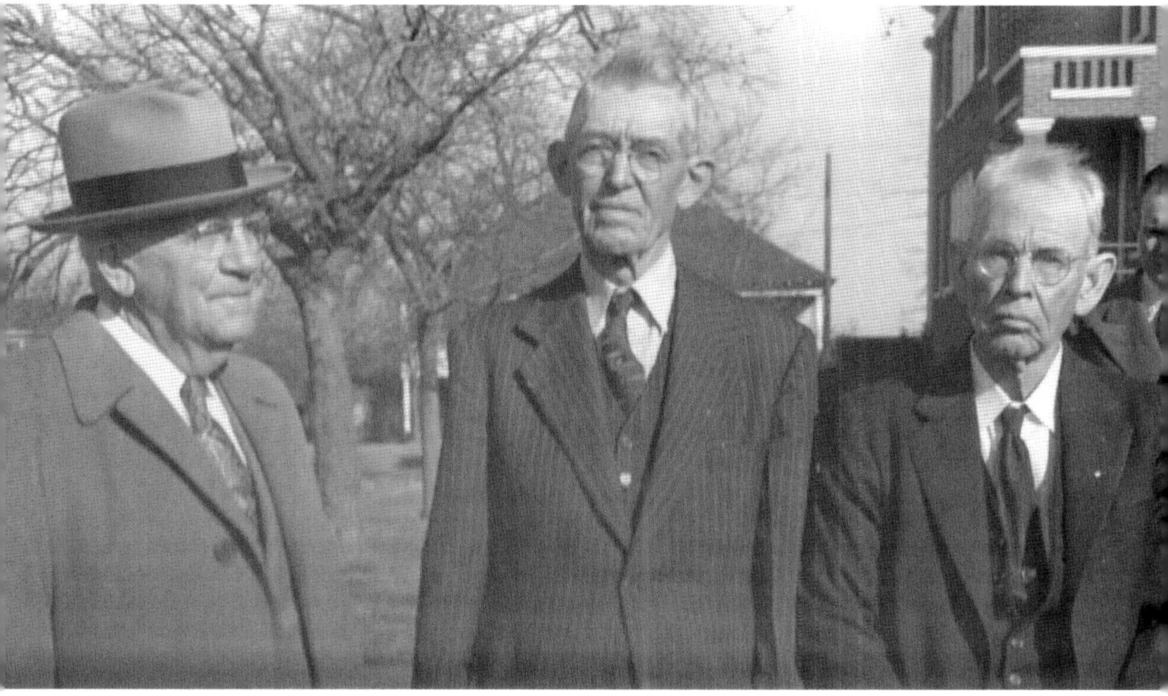

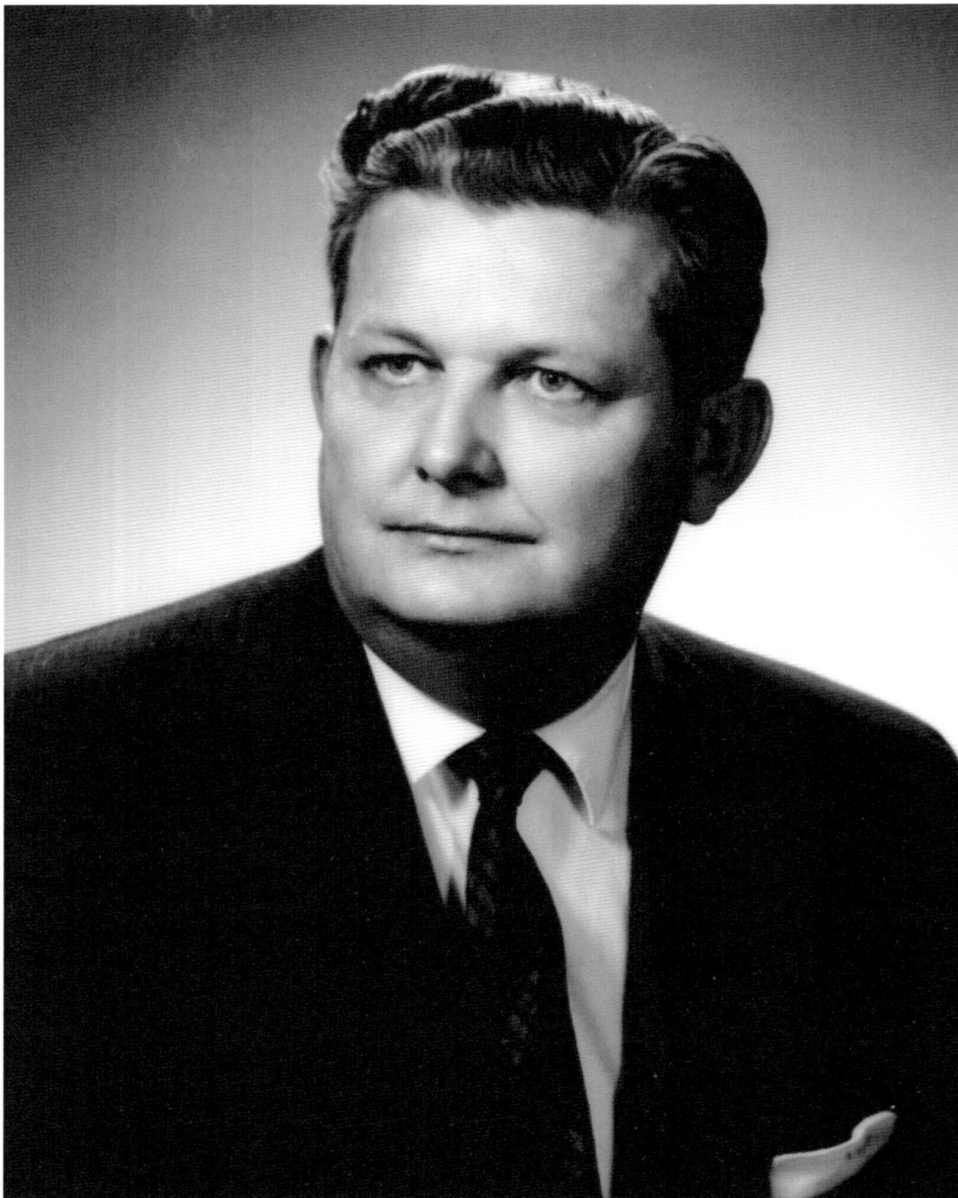

Curtis P. Waggoner

C.P. Waggoner served four terms as mayor of Grand Prairie. His vision for the city's growth came largely through the planning and zoning process. He was an ambassador for the city wherever he went. He helped develop many of the residential areas, was president of the chamber of commerce, chairman of the board for Republic Bank, and served on several other boards and commissions. Waggoner was not one to seek the spotlight, instead quietly serving the community. His wealth and influence earned him the title "Fat Cat," but even his critics admitted he was an unselfish man and largely responsible for Grand Prairie's growth in industry, commerce, and population. A self-made man, he founded C.P. Waggoner Sales Company, with the slogan "Quality Product and Dependable Service." (GPML.)

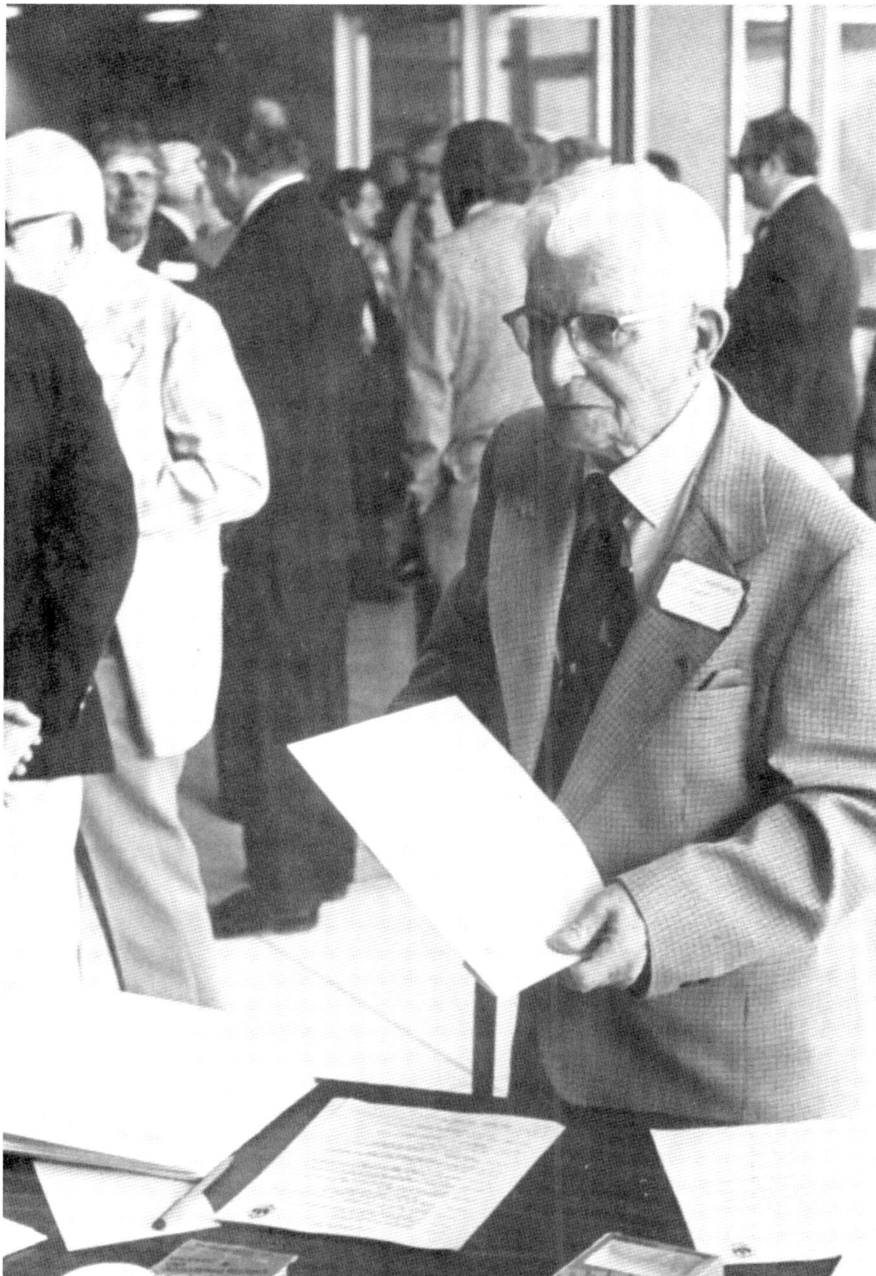

Dr. Charles Daniels Cupp

Dr. Cupp was a longtime resident of Grand Prairie. Born in Coleman County, he graduated from Tulane University in 1912. He began his practice in his hometown of Hillsboro before relocating to Grand Prairie. Dr. Cupp was instrumental in promoting and establishing a hospital in town. He was involved with the land acquisition plans and with advocating to get the much-needed facility built. Upon his retirement in 1976, he was the nation's oldest practicing doctor. He died at the age of 104. (GPML.)

Dr. William Colip and Olga Colip

It is no surprise that Dr. and Mrs. William Colip received a yard-of-the-month award. Olga Colip was a longtime participant and member of the Garden Club in Grand Prairie. She had received a degree in home economics from Texas Women's University and was active with its alumni. She continued her education through trips overseas.

Dr. Colip, one of the town's early doctors, was cochairman for the Grand Prairie Tuberculosis Committee. According to a 1959 *Grand Prairie Texan* article, he considered tuberculosis a "major public health menace." He and Olga were active with the State Health Department, including getting the mobile X-ray unit brought to town on a quarterly, instead of an annual, basis. (GPML.)

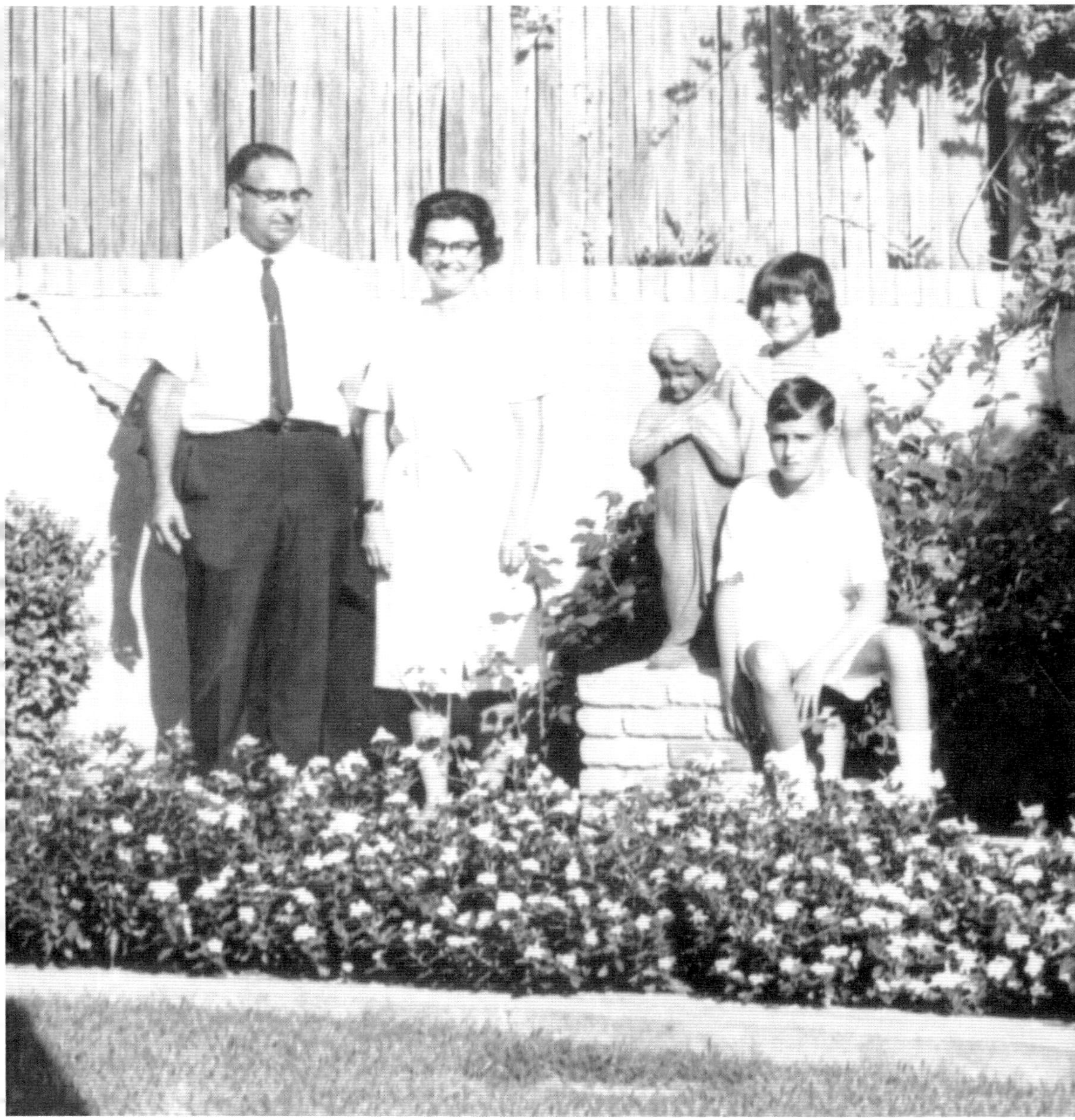

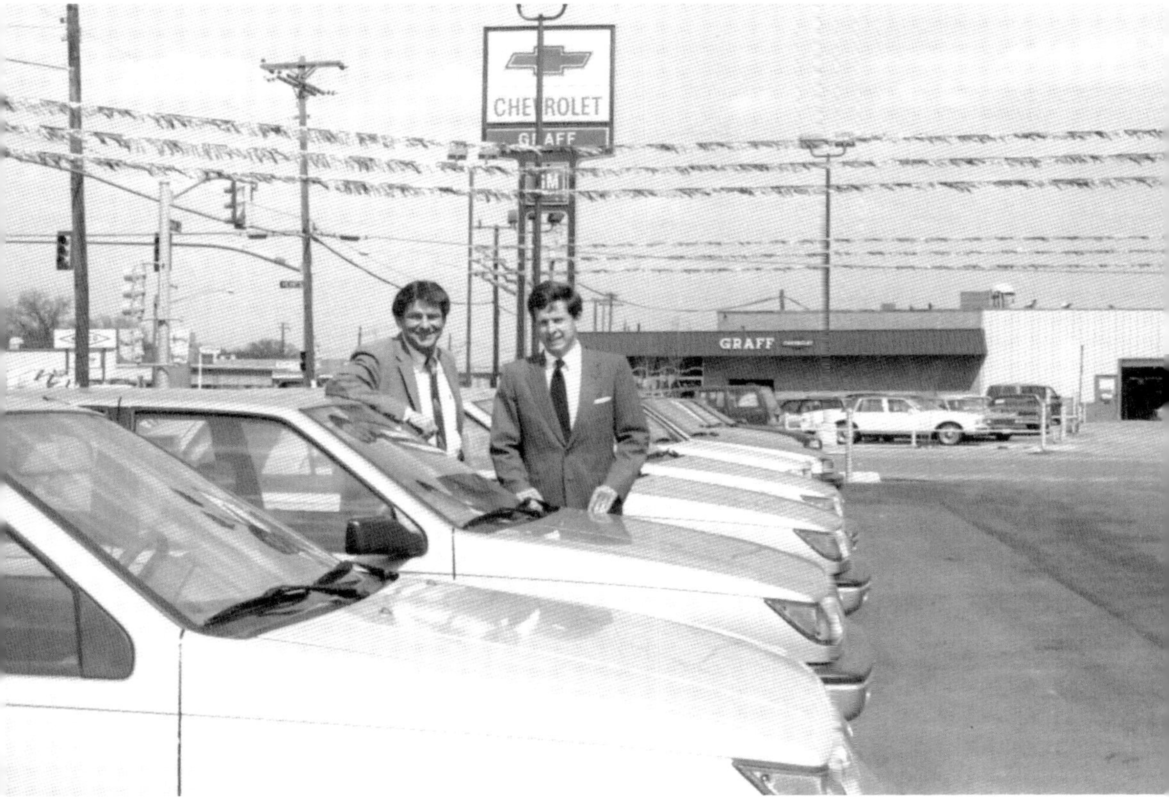

Billy Joe and Judy Erspamer Armstrong

Billy Joe Armstrong (left, with Stan Graff) was a lifelong resident of Grand Prairie and one of its biggest supporters. A car salesman at Graff Chevrolet for 40 years, he coined the slogan "Good people doing good business in Grand Prairie."

He was married to his high school sweetheart, Judy Erspamer Armstrong, for more than 50 years. Judy was a teacher for 11 years and then opened a teachers' supply store called Teaching Tools. She served on both the library board of the Library Foundation and the Grand Prairie High School Alumni Association Board. She was named Outstanding Educator in 2008 by the school's alumni. (Courtesy of Graff Chevrolet.)

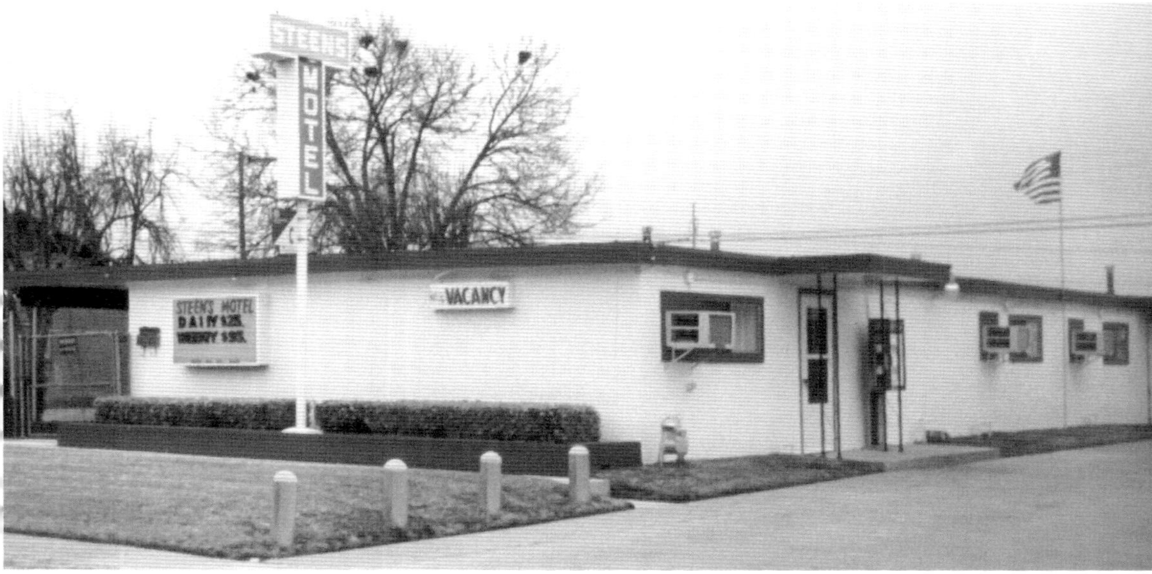

Bobby Steen

During the era of segregation, Bobby Steen designed, built, and opened the Steen Motel in the Dalworth section of Grand Prairie to serve those denied service elsewhere. A place designed to feel more like home than just a place to stay overnight, the Steen Motel was built to make its customers comfortable.

Steen has kept the motel in its original style. The rotary dial pay phone that was in operation in the hall until 2008 was relocated to city hall. He and his wife, Gale, keep the facility in beautiful condition. It includes a homey patio and a community kitchen and dining area, as well as a washer and dryer—all for the convenience of their customers. They have built their business with the support of some very loyal customers, and the facility, which opened in 1959, has earned a historical designation. (GPML.)

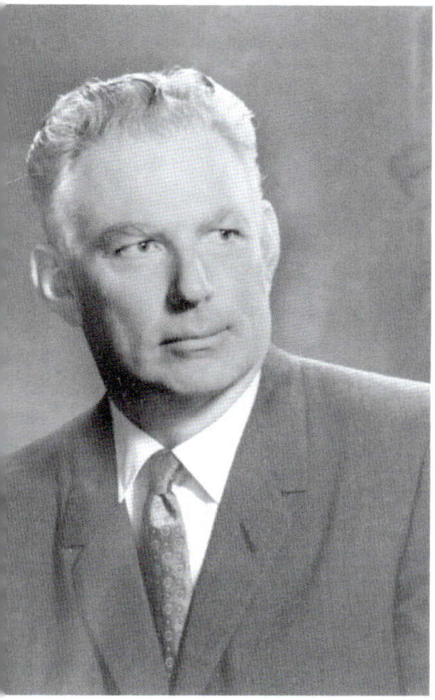

Irving League Taggart

Tag Taggart was running a marketing management company when he decided to build a Texas-scale flea market. Traders Village opened in 1973, and by 1999, it averaged 23 million visitors a year. Instrumental in Western Days, he built the rodeo arena at Traders Village for the annual event. He served as the parade's 20th-anniversary grand marshal and was quoted in the *Grand Prairie Daily News* as saying, "The reason we started this was to generate exposure for the city. It's a good, wholesome way to honor the history of the area."

Taggart was a true leader. He was a past chairman of the chamber board, which recognized him as the Member of the Year. He also was a founder of the Rodeo Club, known as the Wranglers, and was chairman of the Association of Rodeo Committees. Taggart served in leadership roles for the Grand Prairie Visitors and Convention Bureau, the Foundation of Life, the DFW Medical Center, and the Texas tourism industry.

His activities for tourism included serving as chairman of the Texas Travel Industry. He won its Lifetime Achievement Award. He also earned the Texas Department of Transportation Travel Division Gene Phillips Award and A&M's Terry Hershey Award for Excellence. (Both, CofC.)

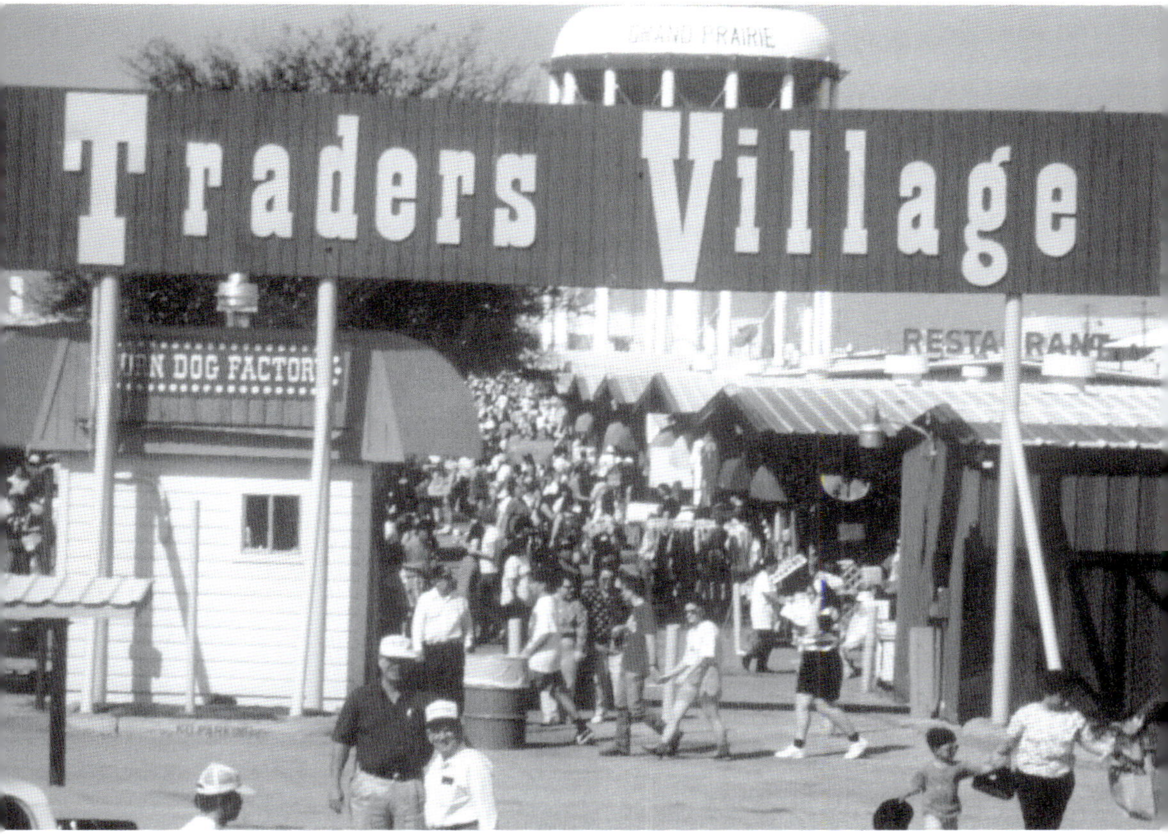

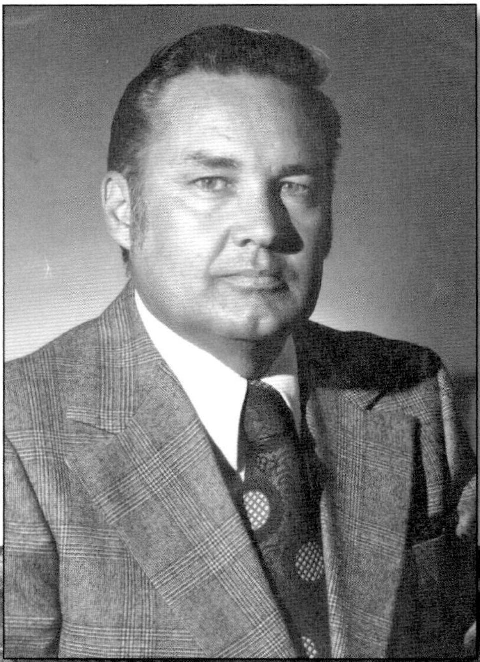

Bill Strong

Bill Strong is the president of Southland Memorial Park in Grand Prairie. He is also the owner of Bill's Pawn Shop, which is where funeral arrangements for a deceased loved one at Southland Memorial Park are made. Strong is a very private individual, but the cemetery has long been a controversial subject. Local newspapers and magazines have reported on complaints about disorganization, piles of tombstones on the property, and, once, a skull that was found.

Strong's love for animals was obvious to anyone visiting the pawn shop. He has kept birds there, and, for many years, a monkey cage occupied a large space in the shop. One of the endearing sights for drivers on the north side of town is the llama farm adjacent to the Strong home. (Right, GPML; below, author's photograph.)

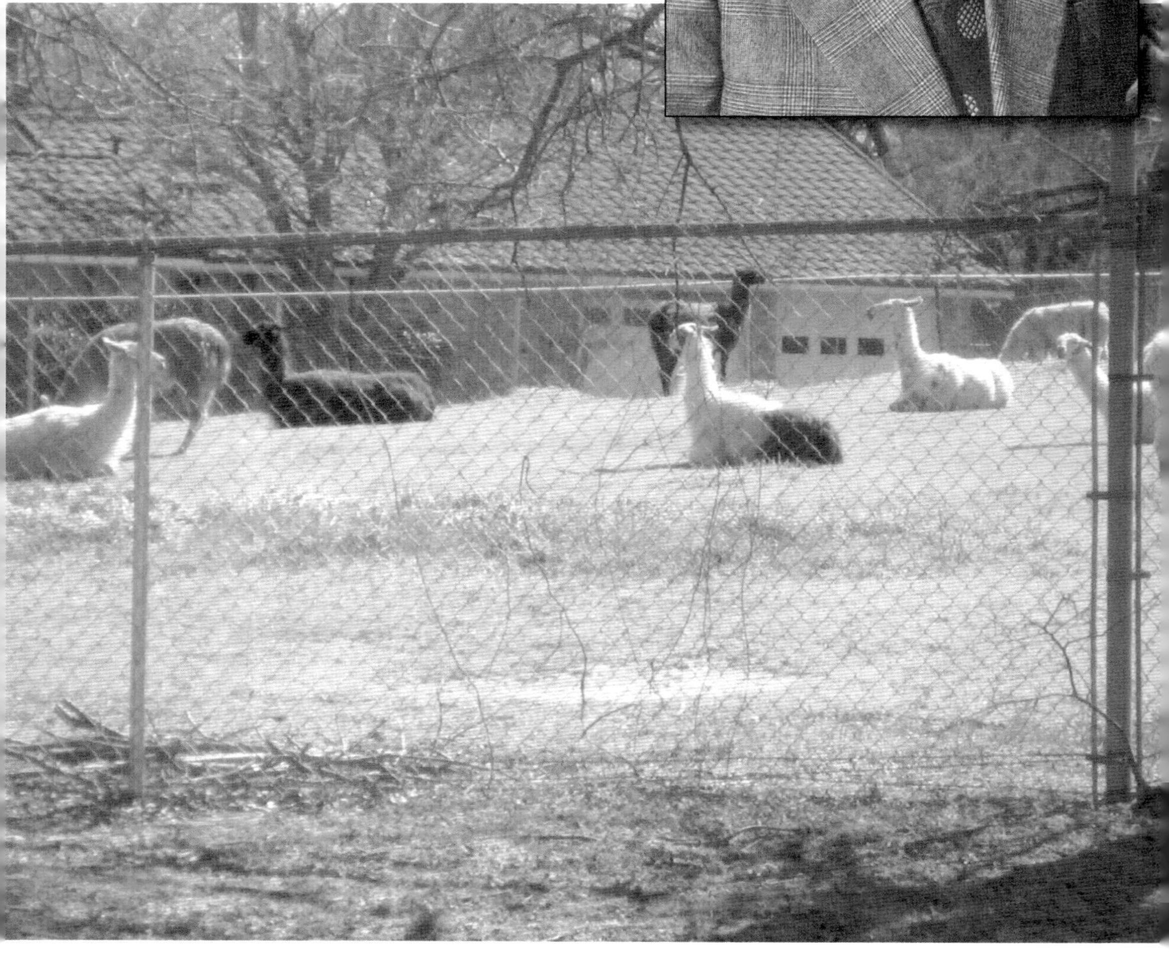

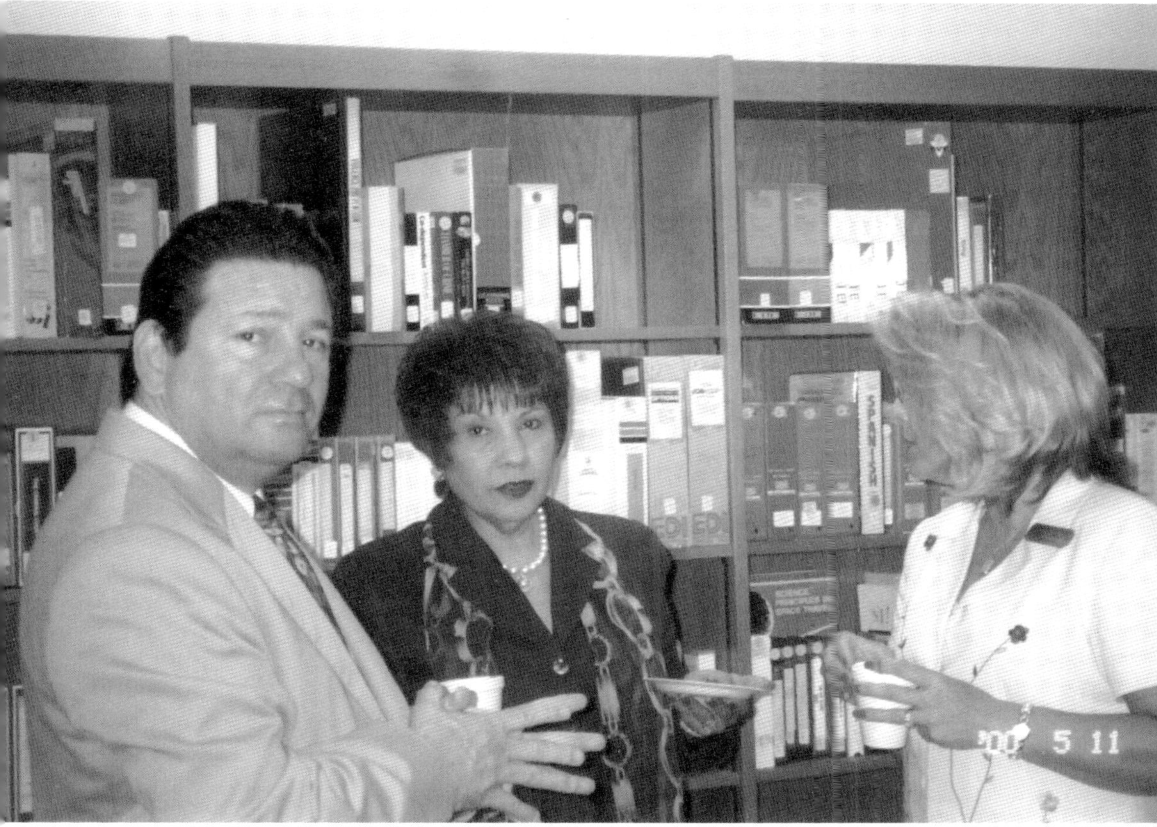

Gloria Carillo

A person of great strength, Gloria Carillo (center) is a businesswoman and an activist. She has helped to promote education in the community and has worked with city hall. Carillo helps to care for her ailing mother while still being active in the community. She serves as head of the Cinco de Mayo Parade committee, has been active in the chamber of commerce, and is vice chairwoman for the Unity Coalition. During the last election, she made an unsuccessful bid for the Grand Prairie Independent School Board, losing to an incumbent. A dynamic woman, Carillo continues to serve the Grand Prairie community. This trait seems to run in the family, as her sister Christina Gonzales was a founder of Lifeline Shelter. (CofC.)

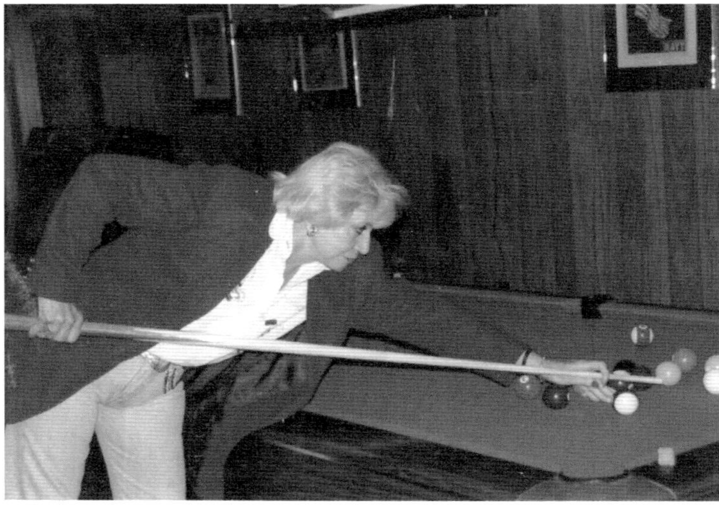

Mildred Walker

At the age of 92, Mildred Walker says, "I've had a wonderful full life." She and her husband returned to Grand Prairie after World War II. They started a small sporting-goods store on Jefferson Street. It was not long before they were in the marina business all over the state. Now widowed, she and her children own and operate the Lynn Creek Marina and Oasis Restaurant at Joe Pool Lake, which is celebrating its 25th anniversary.

Mildred Walker has been involved in leadership and in the foundation of many organizations. She brought the American Field Service to Grand Prairie, sponsoring a student from Norway. She is a past president and charter member of the Women's Club. She is also past president of Business & Professional Women. She served on the Grand Prairie Arts Council, the chamber of commerce, and Children's First Center. Mildred volunteered with the Red Cross for 13 years, served on the DFW Medical Center Board, and ran for the state legislature. She has been honored with the Athena Award, the Citizen of the Year Award, the Entrepreneur of the Year Award, and the Business of the Year Award. She has been recognized by the parks and recreation department, and Mildred Walker Parkway was named for her. (Both, CofC.)

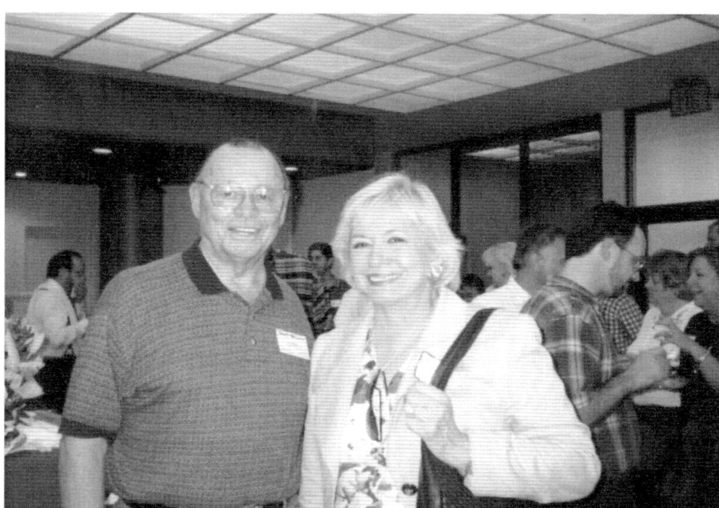

Nelda Jean Hulsey

Jeanie Hulsey had a great love for bowling. She began her career working at Irving Lanes before becoming assistant manager at Triangle Bowl. She then moved over to Golden Triangle as the assistant manager before being made manager. She purchased land in Grand Prairie and built Forum Bowl. She is now retired. The bowling alley is run by her three children, and she is still on the board.

Besides receiving numerous awards, Jeanie hosted the Professional Bowlers Tournament every year. She also cohosted the *Bowling for Dollars* show. She was named Proprietor of the Year by the TX Women's Proprietor Association in 2005 and was inducted into the Fort Worth Hall of Fame in 2004. She is seen here with ABC sportscaster Chris Schenkel (left) and professional golfer Byron Nelson. (Courtesy of Johna West.)

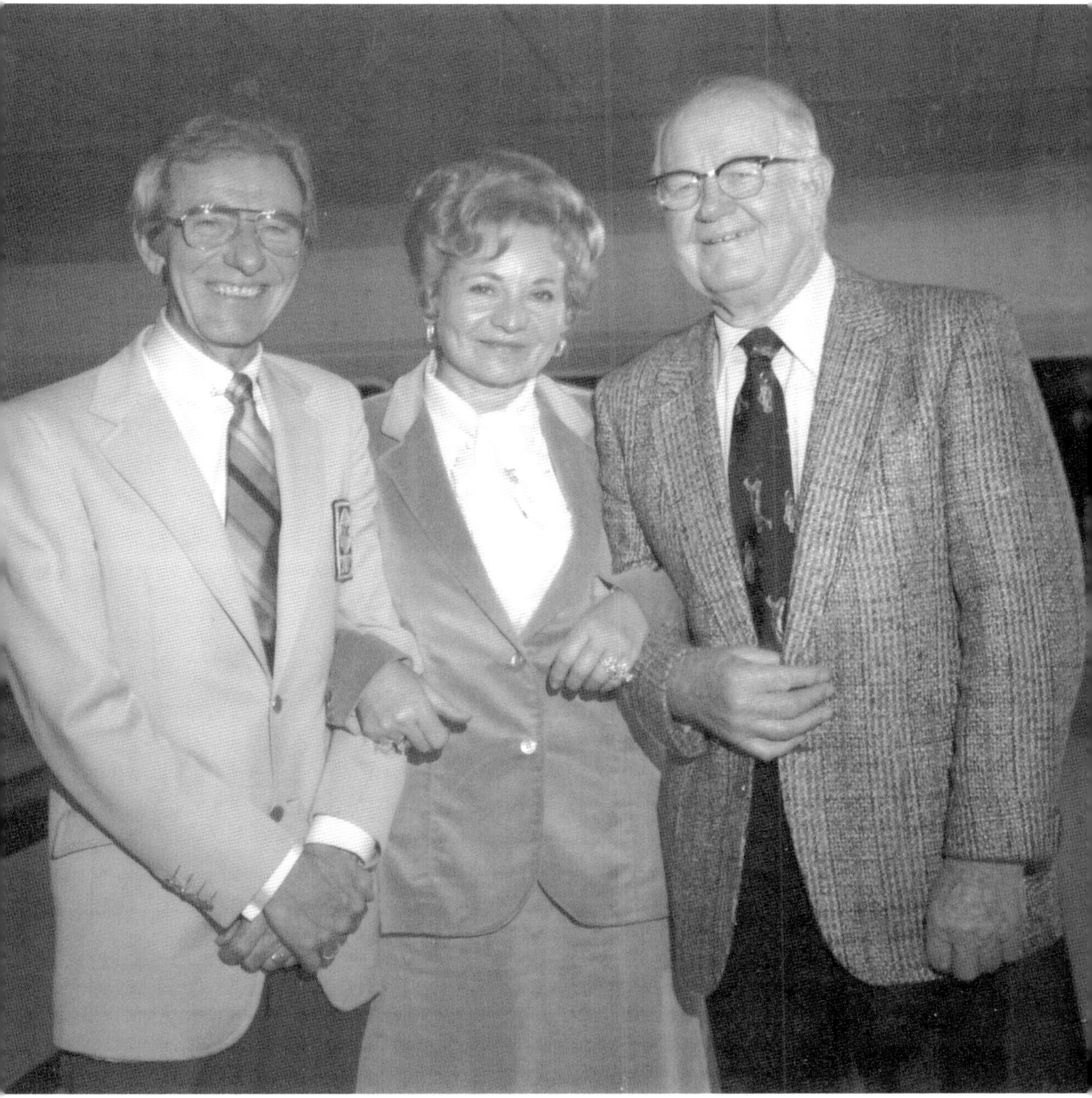

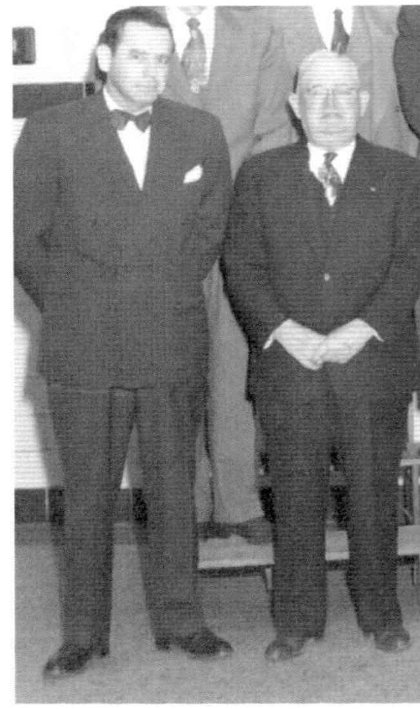

Durwood Sutton

Durwood Anderson Sutton (left, with G.H. Turner), born in 1917, graduated at a time when high school only went to ninth grade. He then attended Byrne College in Dallas before moving to Grand Prairie. He then went into the Army. He met and married his wife, Josephine, while in the service and then returned to his job at Grand Prairie State Bank. Just as he rose through the ranks in the Army he did the same at the bank. When he began at the bank, his responsibilities were wide and varied, including janitorial duties. He retired 50 years later. He was a founding trustee for Dallas County Community College, director of the Dallas Turnpike Authority, and director of the Scottish Rite Hospital for 25 years. He was also the foreman of the grand jury that indicted Jack Ruby. (CofC.)

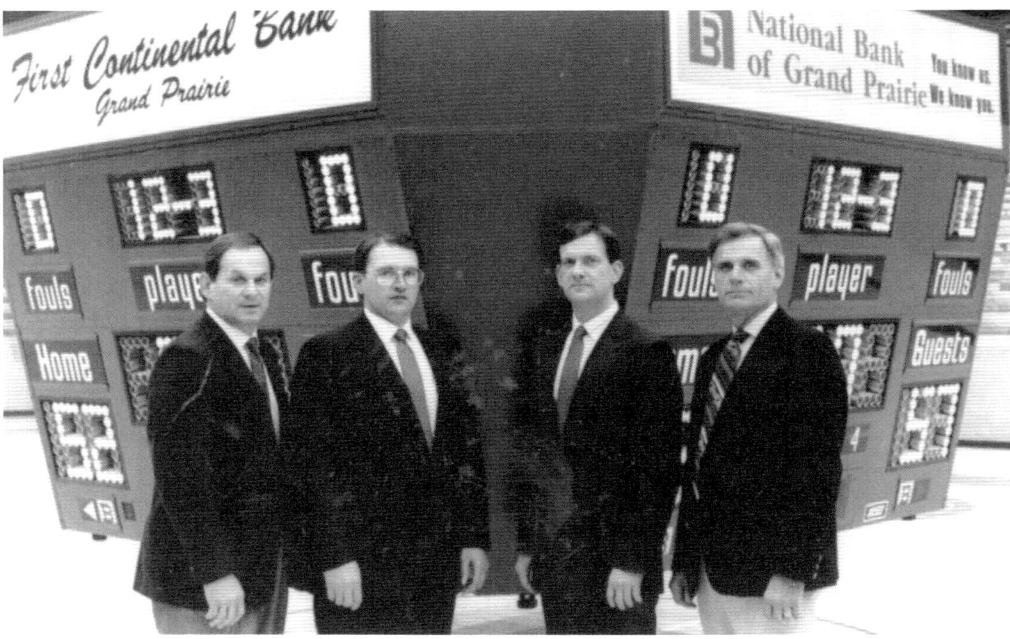

Marshall Sutton

One of five siblings, Marshall Sutton followed in the banking footsteps of his father. He received his bachelor's degree in banking from Texas Tech University and his master of business administration degree from Southern Methodist University. Sutton served 25 years at Grand Bank of Texas, where he was president and CEO. He had previously been executive vice president at Grand Prairie State Bank for seven years. Now president of Grand Prairie State Bank, he owns SuttonCo Banking Consultant. Like his father before him, he serves his community. He supports and is a board member for different organizations, including the Lifeline Shelter and the Grand Prairie Housing Finance Authority. From left to right are Buddy Berry, Brent Johnson, Marshall Sutton, and Marvin Crawford. (Courtesy of Angela Sutton Giessner and Sutton-Giessner family.)

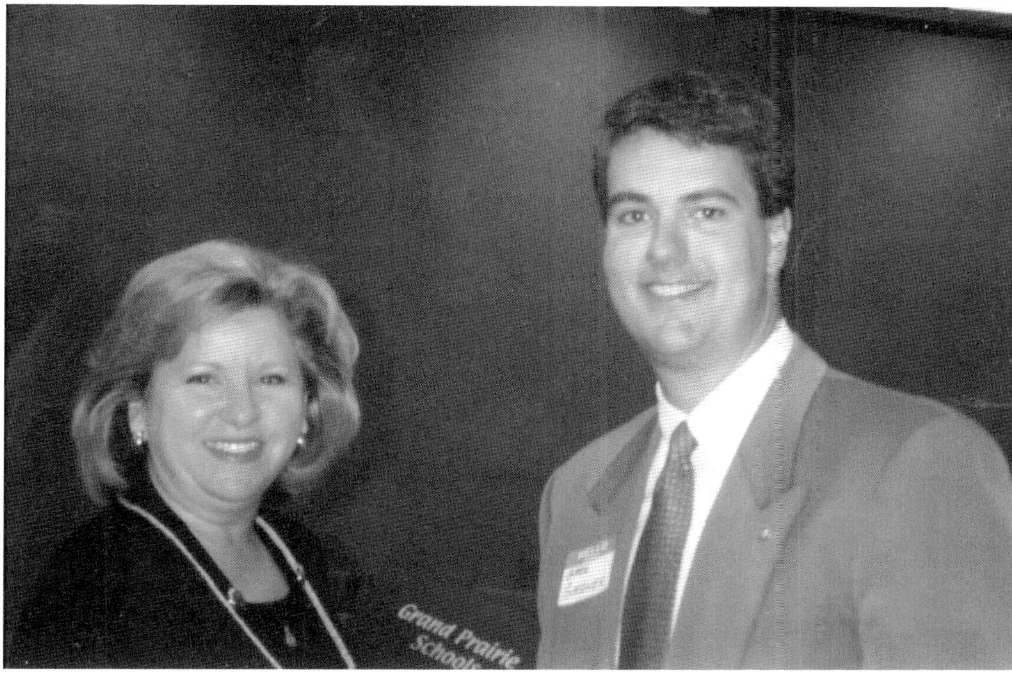

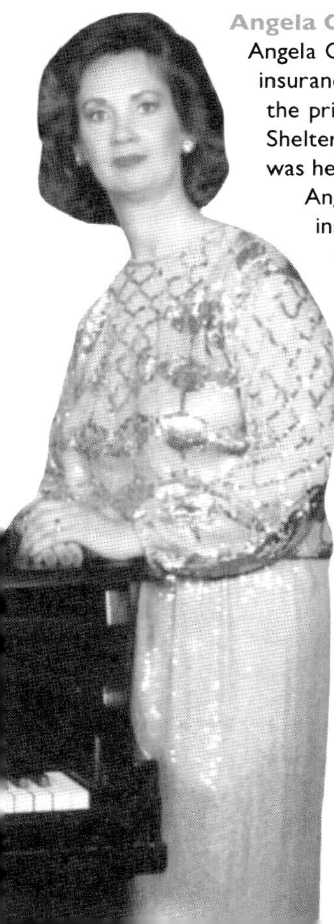

Angela Giessner and Greg Giessner

Angela Giessner (left) carries on her family's legacy for the community. She is an insurance agent, member of the Grand Prairie Historical Organization, and holds the private collection of G.H. Turner's scrapbooks. She is a founder of Lifeline Shelter, which is her passion. The first steering committee meeting for Lifeline was held in August 2003, and by September, it had its 501(c)3 nonprofit status.

Angela's son Greg Giessner is a city council member and partner in her insurance agency. They are shown in the above photograph. Greg and his wife are raising twin sons. (Left, courtesy of Angela Sutton Giessner and Sutton-Giessner family; below, CofC.)

Dr. N. Carolyn Wicker

Dr. Wicker has been a practicing veterinarian in Grand Prairie since 1982 as the owner of the 303 Animal Clinic. She takes her work home with her, as she is the owner of four dogs. Her love for animals is evident. She was recognized by the American Animal Hospital Association with its Excel Award and received Grand Prairie's Woman of the Year, Athena Award. Dr. Wicker is a member of local, state, and national veterinary associations and has been on the board of numerous community organizations, including the Grand Prairie Animal Control Board.

Dr. Wicker believes in giving back to her community. Her most passionate endeavor is the Grand Prairie Independent School District Education Foundation Board, on which she serves. Through the board, she works toward getting college scholarships to students. (Author photograph.)

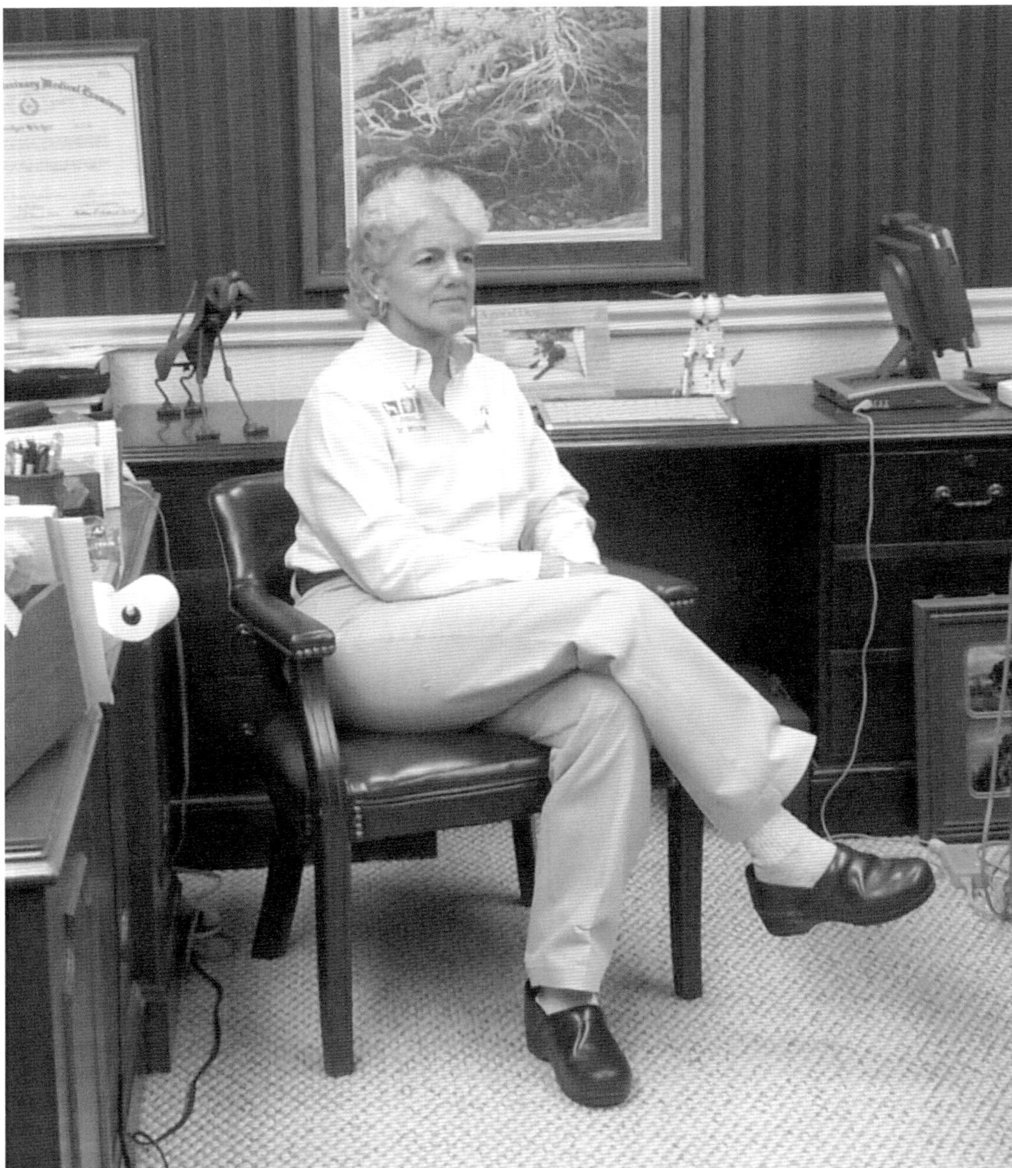

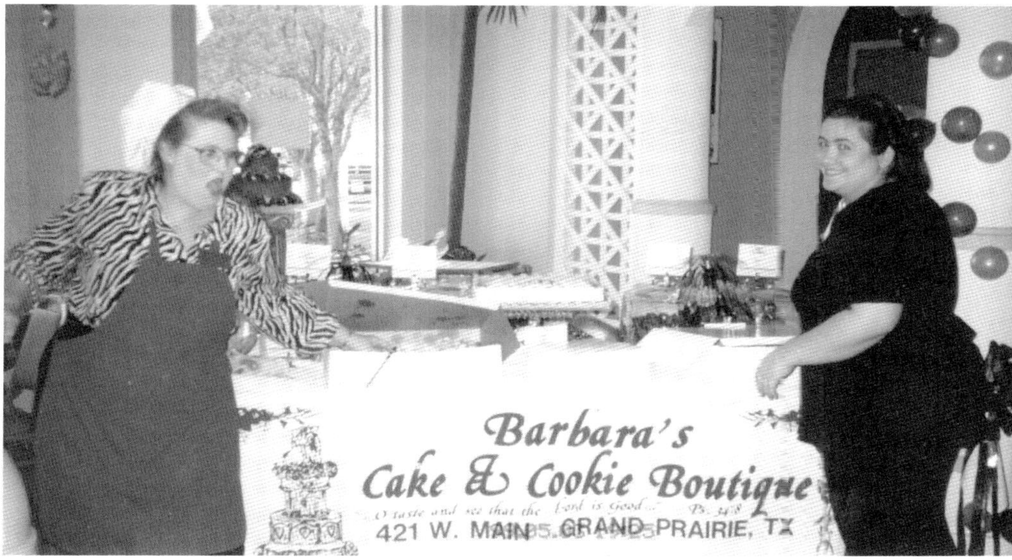

Barbara Owen

Barbara Owen developed a love for baking, winning her first baking contest in elementary school. She married history buff Karl Owen. Purchasing a historic home in Grand Prairie, they researched and landmarked it. Barbara spent many years working in bakeries, teaching, and doing demonstrations while the couple dreamed of opening their own bakery. After many years and prayers, they were able to open their business in a historic building. Their dream and her talent have been realized and recognized. She has received awards from Grand Prairie, Arlington, Channel 8, and Fleur-de-Les Wedding Show, and has won bronze and silver medals for gingerbread competition.

Barbara Owen has also been visited by many celebrities over the years. After one such occasion, her elderly assistant told her, "If we're going to have clientele like that I need to put my teeth in." Barbara is pictured above at left with Deb Townsend and below at left with Wendy Gore. (Both, CofC.)

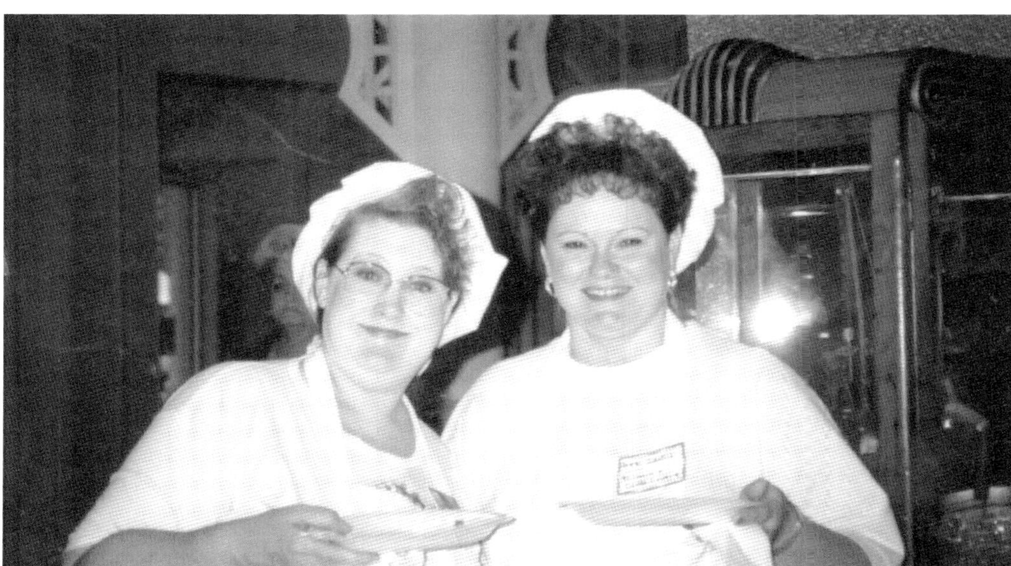

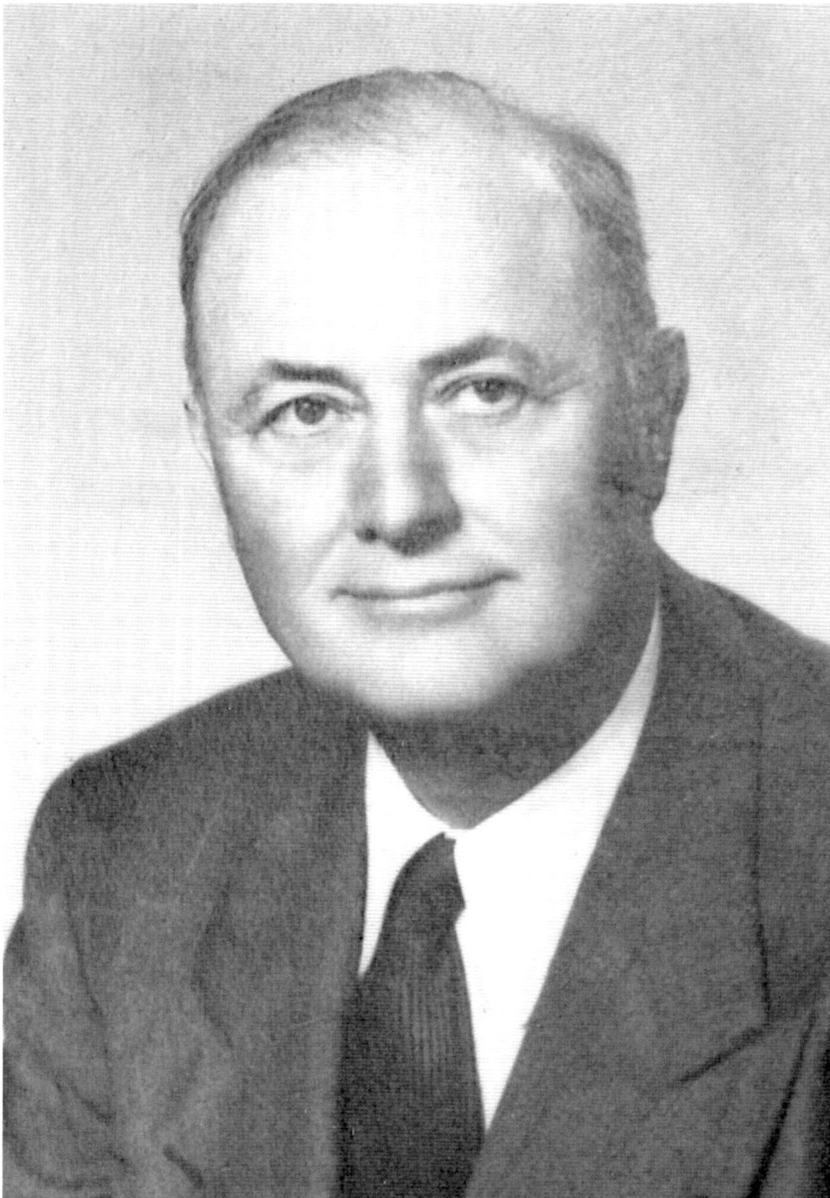

John William Trimble

J.W. Trimble was an active member of the Grand Prairie community and served in a number of ways to promote both business and people. He served on the city council for 12 years. He was also president of the chamber of commerce in 1936, commander of the American Legion, and an elder in First Presbyterian Church. He was also active in Rotary.

Trimble was assistant treasurer for the G.H. Turner Company before he started his own business. In 1953, he decided to establish his own real-estate and insurance business, opening the new enterprise out of his own home. He and his wife, Ruth, had purchased their home on 104th Street from the Mean estate. The Queen Ann–style house is now a historic landmark in Grand Prairie. (GPML.)

ABOUT THE ORGANIZATIONS

The Grand Prairie Historical Organization's (GPHO) mission statement reads: "Promoting and preserving the rich history of Grand Prairie, Texas, by collecting, preserving and interpreting the history through committed volunteers who translate to others while maintaining the highest standards of excellence." It meets quarterly at the GPHO building on Main Street. For a few short years beginning in 1975, the historical organization and the genealogical society were one organization. The divided organization did not work, and two entities were formed to meet the needs of the community.

The Grand Prairie Genealogical Society's (GPGS) mission statement reads: "The Grand Prairie Genealogical Society is an Educational and Cultural organization whose purpose is the fostering of education in genealogical research, encouraging new interest in research and compiling, collecting and encouraging the preservation of research materials." It meets the first Thursday of each month at the main Grand Prairie Public Library. It will celebrate 50 years in 2017 and is a vibrant organization.

Besides hosting informative speakers, GPGS focuses on preservation and acquisition. The cemetery committee has spent the last couple years surveying and recording all but one of the cemeteries in town. The library committee is sorting major collections of books and materials to be donated to the Grand Prairie library and other local library genealogical collections. The board of directors has just authorized a new preservation committee to work with the local chamber of commerce to help name people in their photograph collection and to preserve pictures, newspapers, and other materials currently in storage.

The coauthors of this publication are both past presidents of the society. Their service has included membership in the society and on the board as officers, chairmen, and committee chairmen. Their many years of service and influence is seen in all aspects of the society. (Left, GPHO; right, GPGS.)

INDEX

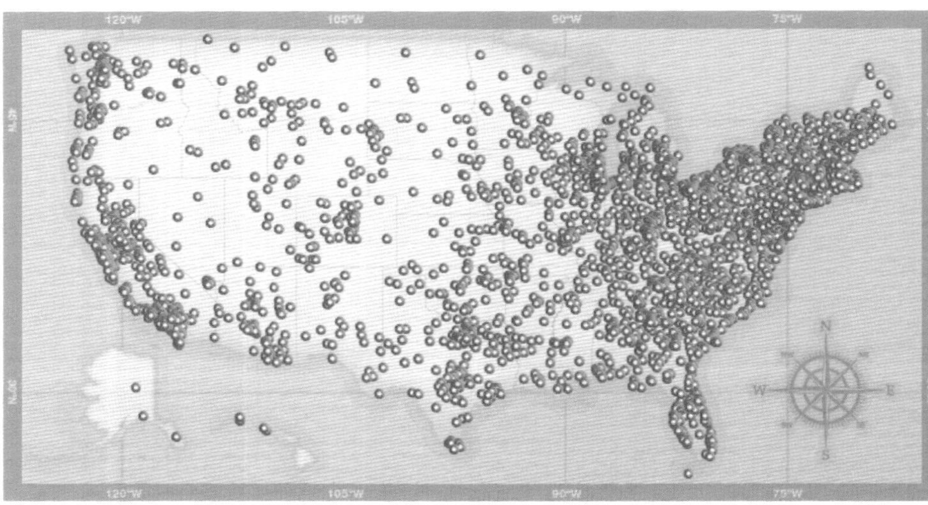